Wondrous Child

Also by Lindy Hough

Poetry

Changing Woman

Psyche

The Sun in Cancer

Outlands & Inlands

Wild Horses, Wild Dreams:
New and Selected Poems, 1971–2010

Anthologies

Nuclear Strategy and the Code of the Warrior:
Faces of Mars and Shiva in the Crisis of Human Survival

Wondrous Child

THE JOYS AND CHALLENGES OF
GRANDPARENTING

For Kathleen

EDITED BY
Lindy Hough

FOREWORD BY
Jane Isay

Lindy Hough
Joanna Biggar

For Kathleen, who's into grandparenting in a big way. Best, Kitty

North Atlantic Books
Berkeley, California

Published by   Cover and book design © Susan Quasha
North Atlantic Books   Cover image © Maggie Taylor, "Small
P.O. Box 12327   possibilities"
Berkeley, California 94712   Printed in the United States of America

This is issue number 70 in the Io series.

Wondrous Child is sponsored by the Society for the Study of Native Arts and Sciences, a nonprofit educational corporation whose goals are to develop an educational and cross-cultural perspective linking various scientific, social, and artistic fields; to nurture a holistic view of arts, sciences, humanities, and healing; and to publish and distribute literature on the relationship of mind, body, and nature.

North Atlantic Books' publications are available through most bookstores. For further information, visit our website at www.northatlanticbooks.com or call 800-733-3000.

Copyright acknowledgments are listed on page 270.

Library of Congress Cataloging-in-Publication Data
Wondrous child : the joys and challenges of grandparenting / edited by Lindy Hough ; foreword by Jane Isay.
     p. cm.
Summary: "An anthology of twenty-nine tender, fierce, and inspiring essays, Wondrous Child explores the complexity of the grandparenting relationship in today's diverse society"—Provided by publisher.
  ISBN 978-1-58394-362-5 (alk. paper)
1. Grandparenting. 2. Grandparent and child. I. Hough, Lindy, 1944–
HQ759.9.W66 2012
306.874'5—dc23
                    2011031278

1 2 3 4 5 6 7 8 9 SHERIDAN 17 16 15 14 13 12

To my older sisters, Susie and Polly—
grandmothers whose warmth, clarity, and spontaneity inspire me

Contents

Acknowledgments   ix

Foreword   xi

Introduction   xvii

Part One: Settling In

Wild Thing Baby ······ Jay Mankita   3

Following Fifi ······ Kitty Hughes and Bridget Connelly   4

In the Order of Things ······ Douglas Silsbee   15

Talking about Race and Gender ······ Joan Steinau Lester   23

In and Out of Step ······ Gloria Avner   30

The Whirling Heart Dance of Grandmothering ······
Saphira Linden   34

Carving Paths in Snow ······ Gill Wright Miller   44

Listening to Leo ······ Lindy Hough   57

Part Two: Balancing Reality and Hope

Evolving as a Grandmother ······ Nadia Natali   67

Grandparenting with a Broken Heart ······ Judyth O. Weaver   72

Professional Grandma ······ Salle Webber   76

Confessions of a New Step-Grandparent ······ Sharon Bray   84

Love through the Distances ······ Keith Dalton   93

Four Generations of First-Born Daughters ······ Donne Davis   102

Twins—Day and Night ······ Joanna Biggar   110

The Accidental Grandmother ······ Karine Schomer   123

Part Three: Grandparents Raising Grandchildren

A Heart's Perspective ······ Avery Bradford   141

An Explosion of Love ······ Joanne Maurits   149

The Grampy Diaries ······ John Lunn   155

A Legacy of Parenting ······ LENORA MADISON POE   168

My Grandkids Keep Me Young ······ JOANN WYNN   177

Being There for a Child Forever ······ KAREN BEST WRIGHT   186

Part Four: Grandchildren Remember

Hark, the Moaning Pond ······ TISSA ABEYSEKARA   195

Calling Clotilde ······ LAUREN ACZON   211

The Collapse ······ DAVID JACKSON COOK   220

Grandmother's Lap ······ NANCY HATHAWAY   229

The Russian Album ······ MICHAEL IGNATIEFF   235

Angels Gather Here ······ VANESSA SMITH   247

Obaachan: What Do *You* Want to Do? ······

STEPHEN MURPHY-SHIGEMATSU   255

Contributors   263

About the Editor   269

Permissions and Copyrights   270

Acknowledgments

A TRIBE OF COLLEAGUES, FRIENDS, family, and children helped me along the path of assembling this book.

I want to thank the contributors, who opened their hearts and wrote skillfully about their experiences either as grandparents or a grandchild with an elderly or dying grandparent. Without you, we would not have the varied age range, geographical variety, and level of serious inquiry *Wondrous Child* has achieved. You kept the book grounded in the details of your families and histories, all over the country and in Canada, often telescoping years and geographical distances into thoughtful, yet relatively succinct descriptions.

My respect and gratitude go to my colleagues at North Atlantic Books for their professionalism. They understood the vision of this book and helped me realize its potential. Janet Levin, Kat Engh, and Roslyn Bullas steered *Wondrous Child* carefully, each bringing their special expertise to it. Laura Shauger contributed wise and careful copyediting, for which I am grateful. The experience of publishing Tissa Abeysekara's *Bringing Tony Home*, with its compelling portrayal of the grandmother, planted a seed in my mind about the importance of positive grandparents. I'm grateful to Michael Ondaatje and Mark White for bringing *Tony* to our attention, and to Mark and Asanka Abeysekara for helping with permission to use this moving excerpt from the story in *Bringing Tony Home*.

Nancy Hathaway was an early influence on including a sense of the sacred in the book. Louise Steinman, Amy Gorman, Susan Halpern, Donne Davis, Joanna Biggar, Saphira Linden, Alia Wittman, Judyth O. Weaver, April Gilbert, Rondi Gilbert, Summer Brenner, Brooke Warner, and Elizabeth Kennedy listened to my questions about intergenerational communication and often responded with bracing talk about how they saw family dynamics, as well as how to portray them in an anthology.

I also want to thank Dr. Lenora Madison Poe, who described not just her own work locally and nationally to bring visibility to grandparents who raise their grandchildren, but invited me to meetings of the Grandparents As Parents support group in Berkeley. Together we found a way to touch on this large and important demographic of kin care for children. There I met JoAnn Wynn, who opened her world to me and became a friend.

I am grateful to my sisters, Susie Doyle and Polly Hough, who shared their understanding, wisdom, and enthusiasm about grandparenting years before it became a reality for me.

To my children, Robin Grossinger and Miranda July, and their spouses, Erica Wandner and Mike Mills—you are the immediate family surrounding me. I'm grateful for your love and stability, as we venture together into being an intergenerational family. The voices of my spirited grandchildren, Leo and Joey, were often in my mind. Finally, the love of Richard Grossinger, my long-time husband and partner, sustains me. He has shared with me this remarkable journey of being a family.

Foreword

MY OLDEST GRANDSON AND I were on our way home from his school when we learned that President Barack Obama's motorcade was nearby. We hurried to the police barrier, excited and expectant. First came the motorcycles and the limos, and finally the square car with the flags. When we spotted President Obama's profile in the car window, we were dancing and screaming with delight. "Was this the best moment in your life?" he asked. "Oh, no," I said, "that was the day you were born."

I wept and then melted when I first held him, as any grandparent would. I also felt a great rush of immortality. I suddenly became a hinge in history. I was born before World War II, and my parents at the turn of the twentieth century. Their older friend, born in the nineteenth century, sang me baby songs she had learned from her mother, who was born after the Civil War. My twentieth-century sons heard these songs. I murmured them to my grandchildren in the twenty-first century. They sing my songs to their younger siblings, and I know their grandchildren will hear these same songs in the twenty-second century. That makes four centuries, the way I count them.

We also become the carrier of stories and values, and we have the chance to give the little ones a great gift in this harried era—time, free time, time without constraints of appointments, lessons, or obligations. It doesn't matter how many hours we spend with them. Grandparents can stop time by relaxing and focusing on their needs and wishes.

It's easier to create grandma space when the parents are not around. It's best to be alone with them. So every week, I spend a morning or an afternoon alone with each of my small grandkids, who range in age from little baby to seven. I find the regimen exhausting and sometimes overwhelming, but I have already seen the second grader long for the company of his friends when he is with me, and I know our alone time is running out. That energizes me to be with the three-year-olds and the baby.

My own kids kept me so busy and exhausted that I didn't have the energy to watch them as closely or enjoy their antics as much as I do the grandchildren. I love to see the development of language, manners, competence, and conscience in the grandkids, and it's fascinating to see their different personalities emerge from within the same family. It makes me understand the generosity of the gene pool my grandkids come from.

I'm raving, I know. But that's my job, to love them completely, to pay scant attention to their flaws, and to be ecstatic at their smallest accomplishments. My kids believe that I have an inaccurately positive view of their children's accelerated development. They are mistaken, of course. And I am right. Realism is for the parents and teachers, not me. In our complete acceptance of the children, we provide what everybody needs: to be loved completely, to be recognized for who we are, to be forgiven for small infractions, to learn how to be a better person, to hear the stories of our family and listen to their own childhoods recounted with affection. The beauty of this connection with the grandkids is that it works both ways. In times of stress and grief, nothing heals me like the complete love those children have for me.

I am lucky to be included in the lives of my kids and their families. In order to keep their doors open, I sometimes have to keep my mouth shut. So when the first grandchild wasn't allowed to sleep on his tummy, I bit my lip. And I have learned to use my cell phone in another room altogether when there's a baby in the house. What did I know? It turns out they were right. All I care about is the welcome mat, wherever the facts may lie.

Now, let me complain about my back and my knees. They kill me when I am on the floor for hours and have to get up and down. Sometimes I feel like a dinosaur, tromping slowly through the playroom. And what about colds? I am constantly getting one. Nobody ever warns me of the green muck coming from the child's nose. It might keep me away from the babies, and the fact that I have a tendency to bronchial ailments hasn't penetrated my children's consciousness, especially when they need me. One time I was too sick to see Benji. He cried piteously. When chided gently by his parents, he responded, "I'm only four. If I were ten, I could handle it." When he's ten, I'll be lucky if he spends any time with me.

My friends and I, grandparents all, complain to each other about how demanding our grown children can be and about their rigidity. We chat about the exhaustion that follows our time together, and about the effort it takes to accept their foibles. But we all know that these complaints fade before their enthusiasm, their attention to our songs and stories, and the hugs we get from those kids. Gifts of this magnitude demand gratitude and are worth the sacrifice.

Another word about sacrifices: If we don't agree with the way in which the children are being raised, we learn that our wise advice is usually greeted with annoyance. So we have to bite our tongues. If we live a distance from our grandkids, we are houseguests—and hostages. We have to follow their regimen, no matter how we feel, and sometimes watch our edgy kids make what we think are serious mistakes. Make a constant fuss about what the little girl eats? Maybe they're making a future anorexic. Fail to calm down the overtired little boy? Is he headed to ADD-land? Too many sweets? No sweets. Too much TV? No TV. It's a puzzlement. As the grandchildren grow up, bigger worries—drugs, serious misbehavior, and problems in school—keep us awake at night. We can't do anything about these dangers, and we dare not discuss them with the parents. We are called upon to make financial sacrifices for the youngest generation, and to put up with insensitivity and annoyance when we don't meet the standards our grown kids set for us.

Tensions with our grown children pop up all the time. But we know that distance is a powerful tool in making us toe the line. You can fight with them and be absolutely right, but then don't hold your breath until the next invitation arrives.

Sometimes words fall out of our mouths that we instantly wish we could take back, but they are etched in the memory of our children. Call the baby nurse, an authoritarian lady in a white uniform, "Hitler" and you're not welcome for years. Murmur to yourself thoughts about spanking or sassy behavior, and doors shut on us.

It's an eternal problem: however grown our kids are, and however old we may be, they are still our children, and they will respond to us as their parents. Their wives and husbands also have families. We compute the amount of time each family gets with the grandkids, and they may be comparing the size of our gifts. We may like the in-laws, or we may not—it doesn't matter, because we have to be nice at all costs. Many sons move closer to the maternal line. That feels natural, but it's no fun for the mothers of men.

Still, the joy overcomes the troubles, and it's hard to imagine life without the grandkids.

Remember the story in the book of Genesis when God tells Abraham to take his beloved son Isaac to a mountain, there to sacrifice him on an altar they build together? Abraham follows directions and binds his son Isaac to the altar. Just in time an angel stays Abraham's hand. This text is hard to understand. How could a father agree to kill his dearest son? My friends and I think that if God had told Abraham to sacrifice a grandchild, Abraham would have replied, "Not me, God. Try somebody else." So much for origins of the Judeo-Christian tradition.

The book before you offers a wide panoply of responses and reactions of grandparents, male and female. Delightfully, it also includes memories by adult grandchildren of the grandparents who meant so much to the writers. Multicultural—inclusive not only of the American rainbow, but the world—*Wondrous Child* is an album of love, remembrance, and commitment.

The first section, "Settling In," is filled with the stories of people getting accustomed to being grandparents, under a wide variety of circumstances: we hear from grandfathers, a grandma taking care of her grandchild with her good friend, the child's godmother. We encounter multiracial families, and stereotypes. We learn how grief can be salved by a newborn, and the reality of guilt and distance. The beauty of this section is that it does not hide the problems and ambivalences.

In Part Two, "Balancing Reality and Hope," we read about the difficulty of setting boundaries with our kids and grandchildren, and what it feels like to be banished from your children's home. We hear from a postpartum doula who now has to be quiet when her children and their babies move in. We watch high expectations from a step-grandparent tumble in a good dose of reality, and hear from a grandfather who learns to deal with his own sense of failure. When four generations of women get together, a grandmothering group appears, with wisdom and humor for all.

There's sweet and difficult when grandparents are given the responsibility of raising their little ones, as we read in the next section. Each of these four stories casts a different light on this situation. Told by three grandmothers and a grandfather, with an overview of the needs and support structures for grandparents raising grandchildren by a renowned leader in the field, these accounts make for sometimes gritty reading. The authors' abilities to share their experiences with honesty and humor make them a great contribution to our understanding.

Part Four, seen from the other end of the age spectrum, contains memories written by adult grandchildren about their grandparents from different parts of the world and eras. No matter what happens, there is emotional deepening—enough that these relationships mean everything to the authors. The play of culture falls down through the generations, not always easily, but giving meaning, and is caught in these descriptions—the Filipino grandmother, rigid in habits, who wants to be American more than Filipino; the Japanese grandmother imported to the States, who can't voice her own desires, so used is she to serving others in her native land.

The great virtue of *Wondrous Child* is range: over ages, situations, cultures, and gender. To read it is to experience the varieties of ways in which love crosses the generations, sometimes accompanied with pain, but always with affection and vitality.

JANE ISAY
New York City

Introduction

WHEN MY SON BECAME A father and I became a grandparent for the first time six years ago, I wondered how my husband and I were going to do this. It was a major passage, wasn't it? A major relationship? The birthing classes for their generation seemed to stress the danger of overbearing grandparents. My son had been on his own for quite a while, and my daughter-in-law's mother had died when she was in college—we all mourned that she couldn't be here for the new child, and I was jumpy about occupying space that perhaps should be hers. It was an intimate thing, to enter their world as new grandparents. But my daughter-in-law had good memories of her own grandmothers, and was welcoming. They wanted this new baby to have strong relationships with his grandparents.

My grandparents on both sides embraced the idea that "Children should be seen and not heard." As the youngest child, I came along when they were much older, but they didn't seem to want to talk to children or play with them. My parents, sadly, were not memorable grandparents to my children—partly because of the three-thousand-mile distance, and partly because my dad died when they were infants. Although my sisters' kids remember my parents fondly, by the time I got married, my parents were divorcing and starting new lives. They seemed less involved in being grandparents—which meant no role models for me, and no image of what loving grandparents could be, for my children.

I looked for collections of grandparents writing about the experience, to hear how other grandparents fared on this possibly perilous journey. I'm a writer and publisher. To my delight, there were few anthologies—a niche not yet totally full! As I planned a possible anthology, I realized I had some goals: to publish accounts that charted the pleasures and difficulties of finding and creating intimacy with this relationship; to discover how being a grandmother or grandfather changed or enhanced our relationships with our grown children; and to give voice to grandparents across a diverse demographic of class, gender, and race.

During this time, about three years ago, my world was enriched by knowing young people who were losing a beloved grandparent. I realized these younger voices would give a view of a grandparent from the other end of the age spectrum, enhancing the tone and variety of the volume. I searched for some of these accounts in published memoirs, and found contemporary writers who, sometimes in grief, but other times with a kind of dispassion, recounted their memories of a strong, positive grandparent.

About halfway through gathering my pieces, I became aware of the significant jump since the 2008 recession of grandparents raising their grandkids themselves—many of them writing about it in online blogs. In 2005, the U.S. Census Bureau noted that nearly six million children, or eight percent, were being raised by their grandparents. Their voices and circumstances are significant, partly because they are raising generations of young women and men who would otherwise go into the foster care system. Many people I spoke to thought the anthology should *only* be about this group. *Wondrous Child* includes grandparents raising grandchildren because they are so important to our cohesive social fabric, and also as a reminder of how hard it must be to take on this much larger assignment.

Early on I was tempted to enlarge this anthology to aunts and uncles who play a significant role in a child's life, often as involved as grandparents are. But we needed focus. *Wondrous Child* might be a prism, but it could not refract light from everywhere.

The accounts from our contributors show a number of factors that determine how the grandparenting relationship will play out. The following are some general truths that weave through the contributors' pieces:

New families want to determine everything about their own parenting. Your job is to support the young family, and be there for their children. Although the generations have much in common, parenting methods differ. You get to look at new methods, and whatever you did will become part of your unspoken oral history.

The nature of being a parent is that you don't always understand your child's methods of separation or the grievances that were hidden in his or her growing up. Things can come up in being around your children's family that feel very old. Small things loom large. Sometimes the tinder seems dry and easily sparked.

Adult children from families in which everyone has had practice in talking out problems as they come up are blessed. In many families, talking about anything "real" can escalate tensions quickly. But intimacy and naturalness are built on trust. You want to be able to count on one another, within reason. Forgiving one another for not being able to be there at a given time is an important way of having each other's backs.

Grown children can use your help and hopefully wisdom, and it's not only as an elderly person that you will need them. People in a family need one another at any age. Families who help one another and do things together because they enjoy each other's company build connectedness. The warmth of the extended family benefits not just grandkids, but adults also, in whatever decade of their lives.

Grandparents live on the periphery of the new family—sometimes closer in, sometimes further out. The more you and your children's family see yourselves as a unit, the more you'll take the time to communicate clearly so that you can handle misunderstandings without tension.

A huge pleasure of grandparenting is seeing your grandkids grow up in a smoothly operating household. To experience close-up the growth of a child over the years is a privilege and joy. This child is part of you. You are giving her or him the gift of your attention, your time, and yourself.

Wondrous Child is divided into four parts. In Part One, "Settling In," grandparents describe how they adjust high expectations to reality. Opportunities and limitations become revealed. A grandmother who knows she's involved in different things than her children's family delights in being herself, as they explore art, Buddhism, singing, and festivals. A new grandchild is the positive bright note for a large family in a year of loss and tragedy. A ski trip with a seven-year-old and a grandma is a hair-raising journey of self-knowledge. A Nana and her grandson amuse themselves by telling each other stories.

Part Two, "Balancing Reality and Hope," deepens into the challenges of being a grandparent. A grandmother opens her house to her children, but holds on to her dreams. Distance and clashing belief systems greet a new grandparent. Children and a wary step-grandmother settle into the pleasures of family life. Distances are spanned through the years, using the mail, phone, Skype, and plane tickets. A postpartum doula reflects on her own children and grandchildren at home, as she works with the families of her clients. Twins are born and go abroad—an enterprising grandmother follows to help and not lose touch. A career woman who never wanted children finds being a lively grandmother rewarding.

Part Three, "Grandparents Raising Grandchildren," is written by grandparents parenting their grandchildren. This can be a perilous business—picking up the pieces, often investing one's all until the parent is able to take care of them, and letting go again, sometimes to fragile circumstances. A single career woman takes her grandchild full-time, creating a safe, nurturing home. A prominent psychologist and national leader in the African American Grandparents As Parents movement describes it and her support group in the San Francisco Bay Area. A father happy in his empty nest, writing full time, is greeted by his son and three young boys on the doorstep, for more than just a visit. Two grandmothers describe raising their grandchildren for some years and then giving them back when their children are able to make a good home for them—a bittersweet experience.

Part Four, "Grandchildren Remember," is written by adults describing a beloved grandparent. A Sri Lankan youth remembers a mysterious grandmother. A Filipino grandmother dies while her granddaughter is at college, and a treasured grandfather dies in the Deep South. A woman with a strong spiritual background envisions spirit goddesses who can listen to a child—and resolves to be one when she becomes a grandmother. A newly pregnant mom remembers her Italian grandmother and her childhood. A son helping to bring his Japanese grandmother to America realizes how self-abnegation is a core of her upbringing.

These pieces are nuanced accounts of warm family ties and intergenerational communication. They spin to shame the destructive stereotypes our culture holds about elders, mothers-in-law, and grandparents. They salute families who enjoy one another's company enough to spend time together and treasure each others' individuality.

Grandparents invest tremendous emotional energy while holding so few cards. As a parent, you hold all the cards. In friendships and love affairs people hope for equity and leave when it doesn't work. Family is forever. The stakes are high, because just deciding not to participate so affects every other family member. Abrupt change can alter everything—a move to another country, ill health, the dissolution of a marriage, family flare-ups. You must become like water, continually supporting this family, assuring your grandchildren you will find a way to keep this relationship true.

May this book inspire parents and grandparents to keep trying, and give insight into how the generations are communicating. *Wondrous Child* is dedicated to the hope that the relationship between grandparent and grandchild will bring depth and meaning to family life.

LINDY HOUGH
Berkeley, California

Part One

· · · · · · · · · ·

SETTLING IN

Wild Thing Baby

JAY MANKITA

When a baby is born, everyone looks at this unformed creature and imagines how he or she will be changed by the "civilizing" influences of parents and culture. Folksinger Jay Mankita speaks to the hope that an untamed quality that can nurture a creative, resourceful individual—a "wild baby" amid other mammals—will not be lost.

Beyond the shopping mall, beyond the TV set
A voice from deep within is whispering, "don't forget"—
You're a wild thing, baby, a wild human being
And there's more to our lives than what we've been seeing
You crawl through the mud and lie in the field
You know every sunrise as beauty revealed
You play in the ocean; you run laughing down hill
You're a creature of nature, a wild thing still
You're a wild thing, baby, wherever you go
Beyond all you do, underneath all you know
The hawk and the deer are your sister and your brother
The whale and the wolf and every living other
Are calling you home in the whippoorwill's cry,
In the call of the loon and the grunting baboon
In the cover of night, the honking of geese in a homecoming flight,
Coyote's howl, the owl, the growl of a tiger, the roar of the lion,
Crying for you to come home and remember just who you are
The secret of life in the light from a star
Reflected mysteriously in the smile of a baby, or the eyes of a cat
You are an animal being, a wild thing, baby,
A glorious human, and maybe, just maybe—
Even more than that.

Following Fifi
·········
KITTY HUGHES AND BRIDGET CONNELLY

*Two women are best friends. One becomes a grandmother and asks
her friend to be the child's godmother. How do these two roles differ?
In this piece godmother Kitty Hughes visits Bridget when she's taking care of her grandchild Fifi … and enters into a Lilliputian world
of mutual fun and learning. In a lovely confection, they describe in
alternating voices the extended world of this lucky two-year-old.*

BC: My granddaughter is napping upstairs in her mother's old bedroom.
I am downstairs waiting to open the door before the doorbell can ring
and wake her. Kitty is about to arrive. She's a close friend, my daughter's
godmother. Kitty, our friend Cheryl, and I are writers. We have an ongoing writers' group and meet often to confer. Kitty has asked to interview
me for her latest project, an article on grandparenting. Usually her visits
with Fifi and me don't have an agenda.

KH: I am about to ring the doorbell when the door opens. The house is
quiet, and Bridget gives me the "Sh," sign, holding a finger to her lips.
We move quietly to the kitchen in the back. There are cookie crumbs
and a sippy cup on the table, and a tin of freshly baked muffins on the
stove. Fifi's high chair is drawn up close to the table.

In the backyard, I see the large swing that fills almost the whole lawn.
That's the swing in the screensaver photo of the two of them on Bridget's
computer. What must it be like to have a child fill up so much of your
life again? It's hard for me to imagine, but if I get a chance at it, I want to
know more about how it is done.

4

BC: Over tea in the kitchen, Kitty, pen in hand, puts questions to me, things I've never consciously considered: Do I have a grandparenting style? Gosh, do I? I mostly do it by heart, by rote, I tell her. What's most fulfilling? What are the challenges?

The truth is, I don't know. Since Fifi's birth two years ago, I've been so busy taking care of her while her mother attends law school that I haven't really thought about what I'm doing. I just do it. I only know one thing: I am in love.

It surprised me: the pure bodily chemistry, the rush of feel-good hormones that I hadn't felt since my daughter was a baby. I had never thought much about being a grandmother, never yearned for it as some folks do. I figured my daughter's reproductive life was her own business. I had always wanted another child. Kate was born when I was forty, a much desired baby, who arrived while I was busy teaching and writing a book that would earn me tenure at the university.

Fifi arrived twenty-six years later, and I am so lucky that my daughter trusts me to take care of her. When Kate handed her infant to me, she gave me only one instruction: Use big words around her.

What values do I try to teach her? We just live—together. I do it all intuitively, on the spur of the moment. We play. The dining room has become her playroom. We make things up. We tell stories. We go for walks. Her grandfather takes her to music lessons every Monday morning. She calls him Papa. My sister comes by often. She brings blocks, three-dimensional construction toys. Fifi calls her Gram-Ella. We visit with the neighbors or their dogs and cats. Friends drop by. Almost every day now, Fifi asks: Who's coming?

Everything is kind of free-floating, with only a few rules. We have stuff around the house that she could really mangle. So, I've tried to teach her the difference between toys and art. When she tries to grab the wire sculpture of a dove shaped like a hand holding a heart, I tell her: No. This is art. It is pretty. We look at it. We don't play with it. We play with toys.

She knows the difference now. Or if she doesn't, she asks. And now, she has an arts-and-crafts table of her own, so she can combine the two categories and make her own pretty things. It was her idea. She asked me for an "arts crafts table" after her mother set one up for her at home.

KH: I can't help but feel a bit envious. This is a mysterious love I have never experienced. I sense but can't quite grasp its unique chemistry. It is like the love we felt for our own children, but there is something bemused, relaxed, and expansive that I don't remember. This relationship seems freed of the hurried morning routines, getting our children off to child care and ourselves to work, and the constant juggling of priorities. I remember all the "how-to" books and articles, showing how to manage child care and work, but rarely do I remember anything about cultivating sheer unhurried enjoyment of child rearing. I think to myself it can't be all that easy.

Bridget, we are not spring chickens anymore. It must be hard at our age for you to take on daily responsibility like this. What do you do when you have a contest of wills? I remember how willful a two-year-old can be.

BC: Fifi is a strong girl. Luckily for me she got up on her own two feet and started toddling early. I am not a young grandmother, and she is tall like her Daddy, Jamal. As she's grown over these last two years, I've had to learn to be conscious that I am lifting an ever-changing, wiggling, live weight and that I must take care not to hurt my back. I have muscles now. Fifi has made me stronger.

And she entertains me. I love language and the creativity of language play. She astonished me when she was about one. Sitting in her high chair, finishing up an after-nap snack, she looked at me, pointed to the door, and said:

"Out, out."

"You want to go outside, do you?"

"Yes."

"Well, I do not want to. I want to stay in the house. I do not want to go out."

Fifi considered my words, then made a complete sentence, straining with the effort of articulating each word carefully and slowly, "I. DO. WANT. TO."

"Good grief," I laughed. "You *do* want to go out. That is a wonderful sentence. Perfect syntax. And you know how to win an argument with your grandmother, the rhetoric professor! You win. Your first full sentence. We *will* go outside."

KH: I have to laugh, too. I am sure you astonished Felice, as well as she you. You, the rhetoric professor, model language and argument for her, and she trumps you. Then you trump her with an unexpected resolution. I have to say you make it look like fun. I do get that she already has a strong will, and I know where she gets least part of it! Tell me more.

BC: Fifi is kind and caring. A few days ago, I tripped over some logs near the fireplace. I fell and landed hard on my knee. It hurt. Fifi came up behind me as I crouched on the floor and put her arms around me. She soothed me, rocking me like a little mother, saying: "Sorry, Ammy, I sorry you hurt. So sorry."

This tiny girl knew how to offer her grandmother bodily and verbal comfort. I heard at that moment my own Grandmother Connelly's words, "Be kind to each other." She used to repeat this gentle instruction frequently to her seventeen children, and my father repeated it to us, articulating an ethic of caring.

You know, Kitty, I think there is a kind of genealogy of parenting: we inherit habits of caring that embody and teach values we unconsciously pass down through the generations. Some of those habits are more bothersome. I am a worrier, descended—I learned while researching my book *Forgetting Ireland: Uncovering a Family's Secret History*—from a long line of famine-stricken Irish mothers whose fretting ways were caught by one of their sons. He was the great Gaelic-language writer Mairtin O'Cadhain, and in his short stories and radio plays, I can hear the cautioning language of my own mother and grandmothers back through four generations on the south Connemara coast. We cark and care. Conscious of this maternal habit, I try to curb the carking.

Fifi wakes up from her nap. She comes downstairs on her own and joins us in the kitchen. She crawls into my lap. She's still sleepy, but curious about Kitty whom she knows and loves. Kitty is the great-godmother who appeared with a flower-print dress when Fifi was just about big enough for it. What does she have today? A notepad and pen. Now that's interesting. Fifi likes paper and pencils.

Kitty refocuses. Looking at Fifi, she asks:

"Who is Fifi?" Fifi looks at me with her eyebrows knit questioningly, so I ask her:

"Who are you?"

"I Fifi."

"Yes, Fifi is my love. She is Felice Amelie, named for her great-grandmother just as I was named for my Gramma Bridget. She calls me Ammy and she calls herself Fifi."

KH: I am the fairy great-godmother, who shows up with the flower-print dress when Fifi is just about big enough for it. Like most good fairy godmothers, I am probably transmuting my own deep desire for progeny, in this case a grandchild of my own. I think of how in the Sleeping Beauty and Cinderella stories the fairy godmothers barely disguise their own maternal needs.

But in my case there is another absorbing attachment, as Bridget and I have been friends for many years. We have been there for each other as our lives have unfolded. My flower-print dress gift for Fifi was another linking of our lives, mine and Bridget's, my son Steve and her daughter Kate, our mutual godchildren, and now Fifi. I like to imagine my being there for Fifi as she grows up and maybe helping her out of some difficulty, like mythical helper-godmothers. It doesn't hurt to have a grandmother and a great-godmother watching over you.

Fifi wakes up and joins us. She looks a little surprised to see me, then nestles into Bridget's breast and studies me across the kitchen table. This is Fifi in her sage and sober beyond-her-years mode. She barely takes her eyes off my face, and listens intently, like a smart, little gnome. I get the odd sensation that she understands what we are saying and is evaluating it. For a brief second, I flash on her psychotherapist grandfather, Hank, who has that same quiet ability to make you feel you are being "read" as you speak. But this is Fifi in only one of her modes. She has many, already at the age of two, and Grandma Bridget knows them all best.

KH: When my son was born, Bridget was full of yearning for a child of her own. She rocked and coddled Steve, and dreamed of her own child. That child, Kate, who came along two years later, has now brought Fifi into the world. I love little Fifi, while longing for a grandchild of my own and wondering if I will ever see the day.

I look at Fifi and see Bridget. She sparkles like Bridget. She plays with words. She twirls around the room, picking up a book here, a toy there—she points, she compares, she looks to you with her intense brown eyes for confirmation that, yes, she has made an interesting connection, has made sense of something in our shared experience. This is all very Bridget.

I almost forget for a moment that Bridget's eyes are ocean blue, while Fifi's are velvet brown. Fifi looks very much like her Korean grandmother, whose photo sits on the side table in the dining room, and she has her father's African American complexion. Bridget likes to say, "Fifi looks like all of us."

Sitting on the living room floor with the two of them, I feel myself drawn into a special space where everything is transformed. A little like Gulliver in the land of Lilliputians, a miniature environment where everything is the same and not the same, compressed and intensified, the Bridget-Fifi microcosm, where the two of them set up their own parameters, and where Fifi runs much of the show, aided and abetted by Bridget, but this is not quite right ... A kind of interactive space where Fifi gets to take the lead, but where Bridget almost imperceptibly guides, enables, provides positive reinforcement. Above all, this is a space created by mutual fun and learning.

BC: Fifi withdraws a little from us, nestling her head into my shoulder. I tell Kitty about my challenges with setting limits: I like to let children (and people in general) have a sense of accomplishment and mastery, a sense of possibility. Saying or hearing "No" all the time is annoying to everyone. On the other hand, I have to protect her. When she started crawling and toddling, she discovered the kitchen drawers. Obviously, she couldn't have free access to all of them—she might hurt herself. So I told her that the big bottom drawer was hers, the top two were mine, and the middle one for all of us to share.

Fifi is listening. She gets down from my lap and goes over to the drawers. She looks at Kitty and points to the various drawers, saying: "This Fifi drawer, this Ammy drawer. This Fifi, Ammy, Papa drawer."

She is fully awake and ready to take charge: "Ammy, we go play now. We go play Legos, go to Fifi room."

KH: Fifi looks at me as she instructs her Ammy. Clearly, I am to follow, too. While another grandparent might think this child is being too bossy, Bridget hears her developing self-confidence and social skills. (I am taking lots of notes.)

BC: As the three of us play Legos on the floor, surrounded by books, puzzles, and blocks, I tell Kitty:

"We like to read stories about grandmothers. There's Little Red Riding Hood who almost lost her gramma when she had a run-in with a wolf; that one's still a little too scary. The story she likes best these days is 'Roti Rolled Away.' She likes to playact the roles."

Fifi goes to the big basket of books in the corner and selects a pink one illustrated with a picture of a dark-haired, brown-skinned girl who lives in the jungles of India. She leafs through it, then gives the book to Kitty.

"Let's play Roti Rolled Away. Come, sit on couch," she says, going to the living room.

"OK, you direct. You are telling the story," Kitty replies. Fifi picks up a ball on the floor and rolls it away toward Kitty. Soon the whole story emerges in the interaction between the book and the ball. The little girl's Nani gives her a round piece of bread—a roti. It rolls away and she chases it until it rolls right into the river and is lost forever. She cries for her lost bread, but when she returns home, she smells fresh baked roti ready from her grandmother's oven.

My granddaughter likes the lost-and-found story pattern. I'm a folklorist. I taught traditional oral narrative in a comparative context at a university for many years, but Fifi taught me a few things about the Cinderella story and its appeal. She likes shoes. We have a beautiful, dog-eared book of fairy tales illustrated by Gyo Fujikawa. It was Kate's book. Fifi likes to look at the glass slipper lost on the palace staircase, then to turn the page to see the conclusion: Cinderella wearing both her shoes astride a horse with the man who found the shoe. I have never quite thought of it that way before. Fifi's version boils it all down: Cind'ella lost shoe, man find shoe. It's not a runaway roti, but a missing shoe this time. She's got the story pattern of loss and recovery down pat. It is reassuring. Such are the great stories of life and its necessary lessons.

KH: When I returned from a trip to Nepal last year, after trekking in the Himalayas and staying in Cheryl's walk-up apartment in Kathmandu, I remember the first morning waking up in my own bed. There was a moment of panic and disorientation, until I realized where I was. The room swam around me, as the bed, the bedroom door, the warm body of my partner next to me, and the pictures on the wall established their usual places. I realized that I had landed in Oakland, and was back to my usual life.

Small children may wake up crying, experiencing that same kind of panic. I wonder if falling asleep and waking is their experience of losing and finding love and comfort again. They leave the familiar world and make their own first private journeys into their dream worlds, then return to consciousness, where the light has shifted in their room, there is a new noise, they are hungry. The world is the same and not the same. If it is as strange as I imagine, how much more critical it is to provide them some anchoring comfort and security.

In our dreams we go to Oz, but we want to return to Kansas. There is no Good Witch of the North (or helping godmother) to guide you back home, no Aunt Em (or loving grandmother), standing by the bed to ease you back to the waking world. When Fifi awakes from her nap, she finds her grandmother again, and that same warm presence that makes the world OK. I make a mental note. As Fifi's godmother, I will make it my job to support her grandmother and give Fifi help when it is asked for.

I wonder if Bridget is bringing up a budding folklorist. Or perhaps the next family historian. Both Hank and Bridget rewrote their family pasts, Hank most recently in a biography of his mother, the Polish-Jewish grandmother for whom Felice is named. Lurking behind these grandmother stories is the story of family linking and continuity.

Fifi cannot help but be aware that her grandparents lead the writers' life together. Her grandmother often writes while Fifi naps, and Papa Hank is up every morning at his writing desk. She may grow up thinking everyone has a set of grandparents like this.

Bridget tells Cheryl and me that her women friends have always been those who lead a life of the mind. Visiting Hank and Bridget, I am always drawn into a swirl of political and literary discussions. Their current interests are usually reflected on the week's coffee table collection. Today it's Toni Morrison's novel *A Mercy,* the *New York Times Magazine,* the *Economist,* Arthur Miller's autobiography, Barbara Cleverly's novel *The Palace Tiger,* web printouts about President Barack Obama and Mad Republican disease, and a collection of small-town stories titled *Dots on a Map.*

Bridget tells me that Fifi often brings a book to read, to get her grandparents' attention when they turn on the TV. Some day I see Fifi writing a book of her own, perhaps about her Grandparents Hank and Bridget, reweaving the family story to better understand who she is. She may recount Hank's adventures at Burning Man, her Grandma Bridget's riding out into a desert on a camel to gather folklore, how she benefited from her grandfather's studies in child psychology, her grandmother's multifaceted career, the magical times she spent with them in the country, her grandfather taking her to music and dance lessons, her grandmother swinging her in the backyard swing, chanting Irish rhymes. This much I know: Fifi already shares her grandparents' enthusiasm for reading and she notices when anyone takes up pen and paper.

I try to sum up for myself the unique relationship Bridget has with her granddaughter. She gives Fifi her full and complex attention. She creates a special shared space, partly by letting her take initiative. She sets limits indirectly, by encouraging her to make choices from the possible options. She wants to make sure Fifi is self-confident, can take initiative, and be ready to take on the challenging world that faces professional women. She listens carefully and learns from Fifi, intrigued, as a professor of rhetoric, by her formation of sentences and thoughts. She doesn't talk down to her, and she engages her in the world of reading and mental exploration. Fifi, at two, is conscious that Fifi is important.

I am struck by Bridget's ability to draw her friends and new experience into Fifi's world for their mutual enjoyment. Other grandmothers might feel trapped and put upon when taking on this much day-to-day responsibility. Bridget limits her vacations and other activities, fiercely guarding their time together. They have their own social life, as friends stop in and become part of the little world they have constructed. Attention isn't quite the word. This *is* love, mutual and reinforcing. Bridget and Fifi are gifts to each other.

No one can replicate this relationship, yet it teaches me something essential. If you see your grandchild as a precious gift, or perhaps if you can remind yourself of this frequently, you have the ingredient for a lively—dare I say magical—shared experience.

Bridget and I have our farewell hug. Fifi plants a big kiss on my face, shakes my hand, and says, "Thank you for coming." I leave the two of them giggling as I go out the door.

BC: Sometimes I do worry (my Connemara side) about what life will bring my little granddaughter. We have come a long way, this family of ours. My great-grandfather Connelly was a Kentucky slave owner. Now I am bound in blood and love to a little girl whose genealogy encompasses the world—Africa, Asia, and Europe. She is an American. Her existence makes me feel more connected with the world and its future. I want a world where she and all its children will remain safe to create themselves in peace and harmony. Her given name is Felice; it means happiness, and it honors her great-grandmother, a Polish Jew and World War II refugee.

Little Felice was crying over something recently.

"Fifi McFee," I said to her, "Do not cry. Come with me. We'll look in the mirror. We'll put on some lipstick, and the whole world will look better."

So, we looked in the mirror. I painted my lips, then hers. We looked at each other. I puckered my lips and smoothed them together. She rubbed her two red lips together and caught my eye in the mirror as she laughed and wiped her tears.

Felice Amelie. May your name be a prophecy. May you keep your sense of humor, your quick thoughtfulness, and your tough resilience.

In the Order of Things

Douglas Silsbee

The arcing of the generational wheel: after growing up with one's own grandparents far away, it's nice to have your kids living closer. Then one child moves in to make an intergenerational household for a few months—further adjustments. This father's transformation into a grandparent is enriched by memories of his beloved grandmother in a large, mysterious house.

—For my father, eldest daughter, and first grandson

I WALK WITH MILES AS he totters toward the creek. He falls down occasionally on the uneven ground, but has become an accomplished walker in the last couple of weeks. I remove my shoes and all of his clothes except his diaper, and hold his hand as we splash and wade into the cool water.

Soon his diaper weighs about ten pounds and is falling off his little body ... I surrender to the inevitable, pull it the rest of the way off, and toss it across the water onto a rock next to my shoes where it lands with a loud splat. We explore deeper into the pools. I help him across slippery rocks, and turn him loose on the sandbars where he alternately digs his toes into, and eats, the fine gravel at the side of the creek.

I stand with Miles at the top of a little slide, and holding both his hands, swing him down into the faster current. The water rushes past his naked round body, and he laughs out loud as I pull him up against the fast current. I laugh, too, delighted in his delight. We do it again. And again. And again. We're both laughing, him because of the new sensations of cool rushing water gurgling all over his body, me because I can't help it. Is it his body in the creek? Or mine? It doesn't matter ... we couldn't be happier!

My grandparents lived on the edge of Rock Creek Park, in Washington, DC, with a big backyard. We'd arrive every spring vacation. Nana would meet us as we piled out of the car; after a cursory hello to my parents, she virtually ignored them. She whisked me and my two brothers into the sunroom filled to the brim with play animals, told us how happy she was to see us, and asked us how we were. It felt like coming home. When Nana was with me, her sun shone on me and me alone.

Forty-five years later I still occasionally dream about the magic of that space … a room down in the basement I'm exploring turns out to be like a giant geode, full of sparkling purple crystals. Mysterious, wonderful, a treasure. Fifty years from now, how will my own grandson remember the moments that we are having now? The house that we now live in after we are long gone? Us, after we're gone? I hope he'll remember our times together as innocent and magical. I hope my time with him will bequeath, half a century from now, a comforting knowledge of what it is to be alive, safe, and loved.

The last time I saw Nana was a few months before she died. She had been in advanced dementia in her apartment for years, living alone. It was a sad concluding chapter to an extraordinary life; she was the shell of a once vibrant, loving, and accomplished woman. Her visits from relatives were sporadic. She had confused who my father and I were for years.

She was rather out of it when I stopped by with my wife, Walker, and my then eight-year-old daughter, Alisia. But when she saw Alisia, something of the Nana I had known as a child came alive. Hunched in her armchair, she beckoned Alisia over with her finger, then bent even lower to whisper some secret for Alisia's ears alone. Clearly, Alisia was the most special person in the world. It was a magical moment. Long unused synapses in the dark corners of her aging brain were touched by the presence of a child. Her aliveness was sparked. There was my grandmother again. It was an amazing moment that I remember decades later.

I carry Miles on my shoulders down to the pond. I like having him up there. Alisia always gives us the red baby backpack when we pick him up for our regular Friday night babysitting gig. It seems rather impersonal though, and I rarely use it. I greatly prefer the intimacy of Miles's chubby legs around my neck, the subtle shifts in weight as his little body continually adjusts to my movements, and even the banging of his hands on my head as he drums to some inner rhythm. We are as one.

We sit in the water at the edge of the pond, Miles on my lap, up to our chests in warm pond water. The fish come around—our big koi Nelson and Bertha, gazillions of goldfish, myriad minnows. Even Fat Albert, the biggest of several catfish in the pond, rises up expecting food. I hand Miles the small scoop filled with fish food, and he dumps it into the water, splashing and throwing water as he does so. Instantly chaos breaks out.

Streaks of gold, splashes, loud sucking sounds as gaping fish mouths inhale small chunks of food. Miles reaches out for the fish, reaching, grabbing, occasionally touching a slippery tail, and laughs out loud. We're immersed in piscine plenty, both laughing at the top of our lungs. The louder he laughs, the louder I laugh, and vice versa. We egg each other on. The fish settle down when the food is gone. He passes me the scoop for more.

It never occurred to me that organizing my life around the small town in upstate New York where my parents lived, in order to have a more regular and in-depth relationship with them, made any kind of sense. My own parents lived far from where they'd grown up; we saw my grandparents on special occasions, once or twice a year. This was simply the way things were. Although I wasn't conscious of it at the time, I thought less of people I knew who stayed put. I saw the worlds of the extended families where they grew up as somehow narrow, provincial, evidence of diminished opportunity. Life, for me, became a quest for meaningful work and personal fulfillment; proximity to extended family wasn't on the screen. It never occurred to me that there was a cost to this quest.

We saw my parents during visits at our place, theirs, or somewhere else, several times a year. Once we took a short backpacking trip in Montana with my wife, our two youngest, and my parents. The morning of our last day we walked out of camp up into the high alpine tundra, looking at wildflowers, and playing in the last of the summer snow banks. Together we marveled at spiders walking across the snow, miniature waterfalls of meltwater, and the splendid views west across the plateau. Witnessing his son and grandchildren, my father took a picture, now lost, of me walking with a child's hand in each of mine, Beartooth Butte in the background. I know that we, and our kids, have provided and continue to provide some of the greatest joys in his life, as my own kids have in mine. In that moment, I was walking between parents and children, oriented, sensing myself in the order of things. While there was nothing dramatic about that perfect moment, it seemed to capture all that was right in the world.

I realize that while my parents were connected to my kids, I also see that those connections happened in vacations or visits, once or twice a year. We got together on planned parentheses, time-outs from the intensity of what we accepted as normal. I know that a deeper connection, vastly more rewarding, was available to us if we had found ways to weave each other into the tapestries of our lives. I wanted my parents to deeply know how Alisia's obvious competence and super-responsibility are firmly underpinned by tenderness and fierce loyalty, appreciate the intertwining of Megan's vulnerability and compassion with her brash feistiness, marvel at the paradox of Nathan's deep thoughtfulness and his laid-back absentmindedness. I wanted my parents to actively foster the unfolding and miraculous complexity in each of my three.

And, I wanted my kids to know the good news and the bad news about their grandparents. I wanted them to sense, and be inspired by, the astounding fountain of creativity that my mother Ann was, in spite of her tightly wound and sometimes judgmental exterior. I wanted them to appreciate Bob's deep curiosity, sensitivity, and thoughtfulness, present even when he is sometimes disengaged and inaccessible. I want my kids to be deeply connected to where they come from. And, I wanted my parents to stand in awe, in the fullest possible way, at the lineage they begat.

My mother passed away when I was working in Taiwan. I called my father, and she was dead. I hadn't been a part of it, hadn't said good-bye, had no sense that it was coming.

After Ann died, we invited Bob to come live with us. It was a genuine invitation, not out of a sense of obligation, but out of a real desire to fold him into the rhythms of our family's complex and fast-paced lives. We knew it would not be without challenges, for him as well as for us. And, we welcomed the opportunity to receive by giving, and to build a life with this remarkable man who had brought me into the world, by sharing our lives with him.

Bob decided to stay in his own town, where he had a community, and not to move in with us. I think he's happier there than he would have been living with us; we couldn't have replaced the rich community that he has where he lives. Still, even though I call him frequently to enjoy coffee together, talking on the phone isn't the same. When he comes for visits, he has a nice time with my kids, and they genuinely love him. Yet, while I'm delighted that he has created the conditions for happiness in his later years, I have a strong longing to be more a part of that happiness than our long-distance relationship and occasional wonderful travels together allow. I know that I am part of what gives his life in these delicious declining years pleasure and meaning, and that gives my life pleasure and meaning.

A few years ago I was talking with Nathan, whom I had introduced to white-water kayaking. I told him, "Nathan, you're better at kayaking than I ever was, ever will be, and ever could hope to be."

"I know," he said. Then, sheepishly, wanting to be sensitive to my possibly bruised ego, he asked "So, how do you feel about that?"

I responded, with gratitude, "I feel great about it. I'm at the stage of my life when my kids are surpassing me in all kinds of things. I'm grateful. It's what's supposed to happen."

My kids are taking their place in the world, and developing competencies and ways of being that I don't possess. Megan's charisma and ease in connecting with people opens countless doors for her. Alisia has managed scores of people and a huge budget in a large and complex restaurant. As they find their way, I want to continue to support, to share, to be involved, to offer them something valuable. I sense the clock ticking. My time is becoming shorter, and I still have so much to give.

Alisia and Chance moved in with Walker and me when she was seven months pregnant. After Miles was born, there were five of us in our home, neatly arranged in three generations. We were the elders; there was a baby in our home for the first time in nearly twenty years. They stayed with us for another two months after Miles was born.

I was surprised at how smoothly it went, at how quickly I adjusted to being part of a multigenerational household of five, including a newborn baby. For us, it was deeply gratifying to support them, to be relied upon, to be a part of the miraculous process of bringing this delightful new baby into the world. For Alisia, I know it was significant to let herself rely on us, to come home after all of those years of being strong and independent and building a life free of us, to let us be there for her. The arrangement felt right, natural, and healing.

When they moved out of our country house into town a couple of months after Miles was born, life became simpler, but also less rich and multitextured. Still, we have it good by grandparenting standards in my family. They live in town, twenty minutes away, and it's easy to stop by and see them on a run into town for groceries or a meeting. And, Miles spends every Friday with us. Walker brings him back from town, we explore around outside, and climb the "Staircase to Heaven," an old set of steps we leaned up against a maple tree in the yard because he likes to climb so much. We play with the dogs, eat, and explore the riverbank.

On these Friday nights, it's usually me who gives him his bedtime bottle. Since I didn't acquire breasts at puberty, tucking Miles in is as nurturing as it gets. We lie together, his head on my shoulder. I stroke his belly as he nurses the warm bottle, his eyes closed. Sometimes I simply gaze at his little face, as his breath moves gently in and out, and I marvel at his minute twitches and nuances of expression. Sometimes I fall asleep before he does.

He sleeps between Walker and me. We know our sleep will be interrupted by kicks in the face, or feeling suffocated by a baby arching his body backward over our necks. Waking up the next morning, groggy with sleep, is a small price to pay to have Miles in our bed. He sits bolt upright, points emphatically at nothing, and laughs out loud. We blink ourselves awake, laugh at nothing, and are happy.

After breakfast we take him into town and meet Alisia and Chance at the farmers' market. If it's our lucky day, they invite us for a gourmet brunch at their house. This is a wonderful chapter of our lives. For now, all three of our kids live locally, and we see lots of Miles. We are pretty interconnected. I would truly be grateful to have Bob, or Alisia's little family, living under our roof, with all the challenges and delights that level of interweaving would bring. But I don't get to decide where they live. Their lives have their own trajectories, driven by ambitions that might or might not make sense to me.

I know that, should they move somewhere else, I'll adjust. I've gotten good, through Buddhist practice, at letting go of attachments. But, this one I don't want to let go of. Having my life so intertwined with my kids and my grandson feels right in ways that I never could have anticipated. I had to become a grandfather to know how important it all is, for all of us: for me, for Miles, for his parents.

Being a grandfather orients me in the world. I sense, more acutely, the passage of time and the arcing of the generational wheel. I feel my own inevitable movement toward the waterfall. I won't be here forever, and I certainly don't get to decide where Miles calls home. Yet, when we are together, Miles and I call each other forth. We each nurture the life in the other.

It is the miracle of these moments, coupled with the certain knowledge that they will not last, that makes them so deeply sweet.

Talking about Race and Gender

Joan Steinau Lester

Imagine that your life was devoted to creating a new racial and social climate, which is now so commonplace to your children and grandchildren that they're unaware of how lucky they are to have these freedoms and cultural ease. In this piece the grandchildren assume a race-blind and gender-integrated world; they are not on the battlements. How we got here is not interesting to them ... yet.

"WHAT DO YOU THINK THE kids make of race?" I asked Che as we hurried toward an exhibit at the National Gallery near his Capitol Hill home. I trotted beside my son—yes, named after his father's and my '60s hero—trying to keep up with his long-legged stride. As a busy dad with several full-time jobs rolled into one, he habitually jogged, but this Mother's Day during my visit he'd created private time for us, suggesting an outing to the Romare Bearden show that he knew I'd like. Any time alone with this father of three was a treat.

"I don't know." Che shook his head, but his tone let me know he was open to discussion. "Everything's so different now." He looked genuinely puzzled.

Back in 1967 when he was born, Che's dad and I were fully immersed in Black Power. We raised Che and his sister on picket lines, chanting slogans like *"No Vietcong ever called me, 'Nigger!'"* By the time they were in Headstart, they were proudly Black—despite their white mother. My daughter, Ruby, two years older than Che, once even refused to talk to her white teacher, saying, "The Black teacher is for me."

"Wherever did she get that idea?" the white teacher had asked me as we sat by the sand table in tiny chairs, our knees touching. She peered across a political divide so wide I had no idea how to answer.

Instead, I picked up a handful of sand and let it trickle through my fingers. Ruby had been asking, when she sat on my lap snuggled into my arms, "Mommy, why am I black, like Daddy? I want to be the same as you." I hadn't known how to answer that, either, except to say, "Black is good," and hug her tighter.

"Do you talk about race at home a lot?" the teacher asked, prodding.

"We are very involved with black liberation," I said. I didn't tell her about the men filling our apartment: Black Panthers, with their ever-present guns; the militant Stokely Carmichael, who bounced Ruby on his knee; Rap Brown, who'd brought a statue for my babies from Ghana; or gentle Ralph Featherstone, a voting rights worker who, shortly after his last visit to us, was blown to pieces by a car bomb down South. I didn't tell her about our friend Mickey Schwerner, bludgeoned to death in Philadelphia, Mississippi, with two other organizers. I didn't tell her we were angry all the time, or that it might be time to "pick up the gun," as many of our movement comrades believed.

"But you're white." The teacher squinted, surveying me, clearly puzzled. "Isn't she part white?"

"Being Negro is a political definition," I explained, trying to still my beating heart. "As all racial categorizations are. She's seen as Negro by our culture. In a racist country anyone with 'one drop' of Negro blood is black. Southern court cases have established that. We want our children to have an identity that fits the one the culture puts on them."

The teacher appeared baffled.

"Well, the culture is fucked up about race!" I grew heated. At a time when biracial identity sounded like an attempt to fade out of blackness, my husband and I were adamant. Our children, in the latest terminology, were becoming African American.

Forty years later, when it comes to my three grandkids, I've lost all certainty. Now I'm the one who's bewildered: my mid-twentieth-century categories don't fit twenty-first-century reality.

Chloe, my nine-year-old granddaughter, and I have created a Chit-Chat Club, the CCC; being a precise child, she times our cross-country chats. One hour and thirty-three minutes is our record. We talk about everything.

"I loved *Hairspray*," this blond preteen gushes. "I've seen it four times."

"Me, too," I tell her, wondering what she makes of the racial clash at the heart of the movie.

"It's so funny when Penny's mother ties her up and Seaweed gets her out!" She giggles, remembering the scene.

Does Chloe understand that Penny's white mother restrained her because her boyfriend, Seaweed, is black? Is this a movie Chloe sees as having no relationship to her own life? Her own great-grandparents, both sets, did not attend my wedding to her grandfather, for the same reason. But I'm not ready to tell her that—not yet.

In a stunning family portrait Chloe drew for me last Thanksgiving, there are my partner Carole and I, pasty-faced, arm in arm. There is her dad, his face colored brown; there she is, beside her mom and one brother, all three colored with pale orange marker, while her younger brother is painted brown like his dad. She's accurately represented the varying color tones of the family. What I am so curious about, what I have to bite my tongue not to ask, is whether she attaches any social significance to the variegation. Does she honestly regard the tones the way I did my brown-eyed sister and my blue-eyed brother, those characteristics devoid of meaning?

I tread lightly. Sometimes I wonder if I should be bolder, the way I was as a young mother, but I'm waiting for a cue. I don't want to create tension or confusion where there is none. When it comes to race, the loquacious radical mom of the past has morphed into the circumspect grandmother of the present.

Likewise with my choice of partners. I lectured my own embarrassed teens once I was divorced and became lovers with Carole, angrily countering their "Mothers can't be lesbians!" with, basically, "You'll have to get used to it!" Today my same-sex spousal status is hardly worthy of mention. My grandchildren have known us comfortably since birth as "Grandma Carole and Grandma Joan," one loving entity living far away in California, who regularly fly in to shower them with affection and gifts.

I haven't told them that their dad didn't whisper to even one person the nature of Carole's and my relationship for nearly fifteen years, although when he did come out, he did it spectacularly, in a public assembly at the button-down school where he teaches. "Don't hide the way I did," he urged the students. "If anyone in your family is gay or lesbian, please come and talk to me, if no one else. You don't want to lose out in intimacy with that family member, the way I did with my mom until I finally acknowledged her in her fullness. And until I understood that the things about her that I didn't like, I'd all put onto her being a lesbian."

Thirty years after Carole and I met, the world is so different that his children would be amazed, were they to hear his tale. But when will I tell them? What am I waiting for?

For them to make the first move. I've grown more humble with age, and when it comes to them, more cautious. Even with the election of President Barack Obama, it's a more conservative era, and I'm aware of my limitations as a grandma who pops in and out every few months, rather than a presence with daily or weekly contact. I try. I regularly send off homemade books I write and draw as souvenirs after our visits, or record tapes with stories I create or sing lullabies they can play at night. I call. I'm part of their family's weekly football pool, boning up on a sport I've always hated to keep up with my grandson Ryan, a football zealot. Last year I even watched the Super Bowl so we could talk at half-time and after the game. "Hey, did you see that amazing 100-yard run Harrison made?" I shouted over the speakerphone at his house.

"Yeah." I could tell Ryan was grinning ear to ear. "That was craaaazy." He has the cutest way of saying "crazy"; that sweet word alone was worth watching the whole game (although I was surprised to discover how much I enjoyed the grace of the sport).

"And what about Holmes, when he jumped so high and landed on both toes over the end line?" I said knowledgeably, picking up my lingo from the announcers.

"I know," Ryan said. "I couldn't believe it."

I hung on to every precious syllable of this child who enchants me.

"With three Cardinals on him. That was amazing." Ryan paused, then said abruptly, as he often does when ending phone conversations, "Here's my dad."

Despite joining the children in every arena I can find, from football to Hannah Montana, I don't feel I have the right to introduce such laden topics as race that could affect them so deeply. Not yet, maybe never. Maybe when they get older, they'll muse on it easily.

Strangers ask my pale daughter-in-law where she "got" her dark-skinned younger son, exactly the way passersby used to ask me the very same question about my obviously "other race" children. So all three grandkids have heard the questioning; they visit their African American grandpa, and half their overflowing bookshelves feature African American characters. Still, I hold back.

About Carole and me, they've never asked either, even when they participated in our lavish November 1, 2008, wedding, held during the five-month window of legality in San Francisco. "Let me see the rings," our youngest grandson demanded that morning, grabbing them from his seven-year-old brother. "I want to carry them." For him, at age four, the glittering gold rings, not his grandmas' union, were the focus of interest. Several times during our vows I heard the rings clatter from his chubby fists, hitting the floor while his parents scrambled to find them. "No," I heard his mother hiss once. "Chloe will hold them now." I pictured the two rings on her lap, tied once again snugly to the tiny black velvet pillows my mother had sewn.

"How should I scatter the rose petals?" our granddaughter had asked anxiously more than once over the weeks before the big event, during one of our long-distance Chit Chats. But not one child queried the fact that two women were getting married. For them it was normal.

One high point of the whole event for me, as nourishing rain splattered the windows, was when Che rose, obviously moved, to tell our friends and family that Carole and I were the model for his own marriage. Back in 1981, could I have even imagined that? Still, I suppose that this too was simply another moment in an altogether fun day for the kids, one whose highlight was undoubtedly our three-tiered cake, not their father's declaration of support for his mom and stepmom. Ryan had stood wide-eyed before the cake, which towered on a table above him, for half an hour before we ceremoniously sliced into it.

As the world has changed, so have we all. That is surely a large part of the reason my relationship with grandkids differs so much from how it was with my own kids forty-some years ago, when they were young and scruffy, back in the grubby '60s. Perhaps the difference is more than a change of era: maybe that particular, unique intimacy of mother and child is not replicable in part-time grandparenthood, no matter how deep my feelings for Chloe, Ryan, and Douglass run. They put endless smiles on my face. I dote shamelessly. Yet at the end of the day, when I leave Washington, DC, to fly home to Berkeley, these three delectable children are somebody else's responsibility. Being aware of that, I am reluctant to drop the potential bomb of race on their doorstep. Instead I await their lead as they guide me into the next decade of the twenty-first century, one whose reigning stance on these old social issues is subtler and more nuanced. They already inhabit their world so naturally.

Race, gender, sexual preference … blurring these categories, as a path to equality, has been my life's work. Now that we're here, I'm not sure how to fit my old mind around the new reality. I wait for my grandchildren to lead, to take me by the hand and pull me on. At the right time I will have much to impart, about the way things used to be, when that social data, intertwined with their family history, is useful to them. Now, as young children, these three precious beings are so engaged in their day-to-day lives that the moment is not ripe. A day will come when they pose a question. "Why," they may ask, crinkling their sweet brows, "did Penny's mom tie her up in the movie? Why did they all march in the street?" Or "Why did you change your name when you got married, Grandma Joan? Our mom didn't."

Oh, I'll be ready to teach. But until then, it's my turn to learn.

In and Out of Step

· · · · · · · · · · · · · · · ·

Gloria Avner

A great gift to our grandchildren is just to be our own creative, eccentric, individual selves. These are wonderful gifts, modestly and confidently displayed; they show a grandchild there are many ways to be. Gloria Avner shows the depth and resonance of sharing different ways of seeing the world and different religious traditions in doing art together. She takes her grandchildren and herself seriously—with marvelous dollops of humor.

I skipped childbearing and went directly to grandmotherhood. My partner had four children when I met him, the youngest turning two, the oldest barely twelve. He did not want any more. We made it so. But as we all grew up and out of our smaller selves, I was as eager for these children's children as any parent could be.

They started coming seventeen years ago; the newest is barely two months old. I knew each grandchild long before birth. I welcomed each within hours of their entry, and it is my belief that knowledge and love breed rights of connection. I almost said, and still may say, possession—though I know all children, grand or otherwise, are ours only on loan.

They are mine as much as they belong to anyone who shares DNA with them. Even when they do something so stupid I would rather not be associated with the act, or when they hold my grandparenty feet to the fire and show me to be not quite as cool as I'd like to think, or not quite the paragon of virtue and good decision making as I might wish, they are still mine. I'll defend unto death their right to make mistakes, tease me, and become who they are meant to be.

The oldest two make fun of my driving. If their perceptions weren't so spot-on, down to how I hold my steering wheel, I'd get upset. The youngest two thrive on pure attention and seem to know intuitively that what they do with me will be in the realm of making art or playing in nature. I was a governess once, for a professor's three-year-old and infant, traveling from the States to England. The wife spoke only French. The three-year-old, when we arrived in England, knew exactly, intuitively, to whom he would speak French and to whom he would speak English. Sometimes I think that our grandchildren are not unlike Michelangelo's sculptures. We are not creating them, but easing them "out of the stone," helping them become what and who they already are.

I teach through doing and making, being and storytelling. We garden, make bonfires, walk dogs, pet cats. We play squiggle while waiting for food in restaurants (one person quickly marks a piece of paper and the other adds to it to make a recognizable picture); we play twenty questions in the car when driving long distances. They help me and their grandfather create displays in our gallery.

My eldest granddaughter and I have played imagination games for years, walking out to our pond pretending we are riding ponies to an Indian powwow, bringing with us baskets that we've made and rugs we've woven. We pound acorns into mush with rocks. We shoot wild turkeys with our bows and arrows and make stew for the elders and the warriors. We play that we are traders, and when I ask her (now fourteen and towering over me, but then between six and eleven) what she would trade her finest goods for, the answer was always the same.

"Puppies."

I am of a different tribe. Unlike them, I grew up Jewish, then looked East to Buddhism for years, and West to Native American spirituality as well. The grandchildren always noticed and fell in love with what inspired awe. They knew names of Hindu gods and goddesses, treasured crystals and heart stones before they went to preschool, and looked forward to baking cookies for the birthday celebration of Ganesh, the elephant-headed Hindu god, every August. They appreciated Buddha statues for birthday presents. Even with raucous football buddies over for dinner, they are respectful on a Friday night when I light Sabbath candles and sing blessings over them. They like matzo balls in chicken soup and brisket with gravy.

We are nothing if not eclectic.

Part of my role, maybe any grandmother's role I think, is to be a holder of memory. I don't hold memories of their parents' grandparents, but I look at the recently sarcastic, always contrarian and articulate six-foot-two football-playing grandchild who loves bodybuilding and contact sports, who gets into trouble way too often through misplaced loyalty, and I see the little five-year-old boy who hid under a bench at his first Tae Kwon Do class. I see the boy who loves baking bread with his mother and advises me on the proper way to make a "bed" of spices for spaghetti sauce. I hear him sophomorically knocking organized religion and am flabbergasted by his insight when he says to me, "Oh, Bubby. You're not religious, you're spiritual."

My grandchildren are my teachers, just as I am theirs. They teach me about ineffables like patience and the meaning of comfort, about what a gift it is to prepare and receive homemade food. I have been taught all the positions on a football team and what their duties are (would that I could remember). They taught me how to work an iPod, how to play myriad games, and how, above all, not to be pushy and interfering.

But what do we do about memory and held resentment? This same oldest grandson, about to turn seventeen, held onto anger well into his early teens over an incident that happened when he was two! He would talk about it regularly, about being brought by Nana, his other grandmother, on her way to work, to spend the day with us when he did not want to. He wanted his mother, and we could not make him understand.

His mother was in the hospital, unable to take nourishment except through an IV. She was six months pregnant with his puppy-loving sister-to-be, had a severe inoperable gallbladder problem, and all grandparents were sharing child care during her challenging last trimester. We could not explain it to him, but only distract him with games and food and paint and love. Distraction did happen, but the inner fury remained. Maybe, someday, it will serve him well, or one of us, his grandparents, will figure out how to teach the art of letting go.

There are three new grandchildren now, all younger than four, all belonging to my partner's oldest and the last to marry, his son. There will be many more lessons I'm sure, for all of us, those who share DNA and non-blood Bubby me. The youngest, named Trevor by his parents, was renamed his first day on earth by his three-and-a-half-year-old sister. She swears that her name is the right one and the rest of us just heard it wrong. "His name is Treasure," she shouts, "like what pirates want." I can't say she is wrong.

The Whirling Heart Dance of Grandmothering

SAPHIRA LINDEN

The new grandchild born amid tragedy to people who have been through grief and hopelessness becomes a beacon of hope—a radiant presence who can bring back happiness. The author describes the rich heritage that baby Xavi is born into: Sufi, Catholic, Jewish, and Protestant grandparents, now reeling at having lost most of their life savings in the Bernard Madoff fraud of 2009. For these grieving elders, this new child is a tremendous joy.

I HAVE BEEN A GRANDMOTHER for seven months. This grandchild has several grandparents, at least four grandmothers and three grandfathers. If I marry again, the number goes up to four grandpas. She also has a great-grandmother, my mother. Our mutual granddaughter is fortunate. She has grandparents with such diverse backgrounds and careers that they could be a Global Interfaith Council.

It was so simple growing up. Two sets of grandparents who we visited regularly, sometimes both sets on the same Sunday. For Passover, we went the first night to my dad's parents' house for the Seder. I remember how fast Grandpa (Louis) Linden chanted the service in Hebrew while everyone talked, and Grandma (Lena) Linden was in the kitchen cooking, yelling back and forth. It was very festive. Afterward, grandma would sneak candy to us after my mom had strongly told her not to do that. She closed both eyes a couple of times in a mischievous wink. This happened regularly. My mother says she made good gefilte fish, chicken soup, and other things. Grandma put her phone in the closet. We told her she wouldn't be able to hear the phone ring if she did that. That was fine with her. She was a character, who made us laugh.

As I reflect on her life now, she seemed to have a great deal of joy even though she came from worlds of family tragedy. The youngest of thirteen children and the only girl, she survived all her brothers, who were killed in the Holocaust. She came from an educated family and pushed her three sons into the best educations and careers. The youngest was a teacher and later a very successful real estate broker. The middle son was a merchant who went back to school to become a lawyer and then became an uncontested judge for many years. My dad was a successful CPA, senior partner in the largest local, primarily Jewish, accounting firm in Detroit. My Grandma Lena married Louis, who was a tailor. He was a sweet, simple man. She was the driving force behind her boys' aspirations and success.

And then there were mom's parents: George and Dora. Grandma Trute was so loved by all. She was the one who seemed most selfless and accepting of all of her grandchildren, who were all so very different. And she also was an incredible cook. (I am told that my father would fill up on her food before he went to his mother's house to eat.) What I remember most was Grandma Trute's strudel. She would take all day to bake her strudel with the thinnest, crispiest layers of crust I have ever tasted. My sister tried to write down the recipe one time, while Grandma was preparing her strudel. Jill said it didn't work because Grandma added a bit of this and a bit of that, and it wasn't possible to make sense out of her process.

When these grandparents moved closer to us and to our school, I sometimes went to their house for lunch. That was very special. My mom spoke about how important education was to grandma and how she supported her children in their journey to go to college in a time when that was not the norm, especially for women. Mom didn't have to do her job of washing the floors in the family house when she went to college because one of her younger siblings took it on. Grandpa Trute had been a blacksmith in the old country. When he came here, he did the same work. When there were no more horses to shoe, he made ornamental metal fences. My new grandchild Xavi's father is a metal sculptor who has created ornamental metal fences. Grandpa Trute's last job was in the automobile industry when we lived in Detroit. It was fun to get him to smile. He often seemed sad, but he was always nice to his grandchildren. But again, it was Grandma Trute who encouraged education.

I had an extraordinary experience when she died. My husband and I were meditating all day with our meditation students. I remember the small room at the Boston Center for the Arts, where my theater company was housed. We had been meditating with different students, offering them practices and guidance for several hours when my friend, another Sufi meditation teacher, came in the room between students. She told me that my family had called to tell me that my Grandma Trute had passed on. I was in a very high state at the time. I closed my eyes and saw her spirit soaring joyously from her paralyzed body that had burdened her for so long. I felt an ecstatic sense of her freedom now. I knew that she was offering me a gift of her inspiring, loving, devoted example and hoped that I could carry on for her in that regard. The experience of that moment has stayed with me all these years.

I can only pray that the spirit of my grandmothers can inspire me with their grace, humor, and unconditional love with this new grandchild and others who may grace this earth in the future.

All of Xavi's grandparents have been encouraged to take on different names so she can distinguish us better. We have Opa and Oma; Grandfleur and Grandgee; Grammie Grahm; and I vacillate between Grandma Saphira (how ordinary!) and Bubbe. My son encourages Bubbe; my daughter-in-law says it's up to me. My mother, her only great-grandmother, is Gee Gee.

It is now twenty-one months into grandparenthood. Xavi is an extraordinary soul. I am not objective. Besides being the most charming, beautiful, graceful little soul on the planet, she is a strong, creative initiator and easily makes her desires and feelings known. She is so fun to be with. She helps me reconnect to my own inner child, who loves to play. My own work in drama therapy is based on play. She is one of my best teachers now, when I'm at a low because of having lost—as so many others have also—a huge amount of my life savings in the Madoff investment scandal.

Her parents are both so attentive and conscious with her on all levels, from food to potty training, from creative activities to letting her needs dictate the family rhythm. Her mother is still nursing, and both of them seem to love it. Xavi's words are developing by the day, but even without them, it is usually clear what she wants.

Xavi had a home water birth. She came into the world in a rented inflatable pool. Grandfleur, the grandma who lived in the area and who had been a midwife, was present. I have to admit I was envious. She assisted the attending midwife. Even though it had been a long time since she'd been a practicing midwife, I was pleased that she was there, but it was hard to be across the country.

When Xavi was six months old, I offered to take her and her mom to a dance concert, when my son was busy. My daughter-in-law remembered that at the Berklee Arts Center there is an unused lighting booth where they let people with babies watch a concert, giving them the freedom to yell or cry without disturbing the audience. We watched an extraordinary dance company from Moscow and held Xavi up to the window, which provided a pretty good view. Sound was piped in through speakers. The dances were varied, with very brightly colored costumes, incredible energy, and vibrancy. Our little one began to move to the music in rhythm as she was watching, with intensity and amazing focus. Her mom and I looked at each other in amazement. So, do we have a Martha Graham on our hands or perhaps a Margot Fonteyn? I guess every grandma thinks like that.

Xavi does seem to be a budding artist, dancer, musician, and actor. Why shouldn't she be? Painting, sculpting, acting, playwriting, directing, dancing, songwriting, singing, guitar playing, creative writing, and even performance whistling are in the experience of her grandparents. Xavi's mom is gifted in a variety of art forms; her dad is a metal sculptor and has been a painter. Together, they have remodeled their apartments. He has built furniture, kitchen counters, fences, and much more; my daughter-in-law has been active in interior design, made curtains and a bed cornester, refurbished a chandelier, and much more.

I have been in theater all my life. From a very early age, I was reciting stories to my imaginary audience, standing on my bed. I seemed to have a natural flare for the dramatic. My family thought they were funny when they called me Sarah "Heartburn." That said, I was supported in my budding talent. By the age of eight, I had taken ballet, piano, and drama lessons. I am grateful for my mother's love of the arts. (She was a singer.) I appreciated how she schlepped all four of us kids to lessons, scouts, and other activities throughout our upbringing.

Three of Xavi's grandparents lost most of their life savings in the Madoff fraud. I call losing all my life savings in the collapse my "Madoff initiation." But it is Xavi, whom I connect to on Skype from Boston and in San Francisco in person, who brings me hope for the future. She was a year-and-a-half old when Madoff was arrested, to the day. This child represents a new generation, after the current major shift in consciousness that we are all a part of. We are moving from the death of the old systems to rebirth of the new. When I watch her in playgroups with other children of many different ethnic and racial backgrounds, she helps me remember one of our Sufi ideals that envisions the whole of humanity as a single family in the parenthood of God. When I am with her, I experience this bright soul as pure love itself, and I feel deep gratitude to have her as a grandchild.

All of Xavi's grandparents have showered her with gifts of different kinds. For me, my favorite gifts were supporting her mom's wish to take Xavi to music lessons and most recently to music and dance class. This has been a great joy. The music lessons I paid for in full. After Madoff, I could only contribute to the payment of the music and dance class. That made me sad, maybe more so than a lot of other losses.

Try as her parents and grandparents have to not be sexist or encourage stereotypical female clothing, toys, or activities, this little girl has always gravitated to jewelry and beautiful shoes, and likes to pick out her own clothes—before the age of two! True, she has her own style; the other day, she chose a crinoline slip that was picked up at a secondhand store, which she put on by herself, keeping the rest of her body nude. Recently, when I Skyped, she was sitting on her papa's lap nude with something around her neck. Her papa moved the computer closer and she showed me: "Necklis," she said, eyeing and fingering her newest treasure.

When I was last with her, we read a book together on colors. Blue seemed to be her favorite. "What color is your necklace?" I asked. "Bluuue," she answered. Yes, one of the favorite colors of our Linden family. At one point, my parents, my four grown siblings, and I, all living in different places, discovered we all had blue cars. On Xavi's great-grandmother's ninetieth birthday, everyone was invited to wear blue, and the restaurant and cake were decorated in blue, her favorite color. Xavi was three months old. Perhaps she was impressed through osmosis.

Ah, technology! Mostly, technology creates more work for me. Now, I not only have three phones (home, business, and cell), but two computers (desktop and laptop) that have to be continually updated to be able to talk to each other. It's like two people of different backgrounds in conflict, learning each other's language. I had an early computer since Xavi's paternal grandfather is a crackerjack computer scientist. He once told me he could make a computer dance. He and his current wife began to use Skype to communicate with Xavi; my son suggested I do it as well.

At last, though not with perfect sound, there she was! How wonderful to see her wave and talk to me in her gibberish language.

I am a number two on the Enneagram, a system of soul and personality types. I love to give meaningful little gifts to people. Over the years, I have come to see that the enjoyment I receive from finding things and offering them can mean as much or more to me than to the recipient. It's a fun pursuit. I shop all year long for the next Hanukkah and Christmas.

Hanukkah is eight days, so I get to give eight gifts, one for each night. My children, their partners, nephews, nieces, other stepchildren, and their kids have all gotten gifts like this. I have a storage closet that is all gifts. A second closet for luggage and holiday paraphernalia holds the overflow. The gifts in my closets are often bought with someone in mind. Once Xavi was born, well ... you can imagine how delightful it was to buy things for this precious little girl. After raising two sons, how fun this is. How lucky it is that I had all of these things already. Since the Madoff disaster, I have been able to find things for her in my own closet, without spending a cent.

Hazart Inayat Khan has said,
>My heart is no more mine.
>It is thine own, my spiritual guide.

I believe Xavi has come in to help heal the heart wounds of our complex family system. For me and perhaps others, she has become a kind of spiritual guide.

We grandparents have a wide range of religious backgrounds. Two of us were brought up Jewish, one Reform and one Conservative that for me evolved into Jewish Mysticism. Two of us were born Catholic, one became Episcopal, then interested in Buddhism, then discovered the Dead Sea Scrolls and got into Judaism, teaching in a Jewish day care, and sees herself as a universal Christian. Another was raised Presbyterian, became a Quaker, and converted to Judaism. Another was born Protestant, and another came from a Catholic mother who was excommunicated when she married a Protestant. She went to a friend's Presbyterian church and, like many of us, later rebelled from organized religion as she knew it.

Many of Xavi's grandparents are formal spiritual teachers trained in the Sufi meditation tradition, and all of her grandparents have been teachers and guides in a variety of venues. Sufism is not a religion. One of the etymological roots of Sufism is Sophia, the wisdom underneath all religions. The Sufi Order that five of us were trained in is an esoteric school that teaches meditation from all of the traditions. It is a universal approach out of which a Universal Worship Service evolved that honors all religions and spiritual paths at the same altar. Candles are lit to honor the traditions of the Great Mother (the many goddess traditions), Hinduism, Buddhism, Zoroastrianism, Native American teachings, Judaism, Christianity, Islam, and the last candle to "all those whether known or unknown to the world, who have held aloft the light of truth amidst the darkness of human ignorance."

From my vantage point, I see that our little Xavi may represent for her many grandparents the light of truth. Like many souls coming in at this time, she reflects us back to ourselves. Authentic spiritual teachers, empty of their limited selves, mirror back to the disciple who they really are, in their essential soul selves. Similarly, as we train Transpersonal Drama Therapists and work with clients, we learn and practice how to get beyond our limited sense of ourselves and mirror the core self back to our students and clients, beyond trauma and early negative conditioning.

In the times I have spent with Xavi, engaged in play with her as well as on Skype, I have often felt her loving, radiant spirit bring me back to that part of my soul self that is innocent, light-filled, angelic, and playful. What a gift.

Many of Xavi's grandparents have hurt and been hurt by others of us. When divorces have been a part of your experience, there is always pain, unresolved issues, and at least an underlying tension.

Having seen each grandparent with Xavi at one time or another in the last two years, I have noticed that every time a grandparent was engaged with her, my heart quickened. I have never seen anything but warm, wonderful connections with each grandparent. Other than feeling sometimes that I cannot get enough of this light-filled being for myself, it has been a delight to watch how joyous and loving each grandparent has been with her, each in their own way. What a treasure this little girl is receiving and in turn offering to us. I can't help but wonder how our world would change if everyone related to everyone else in these ways.

September 11, 2001, was the attack on the twin towers. On December 11, 2008, Madoff was arrested. June 11 is Xavi's birthday. I am writing this on her second birthday. Singing "Happy Birthday" to her on Skype symbolizes, for me, the hope for the future. A Sufi teaching says that music will be the next religion because it is the only thing that goes right to the heart, transcending distinctions and differences that divide us. A child's smile and her own version of making music does, indeed, go directly to the heart.

On my last visit to see her, it was clear that Xavi had learned many new words. She seemed to understand everything (well, almost). Visiting California several times in these two years means coming home to Boston hitting the ground running. This time was particularly overwhelming, trying to play catch-up with work. I often arrange work in California: doing therapy, conducting supervision of my California students, facilitating workshops, and speaking at universities. Since "Madoff with My Money" happened, I was working much harder because I had to let my office manager go. I was trying to do even more work than usual to bring in income, while also sorting through and organizing the piles on three desk surfaces.

My son called on Skype. Funny how all my desk work joyfully goes out the window when they call. We had a lovely talk. After a while, I blurt out, "So, where are your beautiful wife and daughter?" My daughter-in-law yells to Xavi's dad from the other room. I can hear her. "Just move the laptop so we can see each other." Five seconds later, there they are, clear as life, languishing in the bathtub together. They are taking a seaweed bath. Strips of flat green seaweed are swimming on their bodies. Wow! I have been told that I need more seaweed in my diet by my nutritionist. Xavi's mom says that they are having a healthy, relaxing spa experience. How cool is that?

Could any of us have done this with our mothers, the seaweed bath and then for our moms, when they were grandmas, to see us nude in real time? Most of us would say, "Not on her life!"

So, I wave on the computer, as I always do. I tell Xavi that it looks like she is having fun. I tell her I miss her already, which is the truth, even though I had just come home from a visit a few days earlier.

Each of her parents say, "Did you hear what she said to you?"

"No," I answered.

"Miss you," I am told.

"Oh, she doesn't really know what that means," I say. "Cute."

Her parents say in unison, "She certainly does." And to make the point clear, Xavi says it again on her own.

How is it that two words, heartfelt, from a not quite two-year-old, can have such an effect on me? Her loving spirit filled me for the entire day.

Hazrat Inayat Kahn has said,
> My heart has become an ocean,
> Beloved, since thou has poured thy love into it.

Perhaps the most important teaching of any spiritual path is to heal our hearts and learn how to receive and give love, regardless of anything else in our lives. Grandchildren can be the gift given to us as the vehicle to do this. Even though our world and our lives are in crisis on so many fronts, for me, this little granddaughter has been a joyous, loving treasure that helps give me faith and hope for my future and for the possibilities for the next generation.

Carving Paths in Snow
The Learning Curves of Two Generations

....

GILL WRIGHT MILLER

*An outdoor outing takes a turn for the worse, as skis, limbs, and tem-
pers tangle. A seven-year-old learns the consequences of his own actions, and a grandmother learns something about her own behavior.
Three cheers for substantial outings and working toward meaningful
communication with a young person.*

I AM AN ACADEMIC, AND it is December. Every calendar year comes to one
of those overwhelming endings, as final exams slated for the twenty-
first slide in just ahead of serious Christmas complications. What keeps
showing up on television as a "calm and loving family time" proves
instead to be too much to do in too short a time. Once exams are graded,
the days present mainly as complicated scheduling dilemmas with disappointments lurking inside every neatly wrapped attempt at getting
my boys, their partners, and the grandchildren in the same room as a
decorated tree, hot cocoa, and people enjoying each other in bathrobes.

Actually my "boys" are not boys; they are adults now. They have partners with families of their own. My partner, too, has parents who live out
of town. Everyone I love is being pulled in ten directions for the holidays.
I am a border collie when it comes to herding my family at Christmas,
and I can't quite see how I'm going to witness two little grandsons sneaking downstairs in their jammies, wiping sleep from their eyes. It's an
important experience to me, one I am having trouble giving up. In a moment of unexpected brilliance, I yield the calendar date instead, suggesting my little family select December 29 for our Christmas celebration.

Both Christmas and Boxing Day slip by without notice. Four days
later, my children (now ages thirty-six, thirty-four, twenty-nine, and
twenty-four), their partners, and the two grandchildren (ages seven and

four) gather in New York City to celebrate. We have selected New York because three of my four boys live there. The fourth, Chris, lives in Granville, Ohio, as I do, and is coming from Philadelphia with his wife, Mary, and two children, where they have spent Christmas Day with her parents. My partner Jamie and I fly from Granville, extra suitcases stuffed with wrapped packages, and arrive on West 68th Street, take an elevator, trudge down a slim hallway, and slog through a double-locked door to find two small boys mesmerized by Wii tennis on a fifty-two-inch screen.

"Hi, guys!" I shout, a big cheerleader smile on my face, exhausted from the trip but happy to have arrived. I was sure they'd knock me over with hugs to the knees. There was no response.

"Hey," I try again.

Wop, whoosh, bop.

"Ohhhh," voices bemoan something on the screen.

Someone large turns off the TV. Someone small notices the presents coming out of the luggage.

"Can we open them?" Campbell asks.

"Not yet," his father says. "You'll have to wait until after dinner."

The conversation turns to what they had been doing since arriving in New York. It was clear they were feeling apartment-bound and overwhelmed by the city. Having lost his job in the economic downturn, my second son, the only one with children to support, was struggling to feed his family in the Midwest. A trip to New York was a true hardship. I knew what was in those boxes and impulsively thought they might provide a moment of glee.

"Maybe the boys could open one present now?" I half-ask, half-instruct the parents. Before a decision is reached, paper is everywhere and two pairs of shiny hockey skates have been revealed.

"Why don't we take them ice skating this afternoon?" I ask. Rockefeller Plaza seemed the perfect holiday location, but if that turned out to be too crazy, the American Museum of Natural History was sporting an indoor rink made of synthetic ice. The grandchildren were only overlapping with us for one day; this was a perfect intergenerational activity and would give the parents a few moments in New York on their own.

"We're going to a movie," my daughter-in-law announced. "It's too cold outside to skate. Besides, the boys are too tired. They didn't get any decent sleep." I am a bit stunned from all angles. Movies are unimaginative, they are costly, they can be seen in Ohio, they are readily available through the TV, and they have nothing to do with families at Christmas. The antidote to TV-screen tired is physical activity. Ohio living offers openness in both space and time. In contrast, New York apartments are small and contained, and the visitors' schedule is packed with hovering parents. Ice skating—with a grandparent in charge—seemed the perfect offer. But it is not to be.

Feeling disappointed, Jamie and I leave the other wrapped packages for the evening event and walk north on Broadway. We need to check into Hotel Beacon, shop for Christmas dinner for eleven at the Fairway across the street, and do a bit of mental reorganizing. That had not gone well. I feel depleted. I find myself wanting to teach my grandchildren the feelings my grandmother had taught me.

I was raised in a small Midwest suburb of Columbus, Ohio. My mother was legally blind and didn't do one of the main things most suburban housewives did: drive carpool. Instead of carting my five siblings and me off to one lesson or another, she was almost always home, tending to our morning needs, making lunch a special midday chat, and coordinating house chores, dinner, homework, bath time, prayers, and bedtime reading. My mother was always waiting to hear our stories.

My father was equally unconventional in a '50s middle-class neighborhood. Raised as an only child by a single mom, he loved the busyness of the family he had created. In the summers, he came from work to the community swimming pool, put on a diving display for the locals, and then drove us home for dinner. In the winters, he took us skiing at a tiny little resort sixty-five miles northeast. It was my father who did the grocery shopping and my father who chauffeured shopping trips, birthday party carpools, and the annual family vacation.

My parents lived six healthy blocks from my maternal grandparents—far enough to be in different neighborhoods, close enough for us to walk. The union of an Irish Catholic man and an Irish Protestant woman, my grandparents raised their five daughters in the Episcopal Church. We spent every Sunday lunchtime at Mamaw and Grandpa's, with the most well-behaved earning the privilege of riding from church to Resch's Bakery for fresh bread or donuts on the way home. On those special car trips, my grandparents had the opportunity to speak with us about "family."

On birthdays, my grandmother appeared bright and early in the mornings with small presents for everyone. "We are all happy that Gill was born today," she would exclaim. I was as excited for my siblings' birthdays as I was for my own. It was my grandmother who taught me I was part of a family. So, in between those Sunday events and family celebrations, I often trekked to my grandmother's just to smell her house, sit among the lilies of the valley, share my stories, and listen to hers.

It occurred to me that my own mother was not one to pop into my house early in the morning, did not drive my children places one at a time, and had died when my oldest child was just ten, the youngest not yet born. My boys had not experienced the benefit of a grandmother the way I had. My son was not able to meet me halfway because he had not experienced the path; it was not part of his early experience. Perhaps he didn't really know how a grandmother fit into his family.

With Chris, Mary, and the grandchildren back in Ohio in early January, I called Campbell, age seven, and asked him if we could play hooky and go skiing on the first great snow day, just the two of us.

"Yes!" he replied with uncharacteristic enthusiasm.

"OK," I said, "here's what we'll do. You do the best you can to help around the house. Pick up your toys. Eat your dinner. Be nice to your brother. Ask your mom if you can help with the chores. I'll check the weather report and call your parents to see if they will let you go."

"Call my dad," Campbell said into the phone. I smiled, realizing he already knew which parent to ask for which favor.

Campbell is a stellar student, having been enrolled in a tiny private Montessori school since he was three. He is particularly fond of math and science, but ahead in all subjects. His social skills, however, were lagging a bit, given the tiny number of children at his school. This year, his parents had elected to switch him to public school. They placed him in first grade so he would have time and space to learn how to contend with twenty other classmates.

"I already completed first grade," he was the first to tell you. "Now I'm doing it again." He had a bit of a short fuse about this humiliating decision. But it was equally clear that waiting his turn in a crowd was a challenge for him; patience was a lesson he had to learn. Still, missing a day of school was not going to interrupt his spelling or math scores. It would provide him with a day of rest from the crowded classroom. On a Wednesday night, there was a prediction for twelve inches of fresh powder. I called to see if he could miss school.

"Campbell?" his father asked, "Do you have any interest in going skiing with your grandmother tomorrow?"

"Yes!" he answered again. I could hear the twinkle in his eye. Our plan had worked.

"What time do your mom and brother leave for school?" I asked him.

"Eight," he said.

"I'll pick you up at 8:05."

Early the next morning, the air was filled with wondrous large flakes pouring out of the sky like floating feathers after a pillow fight. I arrived promptly. We stuffed extra clothes and blankets into the back of the car and headed north to discover each other on the slopes.

On the drive, we chatted about his new school, his little brother, his karate lessons, and soccer games. I asked him about his favorite winter activity. He asked if we could go skiing every weekend. "Yes," I said, "every weekend there is snow, we will go skiing together." Maybe, we chuckled, we'd even invite his parents. "We don't have to," he said. I let that thought hang in the air, hoping I was hearing him correctly—that he would like having something special with me.

An hour and a half later we pulled into 3100 Possum Run Road and parked right next to the lodge. The Snow Trails slopes weren't open quite yet, but the rental office was just waking up, lights on, a quiet buzz in the air. The park was nearly empty on this school day morning.

Twenty minutes later, boots and skis on, poles in tow, we made our way over to the first lift. It's a bit of an uphill climb, designed that way to make the last run into the lodge much easier. But for Campbell, who hadn't been skiing since last season, it felt impossible. Discouraged and grumpy, he was having one private temper tantrum after the next.

"Ahhh," he grumbled, "I can't do this. I'm just no good. I hate skiing."

I ignored his complaining for the first few minutes. Settling, my grandmother used to call it. Working out the kinks. "No need to respond," she would say. "The child is just talking to himself." Then it got to be too much.

"I'm not skiing with you," I announced matter-of-factly, as I slid beyond him.

"Grama!" he shouted at me. "Where are you going?"

"I don't want to ski with you. You're too grouchy. It's not fun to listen to you. I'm skiing by myself."

"You can't," he insisted. "You have to help me."

"No, I don't," I called over one shoulder. "I don't want to help you. I don't even want to ski with you."

As the gap between us got larger and larger, we continued our exchange. Now we were shouting just to be heard.

"OK," he finally conceded. "I'll stop it."

"I don't believe you," I said. "I don't think you know how."

"I will," he insisted.

Stopping my forward motion, I let his declaration sit in the air a second before I asked, "Promise?"

"I promise. It's just that …"

"Uhhhhhhhh," I shouted, one hand up in the air, stopping him abruptly. "I don't want to know why you're doing it. You haven't been skiing in a whole year, and you think you're going to be as good as you were at the end of last season. It doesn't work that way. You have to give your body a chance to remember. Stop telling yourself it's not working. You have to fall ten times—ten times!—before you're allowed to say you're not good at this. And then, after ten falls, it'll be OK to complain, and we'll try to figure out why it's not working. Right now, this is just about remembering. And you're not giving yourself a chance."

His eyes were full of tears and dismay.

"OK," he said quietly, and made his way over to the lift.

"When you can turn and stop, pick a destination and get there, and collapse to the ground on command, we can go to the next level," I promised on the way up.

"Does that count as a fall? One of my ten?" he asked.

"No," I reassured him. "It means you can get yourself out of a pickle if all else fails." He giggled at that funny expression.

Over the course of the day, we had made our way from the Bunny Hill to the Greens Squares, to the Blues Circles, and on to the (Ohio) Black Diamonds. We had developed a set of games that included taking turns carving paths through the snow, challenging each other on "Follow the Leader" routes through the trees, and chasing each other in a "Cat and Mouse" game, skiing as fast as we could across as many moguls as we could find. Each run we were exchanging high fives at the top and laughing more and more at the bottom. His body had remembered last year's skills, and it was picking up new ones quickly.

Campbell was not quite tall enough to ride the chairlifts so I had to hoist him onto it and fling him off.

"Tips up!" he shouted each time we reached the last post from the tiny lookout house. "Let's go!" he shouted as I thrust him, crack-the-whip style, off the chair.

Six hours later, with only one twenty-minute lunch break early on and another quick stop to purchase goggles in mid-afternoon, the slope's outside lights came on, announcing the end of the afternoon skiing. We had agreed it would be our last run.

We were on the lift near the top of the tallest mogul run, Campbell on my right, when they came on. "Campbell," I pointed across the neighboring runs. "Look."

"Oh," he said, pouty lips, chin in chest, somewhat disappointed. Me, too. We had had a delightful day that had started at 10 a.m. with a grouchy child and was ending at 4 p.m. with a confident skier. "Tips up!" I said, and with that I boosted his little body forward and swung him around to the left. We drew concentric circles in the snow, his a giant arc outside of mine.

I was standing at the top of the hill mapping my path and adjusting my gloves when Campbell, to my right, lost his balance and clipped my knees. He nearly knocked me over. I shouted, "Whoa! Cam!" stretching my arms in an outer-spatial reach pattern, as his skis got tangled in mine. In the next moment—was it to the sound of my voice or the loss of his own balance?—he ripped his left leg from its newly entangled state. But his bindings were caught. His powerful flexor withdrawal snapped my lower leg right sideways at the knee. The thrust itself sent his sixty-pound body careening down the hill. He turned into the line of energy and raced on down, leaving me far behind.

Instantly, my whole body folded in an odd combination of navel-yielding and Babkin reflex, all limbs folding toward the midline. Making a slow, compressing movement with both hands, I cradled my knee all the way down to the snow-laden earth and tried to breathe. I could hear people around me shouting, "Are you all right?" but I was caught in a freeze pattern inside my own little bubble and couldn't respond.

Momentarily, the ski patrol arrived. As we worked out locating Campbell, loading me onto a toboggan, and transporting me headfirst down the hill behind a snowmobile, someone had helped Campbell back on to the lift and he appeared above me on the hill.

"Grama?" his tiny voice asked. It was the first time I heard in his voice what I would call "empathy."

"I'm OK, " I said, "I just hurt my knee." I paused as I took in his sweet face that was beginning to vein like fine porcelain. "I'm fine, honey. See? I'm breathing. I'm talking to you. These men are going to help me down the hill. It's just my knee." As he skied down the slopes next to the stretcher, the energy between us began to shift.

My leg was in bad shape—a broken bone, two Grade Three ligament tears, and a hip out of whack. I was going to be in pain, swollen, and bedridden for several weeks, with a very slow rehabilitation preceding knee surgery and a second recovery period. Meanwhile Campbell was silent about what had happened. His parents couldn't tell if he didn't know, or he just wouldn't say.

Two days later, Chris, Mary, and the grandchildren came to visit me. The boys ran around the bedroom like there was nothing wrong. Every other second I threw up a shielding arm or self-protecting admonition. "Be careful!" I whimpered.

A week later, my daughter-in-law called. "I think Campbell needs to spend some time with you alone. He doesn't seem to understand that he broke your leg, and he doesn't want to talk about it. I want to drop him off after school so the two of you can have some time together to talk this over."

Campbell arrived, books in hand. The snow was still pouring down in Ohio—a record thirty inches in one month, the likes of which we hadn't seen since 1910. Campbell crawled up onto my bed and was stretched out beside me reading yet another book. A holly branch snapped outside the window under the weight of the snow, and we both looked up. Staring at the birds trying to sort through the ice, we were stuck in our own winter thoughts for a moment, and then Campbell leaned over closer to me.

"Grama," he said. "It's OK if we don't go skiing this weekend. We can wait until next weekend." I reached over and gave him a hug. This shy little body that often cringed at physical affection let me in.

Three weeks later, we finally got around to discussing the accident directly.

"I don't really understand why everyone is saying I broke your leg," he asked me. "I wasn't even there. I had already skied down the hill."

"Ahhh," I said, as I started my version of the story from the beginning.

When I got to the part when he lost his balance and I yelled "Whoa, Cam!" before he jerked his leg away from mine, he interrupted me.

"Oh, I see," he said, in a typical Montessori attempt to hold each person accountable. "So we were *both* responsible for this accident. If you hadn't yelled, I wouldn't have pulled my leg out." I had talked my way into a corner. Distorted as his outlook seemed, I saw his point.

"Well," I had to admit, "it's true that my reaction may have caused you to pull your leg away. But I shouted and shouted 'Campbell, stop!!!' and you kept going."

"I thought you meant stop skiing, but I wanted to win the last race down the hill. I didn't know you had hurt yourself."

That last statement was missing the accusatory tone an adult might have. He really meant he hadn't noticed my situation. Suddenly I felt I was in the middle of an Alexander McCall Smith mystery. By tipping the lens, one could see several stories here. It was a genuine misunderstanding. So then he and I had a different conversation, about when hurting people unintentionally and inadvertently still carries the need to take responsibility and apologize.

It was very hard for Campbell to acknowledge that anything he had done was keeping us from returning to the slopes every week there was snow. He hadn't witnessed the fall; he was already on his way down the hill. He didn't know what my screaming referred to; he thought I was keeping him from pushing off. He hadn't noticed I was seriously hurt; I had told him it was just my knee and I would be fine. For all intents and purposes, he was off the proverbial hook. But now he was hearing the village buzz that he was responsible. He didn't understand why he was being accused.

Adults say "I'm sorry" all the time. We know when it is appropriate to say it and we know when we hear it to accept that it was said. But we often fail to forgive. Campbell understood that I was physically delicate—not skiing, in fact—because of some action. He understood he had been asked to apologize for something he didn't think he was responsible for. And he heard me say I accepted his apology. The form was in place, but there was not yet embodiment. There was still much healing to do.

I struggled out of bed a few weeks later to attend Campbell's first grade Toy Fair, an event designed to teach the children observation skills and to practice data collection. As the judge was approaching his tiny desk, I hobbled through the door on my crutches. He peeked around the tall man in a suit, and raised his timid little hand to wave. "Hi, Grama," he whispered, eyes twinkling.

Days later he brought over a handmade card, illustrated with two stick-figure skiers and a caption: "To the best Grama in the whole world." Such beautiful detail. Each chairlift had numbers on the back. The man in the lookout house had a beard. The slope had little rolling hills at the top. The skiers were each decked out in gear, one with poles, the other with none. They both had goggles. My hair poked out of my cap; Campbell's did not.

"This picture," he said, "was just before I broke your leg." He looked up at me, baring the gaps between his front teeth. And we both smiled.

In our culture, we teach children to say they're sorry. The thrust of our argument circulates around the other person's feelings. But we rarely acknowledge the shadow of that conversation: what it feels like to have an apology received. On that day, I realized Campbell had felt the power of forgiveness in his own cells. He forgave me for making him hurt me, forgave me for making him apologize, forgave me for making him contend with himself. But he also *received* my acceptance of his apology, and with it came an experience of empathy, the impetus behind, indeed, the support for, delivering an apology whenever warranted.

Midwestern middle-class grandparents face a certain kind of struggle. We are not to interfere with the daily business of raising our children's children. We don't get to say "Pop Tarts, again? They don't eat enough greens." Or "No wonder they're tired. They stay up too late." Or "That outfit? For *this* event?" Yet we are called upon to babysit or pick up at the last minute, to host Christmas dinner, remember Hallmark holidays, and help offset major expenses like private school tuition or braces—because we are family. That probably means, given enough time, directly or indirectly, we will impart our values to our grandchildren.

Grandparenting is special because in no other relationship do we have quite this kind of opportunity to shape and support another person. Detached from the daily survival needs, we are in the privileged position of seeing a bigger picture. We get to pick our battles from a larger palette. We know that this child is our destiny to love, and we set out, without ambivalence, to foster a bond. We recognize that being part of expanding a child's life with our presence of mind, lack of critical judgment, clear and insistent lessons, and generosity of spirit is a worthy challenge. While often, in this fast-paced, mobile society, it is a lesson learned only with some effort and some sacrifice, we trust the result can be majestic in its simplicity, not just for this relationship, but also as a paradigm for society. If we teach a lesson straight up, say what we are really witnessing, and keep at the relationship long enough to work through the differences in perspective, we might get a big full-body hug, a twinkling smile, and maybe even a handmade picture of doing something together. We might actually experience relational love.

Ultimately, learning to love someone through differences of perspective, even through real physical harm, is a life lesson from which our global community could benefit. Imagine a world where misunderstandings are awarded second tries, where tolerance morphs into unconditional love, and where apologies lift the spirits and embrace the heart not only of the transgressed but also of the transgressor.

Listening to Leo

LINDY HOUGH

Storytelling and improvisation with young grandchildren are rewarding give-and-take with a child. They involve close listening, and stretch one's own imagination. They reinforce in a fun, natural way that the life of the mind and the imagination are connected, and are a great thing about being human. The author writes about storytelling with her preschool-age first grandchild—and wonders how more grandchildren will change this.

LEO RUNS TO MEET ME when I pick him up at preschool. He's four months shy of four; it's April in Berkeley. The teacher says he has trouble listening to others at afternoon group, but she'll mention it to his parents.

We drive the short way home to his house, then play upstairs in his room until I rouse us to start dinner.

"Let's do the story," he says.

"OK, after we eat."

He likes our improvisations. For some months it's been on hands and knees down the hall to his parents' room or to the guest room, me driving the school bus of wooden kids, him flying the wooden airplane to Salt Lake or L.A., places he goes with his parents. We take the kids to a zoo, acting out the little wooden people visiting different animals in places on the rug, which represent different animals. On his striped bedroom rug the wavy blue lines suggest water, a picnic by a lake or stream; we regale each other with our picnic food, listing all the foods we each like. We approve of what each other's brought. The children will like these things.

But now there's also a new story.

It's about Joshua, a sixteen-year-old babysitter who comes to babysit not Leo, but Mama Cheetah and her baby, a large stuffed animal I gave him a while ago who is curled up in the corner on his floor, the baby permanently attached. Who made this up? I think Leo did. Its best feature is that we switch roles, which also involves one of us going out of sight outside the house (his room) and knocking. The door opens and closes; there are suspenseful moments when the door is closed and you don't know what the babysitter is doing inside.

"Want to be the babysitter or the dad?"

"I'll be the babysitter," Leo says. He goes outside his room and closes the door.

Joshua comes knocking. Mr. Grossinger, played by me, is reading the newspaper, answers the door, and explains that his wife is still in the bathtub. Mr. G goes over the instructions with the babysitter—what to feed the baby, what time to go to bed, any other rules. I make all these up, and he follows my lead, devising touches of his own when his turn comes to be the dad reading the paper at home. The food is what he eats, but sometimes it's lunch, other times dinner. The babysitter asks, "Where is Mr. G going?" Leo answers, "Over to the city with a friend." The city is San Francisco, of course, no mention of Mrs. G, who never emerged from the bathtub. Two characters is enough.

I elaborate on some details, he on others. He decides that the babysitter will get them a kite and fly it down by the bay or "at a creek wide enough to swim in." I suggest that the parents are going to Napa, to give a talk—something his dad does often.

We add touches. Instead of driving, I say, "I bet Mr. G can just hop on the back of Mama Cheetah, and they can *bound* up to Tilden and ride on the Little Train."

Leo accepts this without even mentioning it. "And sit up on the engine! And sit in the caboose! But they don't allow cheetahs to ride the train," he says. "Too dangerous. She might hurt someone."

That's the heart of these games—fantasy and reality interweave. Leo is skillful at going in and out of both, as he and I also go in and out of character. He gets up to go to the bathroom, "But that's not Joshua," he laughs. "*He* doesn't need to go."

"And what does Joshua do with his time when he isn't babysitting?" I ask.

"He plays a lot of basketball. And soccer." These are games Leo looks forward to. I remember when he was very little, two or three, at the nearby playground watching him try to get the ball way up into the basket, which stretched much too high—such a valiant series of attempts; it was touching.

My fascination with these stories coincides with the publication of *The Philosophical Baby: What Children's Minds Tell Us About Truth, Love, and the Meaning of Life* by Alison Gopnik. She suggests that far from the young child not being able to discriminate between truth and fiction, as Freud and Piaget maintained, even two- and three-year-olds are very good at telling fantasy from reality, and moving between them. Play is serious business. Gopnik maintains that hypothetical worlds are the way a child makes sense of reality. Entertaining "counterfactual" realities allows a child to learn how to discriminate between alternative courses of action.

Leo's so taken with action figures, who can buzz up to the tops of buildings in a flash, that I find myself at dinner suggesting that I can see through the dining room wall into the next house. He's taken with this, and it becomes a recurring subject: what will we see on the other side of the other wall? In his house, the kitchen, and then what's above, through the ceiling. This isn't fantasy so much as memory, and figuring out what room is above where we sit. But we both have interest in what constitutes the material *between* the ceiling downstairs and the floor upstairs. Then we imagine what's in the neighbor's house to the west. We guess that the kitchen is on the other side of the outside wall, but at what point does the front living room start? To think about what's on the inside of a house you've never been in involves imagining. In the case of his own kitchen on the other side of the dining room wall where we sit, it's a matter of guessing where the stove stops—what's exactly on the other side of my hand here.

A year later, amazingly, this house next door burns to the ground. No one was there, luckily, and the fire was contained to that house alone. Leo and his family watched the fire and the efforts of the firefighters to keep it from spreading to neighboring houses. Now they are having to live through the noisy, dusty demolition with a new baby; during the winter the gaping hole in the ground fills with rain, and a new house is gradually built.

Big doin's tonight. Leo and his parents are coming over to our house to watch the Jets game, on this Sunday night before we all start back to work tomorrow. When Rich proposes this earlier by email to them in L.A., I think they won't want to do it, they'll be driving back and be tired, but they came back yesterday and are up for it. Robin shares Rich's love and faithfulness to the Mets, Jets, and Nets.

In the afternoon I start to get ready and think about Leo. What does he make of coming over to his grandparents, where it's so different from the "alone time" we have? When he's here, he spends his time with his parents, and hardly relates to me and his grandfather at all. The evening goes well. He plays with his toys, crawls all over his mom, starts a game of throwing all the pillows on the living room couches off onto the ground behind the long green couch. Next time I remove the excess pillows so we don't have that to contend with again. Patience, but not passivity. Quiet, steady, abiding love, I tell myself. Do we shrink back, or do we blend with the others?

My thoughts stray to my own paternal grandparents. I think more often of them now that Leo's around. I feel compassion I lacked in earlier years. I'm curious about how my mother related to them. Is it that they didn't know what to say or do with children, or how to be with them when their parents were present? Were they conforming to some behavioral code of grandparents of their era?

Bertha and Raymond Hough ran a dry-goods store in Red Lodge, Montana, when my dad was a boy. Before they immigrated west, my grandfather was a banker in Kirkwood, Missouri, just outside St. Louis. My grandmother wrote novels, detailed stories about people in their midst. Who did she have to talk to about these novels? Enterprising, she loved movies and got herself a job previewing movies for a ratings agency in New York City when my grandfather worked there for a short time in banking—this part of her life is revealed in tiny notebooks in which she wrote down the film, the stars, who directed and produced, and the rating she gave it. This would have been at the turn of the century and the early 1900s before my father was born in 1908. But she never talked about this. Sadly, when we were children, we didn't know enough to ask her about her early life before she was married, or what her early married life was like.

When my father moved to Denver from Montana as a young man after a year at the University of Montana at Missoula, his parents sold the dry-goods store and followed him to Denver. By the time I was born in 1944 they had been grandparents for my two older sisters, living across the street from us until I was about five, then a few blocks away near Cheesman Park.

They were called Dad and Mother—the names my father called them. I remember them being quite silent … but attentive to my dad, who visited them every Sunday. I sometimes came along. We went to family dinners—a roast beef or pork loin on a silver platter, or a baked chicken in a silver soup tureen. Doilies on the back of nubby maroon chairs. My sisters and I used to look at the perfumes and small knickknacks my grandmother had on her glass-topped dresser in her bedroom. Once we were left there when my parents went to Florida, and my sister came down with polio. They came home abruptly and snatched us away for a weeks-long quarantine and plied us with gamma globulin. My sister had a light case—no serious lasting damage, thank God.

Did my mother look down on these homely people, so much less sophisticated than her wealthy family? I don't think so. I know she thought they cared deeply for their son. She encouraged his contact with them and didn't seem to begrudge him fixing things at their house. His dad, the senior Mr. Hough, was the finance director of my father's oil and uranium trade journals. They came over every Christmas and looked on, having coffee and scrambled eggs while we three girls opened presents. We threw a fiftieth golden wedding anniversary party for them when I was six; the photos show a pigtailed Lindy in a short gray corduroy jumper between them on the mantel of the fireplace, before mounds of flowers.

The upshot of these remote grandparents (my mother's side wasn't any better) is that I wanted to see what this relationship could be like, with no models.

A year later Leo strides to me in a grown-up contained fashion when I pick him up, not his more typical mad-dash run.

"We could play outside when we get home—it's so warm out," I say. "You could ride your trike."

"Nope."

What he wants to do is sit on the back of the red couch by the window, feet on the windowsill, and look out the window at passing bicyclists, walkers, cars, the huge, lovely Japanese maple in the front yard, and tell stories.

Our game is something I thought up last time on the way over, a variant of the Richard Scarry book *What Do People Do All Day?* One person thinks of an animal or person and tells about what he or she does all day. Before the telling, the other names the person. Picking out the name is as important as the story. Leo always dreams up a name that doesn't exist yet. I used the name Scooby once, and he sang the song about Scooby-Doo. Last time we did this he acted out the animals, adding a new dimension, closer to real improvisation. This time his stories fall into a definite pattern—an animal or person loses a ball in a lake, and must chase that ball everywhere, down sewer grates and under the ground where it's hard to get it, in mazes of sewers and pipes. There is so much detail that when it's time to cook dinner Leo doesn't stop, but keeps on talking as I edge into the kitchen to start heating the water for his beloved macaroni and cheese.

We pull together much the same dinner as always: some salad, an apple or pear or orange, maybe some black beans, with the mac and cheese. He throws a hacky-sack ball. "You should *make* salad dressing," he says when the salad greens come out and I start looking for a bottle of dressing. He instructs how to make it from scratch, showing where every ingredient is: the oregano in a piece of twisted paper, mustard, salt, oil, vinegar. It's very tasty, even though he pushes away the salad after eating mostly the macaroni.

He plays by himself more now without needing my involvement. He doesn't harangue on the stairs, "Nana! Come up here!" as he would have six months ago. He becomes absorbed with the bubbles in his bath and coats his body with them, standing up with delight that they stick.

After his bath he takes the lifeboat from the huge Lego pirate ship his dad put together with him. He keeps working with it, attaching the oars correctly, putting on finishing touches, absorbed. I see that part of the virtue of this large object is he can take off parts of it and do them over, remastering them until he can do the whole thing. When his dad comes home, Leo proudly shows what he's done. Robin is a wood-carver (since middle school!) and carpenter, and includes Leo often in his projects. Leo will learn how to build and fix things, and so will his new brother, Joey.

In Leo's first years, once Erica went back to work, my husband and I had a regular babysitting stint, alternating weeks. It allowed both parents to work late one night a week. Erica is a therapist, Robin a wetlands biologist and historical ecologist.

It certainly is true that what grandparents want is two things: to be included in the life of the new family and share your own life with them, and to have "alone time" with the grandkids frequently and regularly. At this age, babysitting is the most natural way to do it. When daycare and school come along, there will be other arrangements, I am sure.

Leo's parents value him having close grandparents.

Joey, their second child, was born during the summer of 2010. Leo was brought along during the pregnancy to know what was happening at every stage; he adjusted as they did. One evening he showed me the handsome historical anatomy birth book, and we followed how a baby grows inside its mother, and looked at the pictures of pregnancy and birth through the ages.

Now, a year later, I'm in Maine for four and a half months. Leo is going to day camp for a month in Tilden, and I'm missing it. He'll be six in August, Joey will be one in a few days, and I'll miss being at those birthday parties too.

I know Joey as much as one could at this stage. He is a curious bird, bright and alert, sitting on his blanket on the floor. Earlier this child raised on attachment parenting didn't much like being put down any-where, and there were a few dicey times when the only solution was strapping him on my front, as his dad did to fix dinner. But in a few weeks it got better, and he became comfortable on the floor. Soon he was scooting around, and was a proficient crawler after I left in May.

I will miss seeing him walk, but you can't be two places at once. I know I will push out into a wider definition of who I am in Maine, and it's only three to four months. The dance of grandparenting has been joyful, if at times confounding and perplexing. I look forward to more adventures in grandparenting—a marvelous second story to parenting in these later years.

Part Two

BALANCING REALITY AND HOPE

Evolving as a Grandmother

....

NADIA NATALI

*Timing is arbitrary. Just as the author of this piece was about to go
to graduate school, back home came her daughters, babies and husbands in tow. Speaking up about her priorities and rethinking closeness allowed Nadia Natali to adjust to a new life on the mountain
land where she had raised her daughters and run a Zen retreat with
her husband.*

AS A CHILD MY TWIN sister had a great affinity with our various pets. I was
the one who actually took care of our family animals, but I never engaged with them beyond the necessary responsibilities. My mom as well
as my sister made me feel inadequate about it, implying that I would
never be a good mother. My twin sister married first and had kids.

Back then I didn't feel particularly comfortable as an aunt. Later when
I did marry, I was absolutely certain I wanted children, though I had no
idea where that came from given my earlier fears. When I first learned I
was pregnant, I went into a transcendent state that did not leave me for
many years. My husband Enrico was supportive of my desire to have a
child although he claimed that if it were up to him, he would rather not
add more worries to what life already offered. I remember rather glibly
saying I would take care of everything, not to worry—although I did
worry and wondered if I would be a good mother after all.

I did bond immediately with all my babies. I was in heaven for many
years, discovering myself anew as a mother. All my fears from childhood
were for naught.

I was true to my word about doing everything as a mother. My husband turned out to be immensely supportive of me, which enhanced my
mothering skills—I flourished as a mother and as a woman. We never
had babysitters and homeschooled the children until they reached high

67

school. We lived on a large property in a remote area in Southern California above Ojai, without electricity, phone lines, or TV, and spent years clearing the land, planting trees, and building our home—homesteading. We gardened, I made bread and yogurt, and we ate eggs from our own chickens. The children spent much of their time exploring the property, learning from all the projects we engaged in, which were necessary for living in the wilderness. I also managed to involve them in various activities, some of which meant a drive down the roads to town—gymnastics, ballet, piano, singing groups, and tennis. The children loved to draw, each with a very different style; drawing was the staple of each day. We went to town often, and a typical trip would include lunch, a visit to the library, perhaps visiting a friend, and bringing home groceries. I taught the kids to read, and Enrico taught them math. Reading aloud was a frequent pastime, and each one developed a love of reading.

Children were thus a focal point, even when Enrico and I started our small Zen center. Other participants brought their kids, and we took turns sitting meditation and watching the kids—the children almost had a parallel retreat. At times their friends spent weekends with us. I thrived with all the children around. I felt like the mother in me was a natural part of my existence.

When they became teenagers, I had no idea what to make of these sweet kids acting as if I was now an irritating presence in their way. This period was hard on all of us, and it put a strain on my marriage. I couldn't understand how or why they interpreted my intentions as being against them. I know all teenagers rebel, but somehow given the depth of our trust, I didn't expect the closeness we had to disappear *so* completely.

At eighteen my oldest daughter went to Russia to study theater. She returned six years later with a husband and a new baby. Our second daughter married a man she met at school and had a child. I have to admit that I was expecting our rather unconventional children to have an exotic, adventurous life out in the world and marry late—why, I don't know, except that this is what I hoped for. Never did I expect them to have children so early on, then end up living on our property. What surprised me more was how the two girls became so different in their approach to adult life and their children. What I learned as a mother was one level of awareness, but as a grandmother it has been another story.

It became obvious to me right away that it would be tempting to me to be a mother to my grandkids. I had to quickly develop a whole new set of boundaries that were different from those with my own children. We were all so close when they were growing up. As a new grandmother I found that I had to sort out what that closeness was in order to be appropriate with the grandbabies. I decided to step back and disengage. I was tired of parenting; now that my kids were grown up I looked forward to a really long break. I had gone back to school and was studying for my PhD in clinical psychology, but suddenly both daughters were moving in with babies in tow.

What I ultimately did was a huge surprise—*especially* to me. I drew each daughter aside and confided that I could not be the kind of grandparent I, or maybe they, had expected me to be. I said that I was concerned that they might think I was there to babysit. I admitted I didn't think I would be up to it. I was afraid that my time and space would be used up by taking care of the grandkids instead of studying and learning what I wanted to know now. I said fairly clearly that they should not expect much from me.

This was completely antithetical to the way I had been with my children, which had been to make them the center of my universe, and give and give endlessly for them. I was shocked by my own admission, and even though neither of them acted surprised or disappointed they must have been stunned. I couldn't tell what they thought but I felt at least that I'd been honest.

I knew then that the only way I could build a relationship with the grandkids, in a loving and honest way, was to not feel any obligation and to trust the interactions that occurred naturally. For a while I sat back and observed. I saw each daughter raise her babies very differently, and I wondered about that. I had some definite judgments as to which was the better way. Not surprisingly, the one whose actions resembled what I would have done was the "right way," or so I thought. One daughter, for example, fed her children a closer approximation to what I thought was good food and chose to homeschool them. My other daughter developed her own approach.

After a while the oldest daughter and her family moved to a new home an hour away. As I watched each set of grandkids grow and develop, I noticed something remarkable—that their styles of parenting were mostly irrelevant. What I had held up as so crucial as a mother wasn't true. There is no right way to be a parent, so long as the child feels safe and can trust the intentions of a parent. Nurturing must come from a solid caring. The child must bump up against consistency to learn how to cope with adversity.

Growing up requires learning a series of skills to deal with life. If a child is safe and secure enough, he or she will find a unique way to adapt and move beyond difficult patterns. As I've watched my daughters raise their children differently from each other and seen that both are producing secure, happy children, I've realized the ideas I held so sacred about mothering when my children were small were simply what I came to. They weren't limited, but adequate; but they were one way among many to do things.

I'm beginning to understand that the ways our children rear our next generation demands a bigger perspective than I ever knew existed. We need grandparents who can hold such a perspective, and not demand throwbacks to the way we did things. This understanding has allowed me to feel more relaxed in my role as a grandmother. I am no longer like the mother I was. I know my place is to be totally real and available to my grandchildren without hesitation.

Now I look forward to my time with these children who constantly run in and out of the house. Perhaps my overreaction in creating boundaries a few years back allowed me to see anew what it all means—perhaps I needed to push back and get some perspective in order to be able to change. I am now very much at ease with our growing family. We have had seven grandchildren in eight years, so far. I see them in little groups and also separately. I like to invite the older ones over for dinner, and especially enjoy them one-on-one.

I know I now have a very authentic and engaging exchange with my grandchildren. Being true to myself is the best gift I can give them, and I want them to see that this will be true for them, eventually. My journey as a grandmother carries all that I have been and gone through. A child can feel that. Being a truly available grandparent is valuable enough—you do not need to do much else.

Grandparenting with a Broken Heart

JUDYTH O. WEAVER

The grandchildren are a thousand miles away. Your life is in the Bay Area. Your life's work has been in the exact area of medical care that crops up in a family health crisis, but from an alternative point of view, not regular medicine—the new parents aren't interested in your insights. Judyth O. Weaver faced these two heart-wrenching dilemmas, and has used her Zen training to get through them both.

I WAITED UNTIL LATE TO have my children. My mother died when I was three; being raised by a "wicked stepmother" made me want to make sure I would do better. When I was young I thought of becoming a child psychologist, but found a spiritual path in my teens that led me to a Zen Buddhist monastery in Japan in my mid-twenties. I wanted to be the best mother I could and the everyday life, commonsensical teachings of Zen offered the best training I could find. After several years in the monastery, I felt it was time to return home and raise the family I had always wanted. For many reasons my choice for my husband and the father of my children was not optimal, and I was soon a single mother.

My son, who never knew his father, has turned out to be a very good father. He often complained that he was being raised by "two mothers," his older sister and myself. He now has two daughters and a wife who is as different from me as possible.

I became a body/mind integrative therapist with specialization in pre-natal and perinatal psychology and therapy. When my son and daughter-in-law first became pregnant, I offered them many of my books to read on the subject of preparing for optimal births and the benefits of the natural processes. I was asked to not be in the birthing room and so offered to wait in the hall of the hospital in case they wanted me to bring them anything. After a very long labor with drugs and vacuum extractors, my first grandchild was born with what was eventually diagnosed as the "worst brachial plexus Erb's palsy injury" ever known. In a very short time my daughter-in-law, not appreciating my efforts to help, such as offering osteopathic treatments and homeopathy, demanded that I terminate any suggestions and that I not be allowed to see my little granddaughter except in the presence of my son and only if I kept quiet. Basically, after leaving a full professional life and moving close to them to become a hands-on grandma, I was banished from my granddaughter's life. I quickly had to develop a new spiritual path: keeping my mouth shut. As an outspoken, independent person and teacher, this was very difficult, for I felt I had so much to offer that could help. As a new grandmother I yearned to be as close as I could to the little baby who was damaged and needed extreme support.

I was devastated. There was never any confusion in my mind about who was the mother in this situation, and as someone said to me shortly after the baby's birth, "Grandparenting is like growing another heart." It truly was that for me, but my new heart was broken. My son and daughter-in-law had not been married so long that we had encountered bumps and misunderstandings and developed a way to overcome them. No, this was the first and biggest and forever crucial bump.

I moved back to my work and my home. I offered my support from a distance. I asked permission to come to visit and eventually babysit. It was awkward and unhappy. Every time I was allowed to be alone with the baby I sang a little song I made up, in the hopes that there would be some continuity that she could recognize. And I ached and pined a lot. I also ranted and raved ... to myself.

By the time my first grandchild was one-and-a-half years (just beginning to walk because of her inability to crawl), her mother was ready to birth her second child and I got to babysit for a couple of days. It was wonderful to have some real time with my sweet granddaughter. The second child was birthed as a planned C-section. She didn't seem to me to be really ready to be born, but there she was, healthy, with no major difficulties. As you can imagine, the experiences and temperaments of the two little girls are very different. They are both delightful and precious in so many ways.

And how do I handle all this? How do I take my knowledge and put it aside where it is not wanted in my growing family and continue using it with other children whose parents do want advice and help? It was amazing that many children who were brought to me for therapy and advice were exactly the same age as my granddaughter; but of course they were more developmentally advanced because they did not have her injury. I would do the work that I knew could help them and when they left I would mourn my grandchild's situation. And mine, as I wasn't allowed to offer help to her.

My use of the nonattachment that I learned in my spiritual practice has been very important. If I stand back far enough and keep my view of the "larger picture," I can be calmer in this situation. Letting go of my hopes, wishes, and intentions—all the letting go I worked on in the monastery—is informing me here. Accepting what is and what I cannot do and what I cannot be a part of is very sad for me. How frustrating to be able to see other children benefiting from my work and not be able to offer it to my own grandchild. I must admit this is the most difficult spiritual practice I have ever engaged in!

There are so many ways in which I differ and silently disagree with my daughter-in-law. The toxicity of toys, chemicals in foods, unsustainablity in various ways of living … and if I want contact with my granddaughters—and I most surely do—I must silently accept and support whatever is done in their family. I have to admit I am becoming braver and slipping in a few words and concepts to the little girls that I think are essential, like recycling and composting. And I always bring some "unusual" foods for them to eat. Twice when I've been with them I've even been so brave as to ask them to sit quietly with me for two minutes. We sit quietly and just listen and look.

I am now in the process of, for the second time, giving up my home and professional practice and moving back to where my grandchildren live. I have struggled with this a lot, and it is clear to me that, being in my seventh decade, I may not have much more time with them. At this point I must take every chance I can get to have my presence be a part of their experience too. Flying in once a month to babysit is not enough for me any longer. Rather than see my clients and friends, I am choosing to move again to the city where my son and daughter-in-law live and again start a new life, to have more opportunities to spend time with my granddaughters.

Actually, it feels very much like the sitting I did in the monastery. Just being. Being present for whatever is possible. No expectations, no desires. Just being. Without attachment? Well, that is a hard call. Of course I have great attachment to my grandchildren. I would not be leaving my life of many decades to move in an effort to be closer to them if I had no great attachment. No desires? Well, of course I have desires. I wish my son and daughter-in-law would change. I wish they would care about the safety and education issues that I think are important for their children.

No expectations? Well, I know I must give up all my expectations and just be. Accepting what is, whether I like it or not. Equanimity? I show it publicly, but I don't subscribe when I fuss and rant about things I don't like. Serenity? I've got lots of work to do.

So I think my life will become more meditative. I think I'll have to do a lot of work on myself. Without a busy work schedule, I'll finally get the time to do all the meditation that I've not had space for during the last forty years.

When my grandchildren are old enough and perhaps interested in it, I'll be able to teach it to them.

Or perhaps they'll just get it through osmosis.

Professional Grandma

SALLE WEBBER

Timing. This Santa Cruz postpartum doula was looking forward to more space for her own writing, when her daughter with three children called to ask if she could move back in. Salle Webber alternates this insightful account of her life at home surrounded by three grandkids and her grown children and her life at work (set in italics) with her client families and their newborn babies. Each world reveals the other. She makes it work.

I WAS EXCITEDLY PLANNING HOW I would organize the room I was about to turn into my personal writing and work space. For the first time, one whole room would be devoted to me; there would be no need to work around Leo's clutter, or share the space with anyone. My own creativity could flourish here, and my book would finally get written.

I have worked as a postpartum doula, caring for new babies and their families, for more than twenty years. My mind is rich with memories and stories to tell. I want to be a voice in training the next generation of caregivers. Having a place to write could allow that to unfold, as I share my experience by writing about it.

The phone rang. It was my husband Leo telling me that he was at our daughter Lily's house. Her husband had angrily destroyed the living room and stormed off. She was leaving him, it was her last straw, she was headed home to us with her three kids. Leo spent the day cleaning up broken glass and furniture, and replacing the window broken by a flying potted plant.

The little family, now fatherless, moved in. Fortunately, we had two bedrooms with a bathroom and living room to offer them, and they found immediate security. Our house had always been the center of life for the extended family, with weekends spent enjoying the quiet of our forest dwelling in the mountains of Santa Cruz, California. We tried hard to make the transition less rocky for the children, but our seven-year-old granddaughter was painfully aware of what had transpired at their "old house," where they would never live again. Her three-year-old brother didn't understand the details, but felt the tension. The baby, only four months old, came to bond deeply with his grandfather, who continues to be a strong father figure, three years later.

That was the end of my writing room. It was over before it began. Within six months, our second daughter, her partner, and their baby asked if they, too, could join the extended family living together. It was a joyful addition, with all four grandchildren now together with us. It feels so wholesome, so organic, so like much of the rest of the world, where families routinely stay together in intergenerational living. I enjoy the daily interaction with the kids, and with my own kids. I love hearing the two young mothers laughing together in the kitchen as they make breakfast and begin their day. The child without siblings benefits from sharing with her cousins, and cooperative child care happens willingly. The old guest room is now occupied, and we could really use another room for little Willa, now three. My writing gets done on my laptop at the foot of my bed, and is regularly interrupted by the needs of children.

Have I failed at motherhood, and been sent back to kindergarten? Or am I so good at this that I get to do it again? At a time when I expected to be focused on my own work, I am reading stories rather than writing them, and planning kid-friendly meals instead of quiet candlelit dinners for two. My emotional energy is trapped in their four bright beings. I am owned. Life has become a paradox. I long for room to work, a quiet meditative space. Yet, I miss the little ones when they're gone. My peers, when they hear of our living situation, either respond with great envy for our good fortune, or with horror at the thought of kids ever present. My own feelings fluctuate wildly.

In my professional role as a doula, I recently began assisting a mom whose baby was four weeks old. Her mother-in-law had been with them up until then, but was going home, and now I was stepping in. There were concerns about weight gain and milk production. The baby was lightly dressed, no hat, with just a receiving blanket over him in an open bed. The day was cool. I suggested dressing the baby more warmly. The mom readily agreed to that, as I explained briefly about babies' needs for warmth and the connection to growth. She said that her mother-in-law had suggested several times that the baby needed more clothing, but the young mother had shrugged her off with "He's all right." When I said it, she listened.

Even though the mother-in-law had raised five children, and her daughter-in-law loved and respected her, somehow her wisdom was not tapped. She primarily attended to housekeeping, cooking, and shopping, doing a great job of keeping the home running smoothly as the young parents adjusted. Perhaps she was so welcomed in part because of her ability to not "interfere." But because I was a paid consultant, if you will, they expected me to share wisdom, and they listened to what I had to say.

Going home later that day, I found my three-year-old granddaughter watching TV. In discussion with her father, I made a statement that a lot of television was not healthy for a young child. He said that may be my opinion, but he didn't agree with it. Case closed. I raised my three kids without TV, never hooking up to the cable until the last one finished high school. I've long been convinced of the wisdom of limiting or avoiding television. No matter. It's just my (unneeded) opinion when I'm home. I can play with my little granddaughter, read stories, draw pictures, go for walks, but then I, too, tire and finally succumb to her request for television. How did I manage to keep my own children away from TV? I feel like a failure as she stares at the screen.

At a prenatal visit the pregnant mother of a two-year-old told me that her mother will come for a couple of weeks after the birth. "Will she be helpful?" I asked.

"Oh, yes, she loves to clean, cook, and do laundry," my client responded.

As the discussion progressed, the young woman mentioned that after her first child's birth, her mother was critical of the parents' choice to keep the baby in bed with them. The grandma also felt that breast-feeding was overrated, and pointed out her daughter's nursing challenges as proof that using bottles and formula made much more sense. Her ideas of baby care included leaving a child to cry, holding it only when necessary, and striving to create a convenient schedule as soon as possible. Her daughter and husband felt more inclined toward following the baby's lead, sleeping all together, snuggling in bed for the sheer joy of it, and nursing on demand.

Though there was no spoken acknowledgment of the stress this woman's mother created, the young couple was protecting themselves this time around by hiring me to be their doula. I would present a professional presence, supportive of their choices, and well-informed. My age and confidence with the infant would override the grandma's role as the one who knows best. Once they confirmed that my philosophy was synchronized with theirs, they engaged me as part of their team, with the subtle request to keep grandma under control.

At my house, the young parents like to sleep late on Saturday mornings. Since I am present and awake, I find myself caring for and feeding the kids. I do enjoy this; they delight me with their soft sleepiness, as they bury their faces into my neck and slowly come back from dreamland. Their conversations can be amusing or touching; it is a precious time in our day. Yet, there is a part of me that resents this. Maybe I have something else I want to be doing, but the needs of kids are so immediate and demanding. I can't *not* be there for them if they need me. I'm not perfect. I'm not complete. That's why I'm here on earth, because I'm still working on getting good at life.

Kids expect perfection from their mothers, as well as uncomplaining service. It's always been that way. I observe the absolute dedication that new mothers give to their infants. This is essential, as newborns are utterly helpless without adult care. As they grow, there are many dangers and pitfalls along the way, and mother is expected to protect her young from harm. Yet somewhere along the way, a mother is supposed to stop caring that much, to cease her concern with the child's daily activities and needs. To "let go." A part of me desires to be all things to my kids and grandkids, but I also know that I have other roles to play besides this one. I sometimes feel taken for granted, but also critical of myself for not embracing each moment cheerfully. After all, I am the adult here. Haven't I learned yet to be here now?

One young father, a science fiction writer, was home a lot after the birth of his son. He was very involved in the baby's care, often questioning me about his observations of the child and how to respond. He became very competent at helping the baby become peaceful and surrender to sleep. He once told me, "Everything I know about caring for my son, I learned from watching you." He was a great student. When his mother came to visit, she tried her best to be helpful by doing laundry, preparing meals, and holding the child. She recounted lots of stories from her son's babyhood, and was supportive of the couple's style of parenting, though it differed from what she remembered. Yet, there was a continuous undertone of disrespect coming from son to mother. Unresolved issues about the divorce between his parents, the difficulties facing his brother, and his own independent lifestyle seemed to be coloring the relationship, though the mother tried hard to be unobtrusive and supportive.

My heart went out to her as I observed her son's deep feelings trying to surface. She was doing her best, hoping to move forward out of the past. One day as I was folding laundry, the young dad carefully watched me with his T-shirts. His wife liked him to do his own laundry, but he had never figured out how to fold his shirts. He exclaimed, copying my efforts, that he finally saw how to do this for himself! The fleeting look of disappointment on his mother's face was quickly hidden. He had, again, subtly made her feel like a failure as his mom. He was learning these important little things from someone else.

Since we share a kitchen, which was once my personal domain, I frequently need to surrender my idea of how something should be done.

My daughters are strong-willed and self-assured, a sure sign of my good mothering. I hold back from reloading the dishwasher or adding fruit to the children's breakfast to avoid appearing judgmental or controlling. I try to stay in my room when chaos is reigning among the kids, to allow the parents to handle things in their own ways. It isn't easy. I don't always live up to my own standards. I want to calmly approach each situation with the children and patiently sort it out.

Sometimes, I am with them all and can't stay separate, and too often I respond with stress to their cries and outbursts, intervening and being the cop or the nurse, often overreacting, or so my daughter's look implies. My caring, protective side responds to the hurt feelings and bumped bodies; I want to make everything OK. I don't want them to be yelled at, but to be patiently guided and understood. I know about the development of the wounded child present in all of us, and wish I could spare these beloved babies from the karma of life. At the same time I realize that they've all chosen each other, and it's my place to trust the wisdom of the young parents to raise the children they've been entrusted with.

But I have no foolproof ideas of parenting. I don't know how to get the kids to do what I want them to do, be who I want them to be, think what I wish they would think. I was winging it all those years, and I'm not ashamed to say so, and their parents are winging it now. I tell the new moms, we do our best each step of the way, but the paradox of parenting is that the child is on to the next stage before we have figured out how to handle the last one. Life goes on; parents do the best they can. Get on the river and ride.

One grandmother lived several hundred miles away from her daughter, son-in-law, and their two children. The relationship between mother and daughter was strained by years of hurtful words and periods of estrangement that went on for months at a time. After the second birth, the grandmother tried to reestablish a connection, but it was tenuous. Her previous behaviors had offended her son-in-law, who was often the recipient of his wife's frustrations.

As their doula, I tried to sort through the angry stories and unloving comments, to see where we stood. Soon the grandmother began calling me at night, to discuss her fears and beliefs about her daughter's family. She tried to grill me for information, and shared her perspective on the situation, which was much colored by her distance, age, and the people in her world with whom she discussed her family's affairs. While being polite, I refrained from divulging too much, conscious of my responsibility to honor the family that employed me.

I witnessed the young mother's confusion: she wanted the comfort of her own mother at this trying time, yet feared opening up to this woman who had hurt her so many times. Now the mother of two girls herself, she was mired in conflict, intent on modeling a happy family life, yet in tremendous contradiction with her girls' grandmother. The shame and sadness that overtook her each time her children witnessed an emotional outburst was painful to observe. My role became somewhat of a mother figure to all of them, parents, children, and grandparents, listening to and empathizing with each one's point of view. From this position, it is easy to see how misunderstandings grow and thrive in fertile soil. Each of us is the center of our own universe; it cannot be any other way. We see through our own eyes, we each live in our personal movie, and others play their roles in our drama. There is no agreement on who is the star character.

Meanwhile, back home, my daughter became upset with me for an offhand comment, and I was subsequently told about my cynical tongue, my critical nature, my tendency to make others feel inadequate. Me? I see myself as consistently supportive, sharing all I have, opening my home to seven additional people. I took some time to myself, pondering these accusations. They must be true, I figured, in her eyes, and I want to maintain closeness and trust with my children. I looked deeply to see where the truth lay for me, and how I am perceived by others.

I do have a sharp tongue, and my sense of humor tends toward irony and sarcasm. Sometimes I make indirect judgments, such as "Aren't you tired of watching TV all day?" Or "Have you eaten anything fresh lately?"

How about "The cats would starve if I wasn't here." Or "Has anyone but me ever washed this kitchen floor?" I can see how my attitude could be annoying. I felt foolish, and wanted to withdraw.

Women who have employed me have told me that they love my company, that they will miss my presence when I'm no longer helping out. Certainly, I'm a professional ... I know how to provide care in a friendly and unobtrusive way. But home is where I go to have some of my own needs met, to be free of the expectations of my clients. When the three-year-old pulls me, chattering, toward her game, and her cousin talks over her, in her self-important preteen way, about a wrong done by her little brother as I try to head for the kitchen for an afternoon coffee, I trip over a skateboard. My toes touch something mushy on the floor. I firmly hold the hand that's tugging me in the opposite direction, and I wonder where my energy has gone. I am totally exhausted, though I was the picture of vitality and productivity all day at work. I feel used up, yet there is much still to be done.

Years of meditation and self-reflection have failed to detach my ego from a need for justice for the underdog, for everyone to get along, and for my own efforts to be acknowledged. What raising three kids didn't teach me, these grandchildren seem determined to impart. I'm getting another chance, and with humility I recognize this gift. I've seen so many grandmas who will never be cared for by their descendants, never brought to their emotional knees by witnessing the sadness of a grandchild, never know that sloppy snotty sleepy kiss of a toddler. I know I am blessed.

Confessions of a New Step-Grandparent

SHARON BRAY

Step-grandparents joining a blended family wonder how the children and grandchildren can come to feel like a family, rather than a loose collection of partners and children. The answer is slowly, with sensitivity and kindness to everyone. Sharon Bray abandons her preconceptions and becomes a loving and skillful step-grandparent. The grandkids respond. The process has to begin internally.

MY DAUGHTERS HAVE ALWAYS HAD a knack for surprising me, making choices I don't always understand, yet somehow landing on their feet. When my daughter, Amy, announced she'd met a man "online," I was flabbergasted.

"Online? My God. How do you know he's not some kind of pervert?"

She rolled her eyes, "Oh Mom, you've been watching too many *Law and Order* reruns."

Perhaps I had, but online dating seemed an uncharacteristic gamble for someone whose willowy beauty melted many young men's hearts. Why did she need to resort to the Internet for romance? Despite my concerns, it paid off. Two years later, she agreed to marry the man who had courted her online. We weren't entirely at peace with her decision to marry Michael. He was previously married and had three children, ages nine, seven, and five. The moment she said, "I do," my daughter would not only become Michael's wife, but stepmother to his children as well.

The wedding took place in April on the crystal white sands of a Florida beach near where Michael lived. All three of his children were included in the ceremony. Heather, the oldest, took her place in line as junior bridesmaid while Ashley, as flower girl, sprinkled the path with rose petals. Zachary carried the rings on a heart-shaped pillow and stood next to his father, while Amy was escorted along the petal-strewn path by my husband John to take her place next to the man who'd won her heart. A few minutes later, our family had enlarged to include a son-in-law and three step-grandchildren.

Stepfamilies are among the most common family forms in the United States, but the addition of stepparents and step-grandparents into one another's lives introduces challenges and opportunities for both. A child's readiness to accept new family members is affected by age and circumstance. Although Michael had a loving and close relationship with his children, his interactions with his ex-wife were fraught with acrimony. We were sensitive that his marriage to Amy might produce conflicted feelings among his children.

Zachary, the youngest, was barely a year old when his parents separated, and he was closest to, and very protective of, his mother. According to Amy, when Michael told his children that he was marrying her, Zachary was perplexed. "Why can't you just marry Mom?" he asked.

Zachary's uncertainty was visible at the wedding and captured in the photograph of the new blended family. In it, he stands behind his father, one hand tentatively resting on Michael's shoulder. His sisters sit close to Amy and smile happily at the camera, but Zachary gazes far off into the distance, as if he isn't sure what to make of all the excitement.

We didn't visit Amy and Michael again until five months later. My other daughter telephoned to wish us well.

"Enjoy your new grandchildren," Elinor said.

"They are not *my* grandchildren," I replied. "They already have grandparents."

She was silent for a moment, surprised at my reaction. "Well, have fun with them anyway," she said.

As engaging as Mark's children—Heather, Ashley, and Zachary— were, John and I made no assumptions about our relationship with them. They had two sets of grandparents already. We lived on the opposite side of the country, and despite a joint custody arrangement between

Michael and his ex-wife, their primary residence was with their mother. Warning lights flashed everywhere.

My greatest concern was for Amy and her adjustment to stepparenting, not our becoming step-grandparents. John and I had married several years after my first husband's death, and he became a stepfather to my daughters in their teenage years. There were moments when I doubted we'd ever weather the adjustments. They have forged a strong and loving bond, but it didn't happen overnight. It seemed unnecessarily complicated to foist ourselves as step-grandparents onto Michael's children while they were developing their new relationship with Amy.

Despite all that, I Googled "step-grandparenting" for advice and found no shortage of tips for the newly initiated. More than a few of us were asking, "What *is* a step-grandparent, and where do I begin?"

"Get to know the children," the columnists advised. Better said than done if you live more than two thousand miles away. I read on. It seemed the onus was clearly on us to make the first move while, at the same time, remaining sensitive to family dynamics.

"How do you want us to interact with the children?" I asked Amy, not wishing to create any minefields that might blow up after we left for home.

"Whatever makes you happy, Mom. Go for it."

"Will you play cards with us?"

"Can I sit by you at dinner?"

"Would you read us a story?" Michael's daughters were especially eager to spend time with us. Any resistance I might have felt quickly melted away. I was completely infatuated as the children cuddled next to me while I read to them or offered me dozens of colored drawings labeled "To Sharon, Love from …"

Only Zachary hung back. He rarely asserted himself and seemed to fade into the background in the presence of his gregarious sisters. They had a habit of answering for him even when we directed a question to Zachary. John, normally uncomfortable with young children, was able to draw him out by sneaking away from the rest of us to quietly assemble jigsaw puzzles with Zachary in his bedroom.

"Grandma," Heather shyly addressed me at the dinner table. "Grandma" was what they called their maternal and paternal grandmothers. I felt a twinge of discomfort. Although advice for new step-grandparents said to "let the children decide what they want to call you," I wasn't ready to be called "Grandma" by anyone but my "real" grandchildren. It suggested a level of familial intimacy I didn't have with Michael's children.

My discomfort must have been apparent, because Heather's face flushed pink. "Is it OK if I call you that?" she quickly asked.

"You can call me whatever you want," I said, trying to keep my voice light.

"But ..." I was scrambling to recover from my faux pas. "Just don't call me 'Grandma Bray,' " I said, rolling my eyes for effect. "That's what Amy and her sister called *my* mother. 'Grandma Bray' will make me feel very old."

Heather smiled. Phew. Maybe I hadn't hurt her feelings, but she never called me "Grandma" after that, reverting to my first name, "Sharon." Both of us were apparently feeling our way into our relationship.

Amy slid into her new role as stepmother with aplomb. I marveled at her ability to create equal, yet individual, time with each child. I tried to do the same on every visit to Florida, but it was much easier to interact with the girls. Zachary was still distant with me, preferring to spend time with John.

Meanwhile, Amy's biological clock was ticking loudly. She was nearing forty, and her sister Elinor wasn't married and older by a year. I begin to accept the idea I might never have grandchildren of my own and resigned myself to making the best of step-grandparenting.

"Mom?" Amy was calling from Florida barely a year later. "Are you sitting down?" My daughter told me she was pregnant. I was going to be a real grandmother at last.

"Have you told Michael's kids? Are they thrilled?" I was giddy with excitement.

"Not yet," Amy said, "and please don't mention it if you're talking to them. We aren't going to tell them for a while."

"Mum's the word," I said, wondering how long they could keep her pregnancy a secret. When we visited again, she was five months along and her blouses no longer disguised her expanding waistline. It was time to tell the children about the impending birth.

Michael summoned them all into the living room for an announcement.

"Amy and I have something to tell you," he began. "We're going to have a baby. *You're* going to have a new little sister or brother."

Heather and Ashley clapped their hands and leapt up to hug Amy. Zachary stayed put and leaned back into the sofa. I saw that faraway look on his face, the one I remembered from the wedding photograph.

"What do you think, Zach? You'll be a big brother," Michael tried to draw him out.

"Cool," he said, a half-smile playing on his face. "Can I go outside and play now?"

"Well," Michael said, shrugging his shoulders after the children left the room, "that was anticlimactic."

"Give them time," John said, but I couldn't help wondering was going through their minds. Whatever the children were truly feeling, they kept it to themselves.

Every advice column for the prospective grandparent of any kind was adamant about one thing: don't show favoritism to *any* of your grandchildren, they wrote, and that included your own as well as your "inherited." No problem. I abhorred favoritism in any form, having suffered through my mother's tendency to play favorites among her children *and* her grandchildren. I vowed I would never, ever show favoritism among my children or their children. A noble sentiment, to be sure, but that was before I had a "real" grandchild in my life. Favoritism, I discovered, was impossible to avoid in the case of "real" versus step-grandchildren. As

Amy's due date grew near, I thought of little else. My step-grandchildren became "Michael's kids" again, children who occasionally waved at me on Skype from behind Amy's chair. To be honest, I was so consumed with the impending arrival of a first grandchild, I rarely thought about them.

Any grandparent will tell you that the birth of your first grandchild engenders an instantaneous bond. My heart was in Nathan's tiny fist the moment I took him in my arms. It was no contest. He was *my* grandson and my favorite grandchild, hands down. What I didn't expect were the conflicted emotions I felt toward my step-grandchildren in the days after his birth.

In the week after Nathan's birth, Michael was unexpectedly given a mini paternity leave, a full week off from work to be with his wife and newborn son. I discovered another uncomplimentary emotion: possessiveness. I didn't want Michael there. I'd flown from California to help Amy, and the nine-to-five slot was supposed to be *my* time with *my* daughter and *my* grandson. It wasn't. Michael was on hand 24/7, and worse, *his* children were coming for the weekend. I felt as if I had been deprived of the precious time I'd expected with my newborn grandson, and my resentment spilled over. I informed my daughter I didn't want play babysitter to Michael's children, only adding to her stress.

In hindsight, I'm truly chagrined by my momentary lapse in behavior. I'd read that stepchildren may resent the addition of a step-grandparent in their lives, but nowhere had anyone written about a step-grandparent resenting the inclusion of someone else's children in hers. By the time the children arrived for the weekend, I'd managed to suppress my negative feelings and kept the children entertained and out from underfoot of Nathan's very sleep-deprived parents. It was, I told myself, my duty. I owed it to Amy.

Not long afterward, Michael was given a three-month assignment overseas. Amy was completely overwhelmed with single-handedly caring for an infant while her husband was away, so once again, I traveled to Florida to help out.

Given all that Amy had on her plate, the children's weekly visitations had been postponed until he returned. She felt bad about it, but she was simply too exhausted to care for Nathan and single-handedly manage Michael's children's visits. They had not seen the baby or her for weeks, and it gave me a chance to redeem myself for my uncharitable behavior a few months earlier.

"Why don't we have the kids over for an afternoon," I suggested, "and I'll take everyone out for dinner?"

Amy expressed surprise, no doubt remembering the feelings I had expressed during my last visit, "Are you sure, Mom? You don't *have* to do that."

"I know, but it has to be hard on them to not see you. I'm happy to do it. Honest," I added, in case she doubted my sincerity.

"Oooooh, let me hold him, please." Both girls begged for their turns holding the baby. Zachary seemed content to watch the excitement from a few feet away. Finally, he edged forward and gently, but persistently tapped my arm.

"Can I hold him?"

I pried Nathan away from his doting sisters while Zachary positioned himself on the sofa. He held out his arms, and I carefully placed the baby in them. Zachary's face lit up with an ear-to-ear grin. He nuzzled Nathan's cheek with his own. "Hi, little brother," he murmured. "Hi, there." Something in my heart shifted.

We drove to Ruby Tuesday's for dinner, and all three children took turns holding the baby. Whenever someone stopped at the table and admired Nathan, the children smiled proudly. "He's our little brother," they chorused.

For those few hours, it seemed as if we were truly were a family, sharing time together in unselfconscious fun. When we took them home later, and I stepped out of the car to say goodbye, Zachary surprised me with a quick hug before he ran into the house. Ashley wrapped her arms around my waist, while Heather pressed a note into my hand. "I'm so happy you are here," she'd written. "I love you so much." I look back on that evening and realize I'd begun to find my footing as a grandparent *and* a step-grandparent. My heart had opened to Michael's children, and I think they felt it.

I was back in Florida a few months later for Nathan's first birthday, which fell on the weekend Michael's children were scheduled for their overnight stay. I heard them arrive and walked into the hallway to greet them. As I rounded the corner, Zachary ran into my arms and gave me a bear hug. The girls quickly followed.

"Zach *never* hugs anyone," Amy observed later. "He must really love you."

I had a soft spot for Zachary too; maybe because he was the youngest and needed more drawing out. While I'd learned that each child wanted—and needed—individual time with me, Zachary seemed to blossom most during those moments we spent drawing pictures or playing Scrabble together. He was animated and talked freely about his mother's recent remarriage and the addition of her new husband's son to their family, something he never did with Amy or his father.

"I have a stepdad, Sharon," he beamed, "and a big brother too. I always wanted a big brother." His delight was understandable for a little boy who'd lived in an all-female household for most of his life. Zachary apparently had room in his heart for more than one new stepparent *or* step-grandparent.

"That's great, Zach," I said. "And you know what I like best?" He shook his head. "I like it that Nathan already has a big brother." His eyebrows knitted together as he looked at me, not quite comprehending. "You," I said, touching his nose with my forefinger. "You'll be the best big brother in the world."

"Yeah," he grinned, "I will."

We don't see my step-grandchildren very often. The joint custody agreement between Michael and his ex-wife doesn't include travel out of the state, so they can't visit us in California as Nathan and his parents do. When we visit Florida, our time together is limited to their prescheduled weekend visitations. Michael and Amy are now preparing for a move overseas, and we'll see them less often and will see even less of his children, which is a loss for all of us.

John and I will never have the same relationship as Michael's children have with their other grandparents, or as we do with Nathan, but that won't deter us from continuing to nurture as loving a relationship as we possibly can, whether in person, on Skype, Facebook, or in the exchange of emails, letters, and photographs. The children want us in their lives, however infrequent or imperfect it may be, and we want them in ours.

After Nathan's first birthday festivities were over, I sat in the family room with him, content to have a few quiet moments to play together with my grandson. Ashley tiptoed into the room behind me.

"Grandma," her voice was tentative.

"What, sweetie?" I answered to "Grandma" without hesitation. I was ready to be called whatever they chose.

She sat beside me. "Nathan really loves you," she said, as she watched us play. Nathan handed me a brightly colored ball. I took it and rolled it down his plastic slide, which was our game. He giggled with delight then crawled to retrieve it as I put my arm around Ashley's shoulders. "I really love him too," I said.

"I know you do." She snuggled closer to me. "Can I play too?"

"Of course," I said, "I'd like that." I gave her a hug.

"I love you too," I said.

She leaned her head on my shoulder. "I know you do," she said, and in that moment I knew that we had finally become family.

Love through the Distances

Keith Dalton

*In this account spanning seventeen years, a Canadian grandfather re-
calls the variety of experiences he's had relating to his grandchildren.
Keith Dalton grapples with constructing a strong relationship with
those at a distance, and integrating a new partner. Although he miss-
es the intimacy he had with his children as a parent, this later stage
affords great pleasures.*

IN THE EARLY 1980S MY wife and I moved from our owner-built passive-
solar log home up in the snowbelt near Lake Huron to what seemed at
the time like the banana belt of the rolling wooded hills surrounding Toronto. We were still homeschooling our two daughters, but by the early
nineties our son, Aron, was staying with his grandmother in the city so
he could attend university there. He only came home on weekends. Each
Friday he and I came back from the city together, and each Monday on
my way to work, I drove him back to school.

Aron became involved with a girlfriend named Kim while he was still
in college. Although I warned him about the dangers of having children
too early and how it would limit his options, his girlfriend Kim became
pregnant.

My first lesson about being a grandparent before I even became one
was that things were no longer in my hands.

Initially this felt like a disaster. Bringing children into the world was
to me a huge decision, not something to be taken so seemingly lightly.
It seemed such a waste now for my son to have thrown away so much
care and effort on our part as well as so much of his own potential—just
for the sake of a bit of careless sex. How could they have made such a
terrible blunder? I literally fell on my knees at the end of the bed they
were inhabiting at our house and begged them to have an abortion, for

their own sakes. As I saw it, they were on the verge of ruining their own lives and were going to make things so difficult for their own kids—our future grandchildren, as well as all their descendants on down through eternity.

However, they went ahead with the pregnancy. I was full of my own views of parenthood and its difficulties; my wife and I had carefully waited until we were ready. I had so wished my own children would do the same.

Aron received an assurance of work at an aerospace company before he had even completed his last year at university. They had their wedding that summer up at our house, and we helped them buy and renovate a house to move into that fall. It has been difficult at times for them to have had children so early, but who hasn't had difficult times? They have never taken their childbearing responsibilities lightly and have done a remarkable job.

Kya, Aron's first child and my oldest grandchild, is almost seventeen now, the age her mother was when Kim gave birth to her. She has grown into a wonderfully intelligent, inquisitive, capable, and attractive young woman, as has her multitalented younger sister Bailey.

Being a grandparent is a vast step removed from being a parent. Yes, grandparents have less day-to-day responsibility, but we also have much less intimacy with our children and grandchildren. That absence is painful, sometimes, because it's in such contrast to the closeness we developed through the years of homeschooling. I think it must come as a shock to many new grandparents who are very close to their children during their growing up.

I often feel I have been too distant from my grandchildren, but as Kya reminded me just the other day, even small moments together can matter so much. She told me how fondly she remembers the times I used to take her out to explore the wetlands near our house in the hills to look at the frogs and ducks when she was little. What seemed to me at the time as only a handful of almost minimal and infrequent gestures over the period of a child's life are in fact remembered and treasured.

I often feel just as remiss in my attention to my older daughter's son, Joaquim. He's already four and I've seen him only a handful of times in his life. Zoe and her family live three thousand miles away, on the other side of the continent, and that puts pressure on the rare times we do see each other. The third time I had ever set eyes on my only grandson (the first his birth and second when he was also just a baby), the pressure to connect was almost stressful.

Zoe so wanted me to be the perfect grandfather. She'd built up unrealistically high romantic expectations around me getting together with my grandson. Since I now lived close to the sea on Canada's mountainous Pacific coast, she had conjured up images of Joaquim and me standing at the edge of the great ocean, looking into the vast distances of sea and sky, contemplating the mysteries and possibilities of life with each other. In actual fact this little two-year-old barely recognized me, and had only minor interest in who this stranger was. He was far more interested in running away, climbing sand dunes at high speeds, and escaping the clutches of his young cousins who were also with us.

As much as I tried to reassure Zoe that it takes a bit of time to develop a relationship, even with your own grandson, she felt disappointed and even hurt that Joaquim and I hadn't immediately struck up an intimate relationship at our first real meeting. I felt like a failure as a grandfather.

Around these years I had also begun a new relationship. This was a wonderful event for me, after more than a decade of being single after my wife left our family in search of a life on her own. My new flame was absorbing attention that might otherwise have been devoted entirely to Zoe and my grandson Joaquim. From what I understand now, the relationship between Linda and me unfortunately looked to others much the same way Aron and Kim's relationship had appeared to my wife and me long ago during their early courtship—attached at the hips and lips.

"They're all over each other," Zoe later commented to a friend who had asked if Linda's and my new relationship was serious. Cringe! What kind of grandfather would act in such a selfish, adolescent way?

Thankfully, things have since been repaired. When Linda and I visited Zoe and her family back East last year, it was almost as if three-year-old Joaquim was meeting us as complete strangers.

"They are so nice!" he proclaimed to my daughter later that evening, as if surprised. He barely remembered previous visits because he was so young. Joaquim now accepts "Blondie," one of his terms of endearment for Linda, as a complete member of the family. She is really no more a stranger to him than I am. Since most of my family is dark-haired, Joaquim finds Linda's fair hair a curiosity. One day he surprised Lindy, as he also calls her, by asking, "How does it feel to be blonde?"

Linda's children have also taken some time to accept me. Although her older son felt comfortable with me quickly, her younger son took his time sizing me up. He was surely wondering how I would relate not only to his mother but also his daughter Savannah, Linda's only grandchild—who disliked me immediately. I was an intruder trespassing on her special relationship with her "Nana."

As we left the playground after our first meeting and Savannah climbed into her car seat, this two-year-old glared at me and said firmly "You are not getting in this car!" Luckily I wasn't, so there was no battle. Since then, fortunately, I seem to have won her over. Savannah knows I am not technically her grandfather, but we have a sort of equivalent relationship. Our geographical proximity makes spending time together easy.

Linda and I enjoy a routine of having Savannah spend every Tuesday with us, a setup that helps her parents sort out their complicated, flexible work situations. On other days of the week Savannah stays with other family members—aunts, cousins, and her other grandparents, and there are a couple of days of preschool. Her mom and dad say Linda and I are Savannah's number one preferred destination. Perhaps they are flattering us as a form of gratitude, but there's no doubt that Savannah enjoys being here.

When Tuesday rolls around, her mom tells me she urges them to get her here as early as possible, even when their work situations don't require that they rush her over first thing in the morning. We are told she feels something is terribly amiss if Tuesday comes around and she isn't coming here for one reason or another.

She explodes through the front door every visit, excitedly telling us of her latest experiences or acquisitions. She almost immediately calls for us to join her on the living room floor for a variety of games and activities. Sometimes we just play for hours with the characters in her mega-block building set, or we cut and glue scraps of colored paper into fantastic shapes and creatures. Other times we draw, do puzzles, or read, something she loves because she values information so much.

She's fascinated by the information contained in signs of all kinds, instructions that come with various toys or appliances, and, of course, her encyclopedia. We chuckled as she told us one day that, "I don't know everything, but I do know this ..." I forget the issue exactly, perhaps the fact that ladybugs have white eyes or some other bit of information that I did not know about but which we were able to confirm with the help of Google. I'm amazed by how ready she is to learn. And also how much she, and all my grandkids, have to teach me.

As sweet as she is, Savannah knows she has us both wrapped around her little finger. There are minor power struggles during the day, mostly over which direction a game should go, for example, which she generally wins. The more she is able to have her way, the more generous she seems to become over the course of the day. She can sometimes arrive quite tired and grumpy, having been roused from her bed so early, but a little bit of getting her way soon restores her sense of balance. Just as I did when homeschooling my kids, Linda and I reserve our resistance only for what is truly important. That seems to get respect from her when we use it sparingly. The force of our adult power and authority when necessary can then be quite gentle, requesting her cooperation rather than demanding it.

It might seem contradictory—but by our recognizing her own power and permitting it, and supporting what she is interested in, she seems more able to also give our logic her full consideration and cooperation. By the time the day is over, it feels like we're dealing with an adult rather than a four-year-old. Savannah can hang around the house all day and play the games she loves, breaking only for a lunch of Linda's delicious fruit crepes in the breakfast room and, sometimes, even having a sleepover. When we have her for full days, we include her in shopping and lunch, where we can share our enjoyment of her with friends.

On sunny days there's the playground and a walk, perhaps along the "secret" path in the park on the lake, or to the elephant tree in the park with the stream. In summer we often head up to our favorite lakeside beach with a picnic to cool down; on cold rainy or snowy days we drop in on the nearby hot springs pool.

One game we play at the pool is the bee game. Savannah collects a bunch of small blue Styrofoam floats and distributes them around the edge of the pool, pretending they are "flowers" that we can swim to and collect the nectar from—we're bees. She climbs on my back, hanging on to my neck as we swim around gathering the nectar. I make buzzing noises in the water with my lips, and she directs from my shoulders which flower we should go to next. As we collect our nectar, one flower at a time, we take it to Linda, who is playing Queen Bee back at the hive, to make honey for the winter. Other swimmers are birds or butterflies in our imaginary landscape.

Once, as Savannah stepped onto the edge of the pool to collect the nectar from one of these flowers, a couple who were relaxing and watching us asked Savannah what we were doing. She explained the game in great detail, including the fact that Linda was her Nana and I was her sweetheart, and then she jumped back on my shoulders, banging me on the head in the process.

"Oh, you hit your Daddy's head!" the woman said, laughing.

"He's not my Daddy. He's my Nana's sweetheart!" she said with an "I already told you so" assertiveness that gave us all a good chuckle.

"He is a sweetheart to play like that with you," replied our new friend, a comment that, I confess, gave me a secret pleasure. I do like to notice when I do this grandpa thing well after all.

This level of grandfatherly intimacy with Savannah comes a little closer to the relationship I had with my own kids. Initially it surprised my daughter Zoe on that first trip out West to visit us. Not only did she have to share attention with my new partner Linda, but the grandfatherly role Zoe had foreseen her own son getting had already been developed with someone else's granddaughter! I understood how this level of intimacy with Savannah and Linda could surprise Zoe, just as she was so carefully trying to forge a wonderful relationship between me and my only grandson, despite the enormous geographical distance.

I remember so little of my own grandparents, but my own parents were important to my kids growing up. My parents' loving influence on my children is a lot to live up to, and I often wonder if I am up to the task. I can no more easily accept a fixed role of grandfather than I accepted the role of father with my own children. These relationships are created in the living of them, not preordained roles we must fit ourselves into.

I was amazed when even my own father, an otherwise rational man, expressed his disappointment when my only son Aron, who had fathered two daughters at a very young age, decided that two children were enough and had a vasectomy. That thoughtful choice distressed my father. It meant that my father's family name, Dalton, would not be passed on to future generations beyond his great-granddaughters' lifetime, since my other two children were daughters.

To me, this seemed a trivial issue in the greater scheme of things. However, my daughter Zoe saw her beloved grandfather's wishes as so important to fulfill that she retained the family name for herself and included my father's first name as Joaquim's middle name. So her son's name now includes his great-grandfather's first and last names, Robert Dalton, as part of his own name: Joaquim Robert Dalton Pereira! It was lovely that Zoe also wanted the thread of memory to continue, at least for one more generation.

The power to generate such a loving response is not easy to live up to. I often feel I am failing to meet the high expectations created in my children's minds by their intimacy with my own parents. Thankfully, however, my kids are positive and mature, and they help forge very strong links between me and my grandchildren, despite long distances, emotional as well as geographic, which threaten to hold us apart.

Gradually, Linda and Savannah have become absorbed into my family, just as I am absorbed into Linda's. The more we all cross paths, we become less strangers and more members of each other's families. Savannah is starting to feel like another little cousin to my grandchildren rather than a competitor. She is more accepting of my children and grandchildren as part of the large family she had before she met me. Each of her grandparents had split up and remarried, so her family now includes not only two official grandmothers and two official grandfathers but also each of their new spouses.

Savannah now has four females playing a sort of grandmother role and four males, including me, playing a degree of the grandfather role. That's not even mentioning all the children and relatives of these pairings and the ever-growing number of cousins, to which I now add my own grandchildren. As complicated as it might sound, these partner split-ups and repairings are beginning to seem normal in our grandchildren's world.

I take pride in my ability to relate well with children, though my approach doesn't necessarily fit the often patronizing adult-child model. I enjoy children. Some say I become a child like them, but I prefer to see it as listening to them and taking them seriously. I ask that they relate to me similarly in return. They are larger in my world than their diminutive bodies might suggest. Kids like it when you respond to them as complete beings, even if they still have something to learn. They respond well.

At the drugstore photo counter the other day, while getting a bunch of photos printed for various members of the family who would soon be gathering for the holidays, I suddenly realized I was bragging to the clerk behind the counter about my grandchildren. There was Savannah in her princess outfit and ballet tutu, Joaquim Robert Dalton Pereira in his knight outfit, the older girls participating in the cross-country Olympic torch relay, Kya bungee jumping, Bailey cooking up a storm and singing in her musical production, all of them horseback riding. I am so full of love and pride for all of them.

Grandparenting is a new way of relating. It takes time to learn how to do it well and to adjust expectations. Many of us have to bridge geographical and emotional distances, adjusting to a lesser intimacy with our grandkids than we enjoyed with our own kids. Assuring my children and grandchildren of my love and acceptance of who they are is the greatest success I can have as a grandparent. It's also the greatest gift I can pass on. After that, all I can do is let go, as one generational wave gives way to the next. I hope I did my job as a parent well, because my chance to improve on that is disappearing over the horizon as I grow older. The rest of this mysterious journey of life will soon be up to them alone. Remarkably, thankfully, they all seem to be up to the task.

Four Generations of First-Born Daughters

DONNE DAVIS

The founder of the GaGa Sisterhood, a national grandmothering group that started on the Peninsula south of San Francisco, describes how she's been able to continue the intergenerational contact she grew up with by including her elderly mother in visits to her grandchildren. She and her daughter clear up misunderstandings, and she learns from her mistakes. We aren't privy to her daughter's thoughts, but it probably goes both ways.

WHEN I WAS GROWING UP in San Francisco, my grandparents came over for dinner every Thursday night. I could hardly wait to get home from school to play with my Grandma Amelia.

As soon as I saw her, I'd pull her down on the kitchen floor and we'd play jacks while my mom cooked dinner. "Come on, Grandma, I want to teach you Chicken in the Coop. I just learned it!" She was a good sport, and always played the new games I taught her.

Spending the night at my grandparents' apartment was even more of a treat. They lived just twenty minutes away in a second-floor apartment in the Richmond District, where my grandma and my mother both grew up. At bedtime my grandma made up the Chesterfield with crisp laundered sheets that felt cool when she tucked me in. She sat with me until I fell asleep, telling me family stories about growing up in San Francisco. I loved hearing her describe how she and her parents had to camp out in Golden Gate Park right after the 1906 earthquake.

That bond between my grandma and myself forged my model for the grandparent-grandchild relationship. Although I never consciously imagined myself as a grandma, I *did* imagine myself as a mother and always knew I wanted to have children.

Two months before my daughter was born, my husband and I moved from San Francisco to Southern California for an exciting new job he had accepted. When I called to tell my parents, they were devastated. "Couldn't he find a job in the Bay Area?" my mom asked, already feeling the anguish of her first grandchild living so far away from her. From her point of view, I was leaving the nest and taking their first-born grandchild with me. With that move, our dreams of weekly family dinners were shattered and the tight bond between my parents and me was about to be tested.

For eighteen years we adapted to the distance and settled for visits every other month instead. We drove up Interstate 5 to my parents' house and stayed with them for several days, or they flew down to Southern California and stayed with us. It wasn't anything like the model I'd grown up with, but we adapted, and they got to see their grandchild.

When I became a grandma in 2003, I more fully understood the pain my parents must have felt as long-distance grandparents. Even though my husband and I live only 135 miles from our two granddaughters, it feels like a long way for all of us. We can't just pop over whenever we feel like it. But since we're both retired, we have the flexibility to visit any day we want. We've found that two visits a month works well for all of us. We pack our bag and drive two hours on Interstate 80 to Sacramento for a two-night stay with our daughter, son-in-law, and two granddaughters. We sleep in the guest room of their three-bedroom home and participate in the whole cycle of daily routines and rituals.

Once a month we pick up my eighty-eight-year-old mother in San Francisco and bring her with us. Dressed impeccably, she always waits in the lobby of her retirement community with her green duffel bag, eager to see her grandchildren and great-granddaughters. We've all kept this commitment for the past eight years because I want my granddaughters to bond with their grandparents and great-grandmother the way I did with my grandparents, and my daughter did with hers. We are four generations of first-born daughters born to first-born daughters. The strength of that mother-daughter bond is valued by the women in our family who are proud of not just this fact, but of the quality and depth of our relationships.

One of the reasons these powerful matriarchal bonds have been possible to forge is because of the men we've all married. My grandfather, father, husband, and son-in-law also came from loving parents who fostered and nurtured the importance of family and traditions. Without their support and shared values, we wouldn't have been able to maintain the commitment to building the grandparent-grandchild relationship.

If all this sounds easy and idyllic, I assure you it's taken a tremendous amount of conscious communication to nurture these relationships. We have made countless mistakes and apologies in learning how to get along under one roof—but the payoff is so great we all make the effort. There is no better feeling than pulling into our children's driveway and watching our two granddaughters come racing out the door screaming with joy. I can barely open the car door fast enough to catch them in my arms.

Yet, even in that arrival moment I've made mistakes that illustrate the constant learning process we grandparents face. We used to announce our arrival with our signature honk on the horn ("Shave and a haircut, two bits"), until we woke up the little one during her nap. Now we arrive without the fanfare!

I made another mistake when my granddaughters were little. In my excitement to see them, I often rushed right past my daughter, standing in the doorway. After repeated blunders of this type, my daughter finally complained to me, "Sometimes I think you just come up here to see the girls, and not me!"

I realized she was telling me I wasn't giving her the attention she needed. During that visit it became clear to me that our mother-daughter relationship frequently got relegated to the back burner. The tension continued to build, and by the end of the second day I suggested to my daughter that we go for a walk the following morning—just the two of us. I had trouble falling asleep that night as I tried to think of the best way to bring up my concerns.

The next morning during our long walk, my daughter and I each took turns sharing some of the feelings that had been building up. The tension vanished, like releasing the air in an overinflated tire. Suddenly, we were laughing and joking, and the lightness that had been missing over the past two days returned. We both felt relieved and realized the importance of making time for each other.

I also realized that no matter how much fun it is to play with my granddaughters, it's equally important to make time to connect with their parents. We've found the best time to talk with our daughter and son-in-law is after the children go to bed. During those late-night conversations we've discussed holiday and vacation plans, the projects we're working on, or we resolve the communication errors we've botched.

The most difficult lesson I've learned as a grandma is to keep my opinions to myself and weigh my words very carefully. I jokingly tell my grandma friends that I always roll out the "eggshell carpet" before I walk into my daughter's house. When I was a young mom, I didn't appreciate my mother offering her advice—I still don't—and my daughter definitely doesn't want mine.

As a new mom, she embraced attachment parenting with a passion. She constantly carried the baby in a purple Moby wrap. Even though she looked adorable swaddled against my daughter's chest, I just didn't get it. I used every ounce of will power to stifle my comments until she complained about how tired she was. I responded, "Well, duh, if you'd put the baby down once in awhile, it might help!" I regretted that comment for weeks.

More recently, she was venting about the mean girls in my granddaughter's classroom. Without giving it much thought, I replied, "Oh, that's what kids do in the first grade!"

In my offhanded remark I blew it on two counts. If I'd taken a moment to breathe before responding, I might have remembered the lesson my daughter has repeated to me over and over during these past eight years, "Mom, I don't want your *advice*. I want your *empathy*. I want you to understand how I'm *feeling*."

As simple as it sounds, I should have said, "It must be so hard for you to watch that mean behavior." I could have also commiserated with her, instead of minimizing her feelings: "I remember when you were little and the kids teased you. I felt so helpless; I didn't know what to do."

After all the mistakes I've made, I've gotten good at apologizing. When my daughter told me she was planning to homeschool my granddaughter, I said, "Wow, that's a *big* responsibility!" The next day she called me and said, "It hurt my feelings when you said 'homeschooling is a big responsibility.' I wish you'd followed that with: 'and I know you can do it!'"

I also wish I'd said that. But sometimes the words just slip out unfiltered before I realize the impact they could have. My daughter knows I have confidence in her parenting skills, but sometimes I forget to make a point of complimenting her on them. I've learned to look for opportunities to acknowledge all the hard work she and my son-in-law do in raising their daughters.

I know that our learning curve will always be there, but it's not as steep as it was in the first few years. My daughter and I value our relationship and look for ways to improve our communication. When stressful situations arise, we try to go in another room together and talk about what's bothering us. This quick "time out" often diffuses the tension and prevents anger or hurt feelings from festering.

The payoff for all this work is that my daughter and son-in-law trust us. We respect the rules they've established, and try to follow them. Our reward is getting to take our granddaughters to parties, playgroups, and library story hour in Sacramento. Our older granddaughter started spending the night at our house just after her fifth birthday, a visit that was a major milestone for my daughter. Time and trust have eased some of her concerns. She's already decided the younger one can visit whenever she wants.

When my granddaughter comes to visit, I make play dates with some of my good friends and their granddaughters. On one of those visits I got so excited making plans with my granddaughter that I told her we were going to Golden Gate Park to rent a bicycle boat on Stow Lake.

"Mom, I wish you'd asked me first," my daughter complained. "I'm not sure I want her going in a boat. But now that you've told her, I don't want to be the bad guy and say she can't." We agreed that in the future, I would discuss plans with her first.

When I visit my granddaughters in Sacramento I'm often struck by their almost old-fashioned childhood. They are growing up in the same house where my son-in-law was raised; they ride their bikes and scooters over to the same neighbors their father visited when he was a boy to get treats or permission to play on the rope swing. They plant organic vegetables and strawberries in the raised beds he's built. They climb and swing on the used playground set that their parents sanded and refinished for them. The sisters enjoy playing together, despite their four-year age difference. My daughter and son-in-law have taught them how to speak lovingly to each other. When the girls do argue, their parents help them use kind language to resolve their misunderstandings.

As the girls have gotten older and their interests have broadened, it's been easier for my husband to find activities to do with them. They've always enjoyed reading with him, and now he's taught the older one to play checkers and chess. The two sisters love to sing, so we gave them our piano. I taught them to sing "God Bless America," and he wrote the notes on sheet music so he could teach the older one how to play it. Sometimes before we leave, he'll hide a drawing for them to color and leave a series of clues around their room to help them find the drawing.

Cooking is another activity we all enjoy, especially my mom, who has a tiny kitchen in her apartment. She used to make her own cookbooks by clipping recipes from *Sunset* magazine and pasting them into a binder.

I followed her example but expanded my resources, and now my daughter gets many of her recipes from television cooking shows. Although we've all emphasized healthy ingredients over the decades, my daughter has taken it to a new level with more grains and legumes and less meat protein. We all love vegetables and often make a stir-fry together. The girls help cut up the vegetables and tofu, while my mom carefully trims the strings from the pea pods. During our summer visits we always take home a big bag of homegrown tomatoes, cucumbers, and chard.

Our family has come a long way in our ability to discuss our hurt feelings and disappointments. I don't think I could have achieved this level of insight without the help of other grandmothers. When I first became a grandma, I was surprised by the complexity of my new role. My own grandmas made it look so easy. I felt so many new emotions, and wondered if I was normal for having them. I wanted to ask other grandmas if they ever feared they'd drop the baby or felt envious of the "other" grandmother.

I wanted to find out what other new grandmas were experiencing and get some advice from more seasoned ones. I decided to start an organization for enthusiastic grandmas like myself and called it the GaGa Sisterhood. In December 2003, seven months after my granddaughter's birth, I invited all the grandmas I knew to my house to begin a conversation about what it means to be a grandma today.

We sat in a circle in my living room and told stories about what our grandchildren call us and how we got those names, the great lengths we go to, to see them, all the roles we juggle to make time for them, and most important, how we get along with their parents. There was so much to share and not enough time to dive into all of it. We all agreed we wanted to continue the conversation, and we've been meeting for the past eight years.

Our sisterhood has grown into a national social network of grandmas sharing both the joys and challenges of their roles. Local members meet every other month in members' homes throughout the San Francisco

Peninsula. Remote members receive my monthly online newsletter summarizing our meetings and discussing topics related to grandparenting. In 2008, I started blogging about some of the lessons I've learned as a grandma.

At our meetings we cover a wide range of topics, from enjoying art and travel with our grandchildren to storytelling and discipline. One of our most popular meetings was a discussion about "When being a grandma isn't so grand." Everyone present said they felt comforted knowing they weren't the only ones with daughter-in-law challenges or who were facing competition with the "other" grandma. Through our discussions we try to inspire each other to continue growing so we can have lifelong, meaningful relationships with our families.

I've come to appreciate that grandmas are a fascinating, multidimensional group of women engaged in many different aspects of life. They're joyful about this stage of their lives, fun to be around, and committed to being the best grandmas they can be.

Getting to know so many different grandmas and hearing their challenges has given me a greater appreciation of how unique the bond is that I've been lucky enough to form with my two granddaughters and their parents. The frequency of our visits and the physical distance between us is different from the weekly dinners and overnights I had with my grandparents. But we've evolved and adapted to a model that's satisfying for all of us. At the heart of our relationships is the same deep love and devotion to each other that has linked our families for the past three generations.

Twins—Day and Night

Joanna Biggar

*Twins. For a grandmother, it can mean much more work, but also
a tremendous delight and challenge. With her characteristic good
spirits and wry humor, this traveling granny helps where she can,
with the twins and her other grandchildren. When the family was
transferred to Indonesia, off went Granny Goose to Jakarta.*

WHEN MY SON-IN-LAW AND DAUGHTER called from the doctor's office with
"exciting news," I thought I was prepared for whatever was to come.
After all, I was already a veteran grandmother of four granddaughters,
ranging from a newborn to a five-year-old. But when I asked, "Is it a boy
or a girl?" they both said, "Yes." Then Kevin added, "Remember how
you stay a month when a baby is born? Better plan on two." We were all
entering a new universe.

Twins do not run in either family. Heather had not been taking fer-
tility drugs. The surprise pregnancy was now a double surprise, which
would add a boy and the fifth girl in our family. It would make Heather
and Kevin parents of three babies under two—their little girl Tatum
would be only twenty months old when the twins were born.

This event was going to reset my grandparenting compass. It represented a new phase in my "flying granny" life. My husband Doug and I
live in the Bay Area, and three of our grandchildren live in Sacramento.
It's an easy hop to them, and we go back and forth often, can be on
call for emergencies, and be counted on for last-minute plans. But for
Heather and her husband Kevin, who lived near Washington, DC, we
had already established a commuter relationship, which traded shorter
"full-immersion" visits for spontaneity and made up the gap with phone
calls and Skype chats.

Previously they could occasionally fly west. But now with three babies, traveling would be a logistical nightmare. Everything, in fact, seemed like it would be a logistical nightmare, and for some time the commute was going to be one-way.

From the moment I absorbed the news, I asked myself two flying granny questions as I looked at the changing landscape: How could I help across such a distance, and how could I become part of the babies' lives?

In the first instance, there was so much to be done. Two new babies would upend my children's world well before they arrived in late December. They required baby things in duplicate, a new car to accommodate new car seats, a new room. One way to be useful, I figured, was to simply lend a hand. So months beforehand, my husband Doug, who's handy with carpentry, and I visited to help with projects of building, rearranging, moving furniture, and making a new nursery. It was the Fourth of July. I remember sitting on a low chair outside the house with Tatum on my lap watching the local parade march by in the full heat of Washington summer, trying to imagine how different everything would be by December.

Heather, a slender woman who was already large with the twins, brought lemonade, and glanced back at the house. "Think we'll make it?" she asked. And I thought of the mounds of clothes and equipment friends had donated that still needed sorting—my task—and myriad other unfinished jobs. She planned to work as long as possible because they were stretched financially as well as all other ways, and there would be other unresolved problems that lay before them, like child care. "Of course we're going to make it," I answered, including Doug and myself in the collective. It seemed the right and only answer.

By mid-November, increasingly immobilized by the weight of her pregnancy, Heather was working from home, and knew she needed help to manage the last few weeks even before birth. Looming large was that this time she was certain to have a C-section and spend time in a hospital.

Much as she would have preferred the "natural option," which she'd followed so successfully with Tatum, this was her reality: both babies were breech and had no room to turn. When I arrived for my long winter stay, she turned sideways to present her full profile. "Look, Mom, I'm an elephant," she said, and we hugged each other, laughing hysterically.

I began my role of slipping into their lives as helper again: taking care of lively Tatum, reading her stories, ferrying her to and from day care, shopping, cooking, cleaning, and wrestling the endless mounds of laundry. Kevin came home in time to put Tatum to bed, and sometimes we'd share a late glass of wine in the kitchen, while he'd confess his anxiety and excitement. "I just can't wait" was his usual refrain.

As Christmas Eve 2009 fell cold and snowless, stars making patches in the dark sky, we all felt the same as Kevin. Doug had arrived from California, and Heather was beyond ready. We adults knew what was coming, and it was not Santa down the chimney. While hanging up her stocking, we told Tatum her baby brother and baby sister were about to come.

Heather was scheduled for surgery at 7:30 a.m. Christmas morning. Soon after midnight, however, the twins showed they, too, had surprises of their own, and she began labor. Once at the hospital, she quickly went into surgery, and Finley (who would be called Finn) was born at 1:22, while Clara followed a minute later. Kevin called from the hospital with the great news that all was well.

For me, the exciting and unknown part of my commuting granny's journey was about to begin: getting to know the twins. From the earliest hours of the babies' lives, from my first view of them in the hospital, what struck me was how markedly different each seemed from the other. "As different," one nurse said, "as day and night." Clara was small and delicate, with startlingly blue eyes when she opened them; Finn, robust and hungry, given to letting loose with lusty cries, was a half inch longer and a half pound heavier than his sister. His eyes were already turning dark.

Heather was radiant—propped up in bed as one, then the other tiny child was brought to her; Kevin's boyish grin beamed pride and a measure of disbelief. They were relieved. With multiple births, there are so many risk factors. Everything, even the C-section, had gone as well as hoped.

But within a few hours of their birth, the specialists and nurses began to suggest that the differences between the twins were more than just size, gender, and coloring. Clara seemed to have slight trouble breathing and latching on, and her skin appeared to be the skin of an infant born too soon. Finn, on the other hand, had the skin and attributes of an infant who had been in the womb too long. Clara went into a special respirator for a couple of days, and Finn nursed mightily for both of them. The reason for these disparities, the experts said, could be attributed to the fact that the babies weren't actually the same age, that there was about a three-week gap between them, that they had been conceived at different times.

There is a medical term for this occurrence: superfecundation. While rare, it has been documented many times. Heather and Kevin, still grappling with the fact of having had twins born on Christmas, were stunned and slightly anxious. What did this mean? They felt protective of little Clara, who still wasn't nursing much. Heather, who worried all along that Finn's busy feet had kicked at his sister's head before birth, had a new concern.

In the end, it was a condition that brought no harm, but was a new way to view the disparities between the babies. It proved to be just an interesting fact, but one that underscored how complicated, and worrisome, life with two at once could be. Within days, Clara was eating better. Both babies and Heather were doing well enough to come back to the house where we had not yet celebrated Christmas. Wrapped in layers of "swaddling clothes," Kevin and Heather laid the twins beneath the tree—tiny, elfin, sweetly sleeping. Doug took pictures, and I stared in wonder. There never had been before nor will be again in my life Christmas gifts to compare.

As the intense moments of joy and sense that a miracle had visited the household settled over us, so did the reality of life with newborn twins and a toddler. That first afternoon home, Tatum, who had been very much missing her mother, begged Heather to pick her up. Because of her incision, Heather offered instead to hold Tatum on her lap. Unmollified and sensing that some deep shift had taken place in her world, Tatum went into the kitchen, turned her face to the wall and cried bitterly. Heather followed, trying to comfort her, but Tatum pushed her away. Heather then began to weep, too, and turned away from me when I went to console her. At the end of this intergenerational line of despair, I understood viscerally what I'd prepared for intellectually: this was going to be different. This was going to be hard.

Understandably, Tatum did not like the change taking place in her world. With Heather preoccupied and confined upstairs to recover from her surgery, Tatum knew, as I did, that I was taking on the role of her mother. She pushed me away. But slowly, in my deepening place in the day to day with her, she came to accept me, to laugh and roll on the floor with me, to want to come with me in the car, and to read stories with me in her room. By day, with the help of an army of generous friends and neighbors, I did what I could to keep the household more or less running and to keep Heather supplied with good meals and company. By night, I was ready to fall into bed.

But Tatum was still waking up at night, and Kevin and Heather were juggling the demands of two nursing newborns. Kevin had returned to his job at the World Bank with dark circles under his eyes. Everyone was exhausted. There was no time for real rest in that frantic cycle in which the children never slept at the same time. Doug had gone home, and I knew I could alleviate some of my children's exhaustion by taking on night duty, too.

Each night then, with bottled breast milk at the ready, I took one, then the other, of the sweet, fragrant little baby bodies down into my basement guest room, and we settled in. Sometimes they slept with the abandon of a drunk, hours on end, inside the bumpers on my bed. Sometimes they took the bottle happily, burped, and slept again. Sometimes they didn't, and I walked or rocked with them until dawn, inhaling that newborn smell exuding from their bald scalps, while they nestled against me, wrapping a tiny fist around my finger. Clara made her mewling sounds like a little kitten. Finn cried out loud and clear until sated. I got to know them through that deep, physical bonding that is usually the province of mothers, and often fathers. And in those dark hours, I sensed, too, as Heather did, that Clara really was younger than Finn, and wondered what it meant. I knew I was way beyond the norm of my helper's role, but I'd found an amazing way to get to know the babies. I felt grateful for the privilege.

I left in the snows and winds of late January, having been with my little family for weeks. It was time to resume my life. Heather was able to run the stairs, drive, and lift multiple children. She had hired a part-time helper and broken her into the routine. Leaving was painful, wrenching. Unlike after Tatum's arrival, I wasn't assured that my daughter was fine. Returning to her work seemed like a distant mirage. Now, instead of resuming work doing research in early childhood development, she was living it. But I knew she was strong, and would find a way to step into the exhilarating, if overwhelming, role of mother to three babies. I would find a way to be a continuing presence, a flying granny, by slipping in and out of their lives.

That first time, I had stayed long enough to see first smiles and laughs, to witness Clara's deep dimples and Finn's excitement at grabbing things, and to help preside at the first baths. I knew I wouldn't return for months, and accepted that by then the twins wouldn't know me. But to my surprise and joy, when I did come back, both of them came to me easily, nestling their heads against my shoulder in a gesture of familiarity. I fancied then that in those long winter nights we had bonded in a wondrous, primitive way, and they remembered my feel and scent.

During my shorter visits that first year, I witnessed everyone in bloom, and tried to make my helping role fit shifting demands. I brought wine, of course, did lots of driving and cooking, even for crowds to repay the kindness for many friends, and lots of walking the flower-lined streets with strollers. Heather and Kevin continued to grapple with the extremes of their lives—from exhilaration to stress to the realities of being outnumbered by kids. They accepted permanent fatigue with a shrug. Tatum got used to her new role as the big girl. Her inseparable companions were two little dolls, one in pink and one in blue, named Clara Doll and Finn Doll. Sometimes she would cover them in blankets and walk them in her doll stroller; sometimes she'd bash their heads in.

I was fascinated to watch the babies, who transformed almost daily. It wasn't only their emerging personalities I wanted to witness, but that mysterious, ineffable, yet very real entity, the twin relationship. Even as they continued to appear startlingly different from one another—he stocky, big-fisted, dark-eyed, and with a huge grin; she compact, fair, dimpled, with a rosebud mouth and eyes of transparent blue—they still shared a bond that had connected them, head to foot, in the womb. As infants, they often reached out to grab the foot, leg, or hand of the other as if it were their own.

When they got to the stage of rolling over, Finn would often roll until he bumped into Clara, and then keep on going, despite her protests. In time Clara began to do the same, though hulky Finn was something of an obstacle to surmount. They giggled out loud together, shared things back and forth, bumped heads.

When they could sit, they began to tussle over toys. Finn, already showing his devilish side, would often grab whatever she wanted, and wait for her to squeal. But Clara responded with her own stealth. I watched her wait for him to lose interest or loosen his grip, then she made a grab for the toy and put it out of his reach, without his even noticing. In their side-by-side high chairs, they reached over to the other's chair to raid some morsel, but just as often offered a half-chewed delicacy in return.

116

I imagined what it would be like over time to have a lifelong shadow.

By the time they were one, Finn was a fairly well-developed clown. His large head and legs were like little tree trunks, as he swaggered side-to-side when he walked. Just watching him made me laugh. He climbed, raced, made loud noises, and crashed into things at dizzying speed, which he found hilarious. He liked making others laugh, too, and would obligingly do a lopsided dance for applause. Gregarious, open, and trusting, he took to other people easily, and everybody took to him. One little girl of three at his Sunday school was so crazy about him, she announced one Sunday she was willing to go "if Jesus and Finn are going to be there." "Everybody wants a piece of Finn," Heather commented.

Clara, meanwhile, remained quieter, more sedentary. She could crawl, walk, and climb as well as Finn, only she started later and seemed less interested. She could sit for unusually long periods engaged in playing with a toy and observing the world go by. She appeared to be really thinking—I wanted to know about what. Yet in addition to her stillness, Clara was developing another, louder side. She had long had a giggle so deep and heartfelt it was hard to resist giggling with her. But over the year, her cry had developed—loud, clear, and demanding. While Finn was outgoing, she was reticent with strangers. If someone she was attached to, such as her parents, left the room, she could break into heart-rending sobs and not be consoled. She moved with lightning speed from one mood to another. "Mercurial," Heather called her.

During the stretches between visits, we tried by phone, photos, and our Internet talk to keep up with all their changes. By the end of the first year—the "terrible year" for twins, it was frequently said—I was relieved, as I'd predicted long before to Heather, that we'd all made it. The twins were thriving, Tatum was queen of the nursery, and my daughter and son-in-law, though tired, had come through the toughest year with sanity and humor intact. Even I, in traveling granny mode, had found a way to accommodate the intensity of my visits and their revolving demands with the periods of less contact. I'd found ways to be helpful, part of the conversation as well as the action; and I'd been able to get to know all the children despite distance. "We can do this three-thousand-mile thing," I announced to Doug.

But then came an entirely new calculation of nearly nine thousand miles. Kevin had done many projects in Indonesia and was to be transferred. The family would be moving to Jakarta. In July 2010, they arrived in San Francisco, en route, to spend a week with us. It took two large cars to ferry them and their mountain of luggage—nine suitcases, two cribs, three car seats, a double stroller, and everything else they needed to begin life abroad—from the airport to home. Doug called them the traveling circus.

It was the twins' first visit to us, and at one and a half, they found much to like. Clara, still wary of new adults, took instantly to her three cousins. Finn also enjoyed the other kids, as well as the swirl of picnics, parks, barbecues, and train rides that defined the week. But he also liked the company of his dad, granddad, and uncles, and playing with a fleet of trucks we had on our patio. Among them is a wonderfully crafted wooden one, a miniature tro-tro, acquired more than thirty years ago when my children were small and we lived for several years in Ghana. Seeing it there and watching our only grandson play and ride on it made me realize how the cycle of long-distant grandparenting was beginning again, but I had a different role. In my own parents' time, there had been no cell phones, emails, or Skype—only the uncertainty of long-distance mail to keep us connected. Heather had been just three, Tatum's age, when she went to West Africa. She was repeating a cycle as an adult from her own childhood.

The week's visit had again been a time of intense togetherness, but it was also a transition, a time of bonding anew with the children before once more letting them go. A distillation, really, of the whole commuting experience. It was bittersweet to watch their plane take off west into the endless night—a trip of twenty-four hours best forgotten. I was truly excited at the adventure and opportunity ahead for them, but sad at the ocean of distance that would now separate us. When the first email came that they had arrived safely, if mostly sleepless, we were relieved, and began setting our internal clocks to calibrate the fifteen hours between us. Their day had become our night.

The first few months of their new life we followed on Skype: from living in a hotel to adjusting to harrowing traffic to moving into their spacious if sparsely furnished house in a quiet, garden-filled neighborhood of noisy Jakarta. The twins were just beginning to talk using many words, and they excitedly held up things for us to see, or taste, though sometimes what they said was now in Bahasa Indonesian, the national language of Indonesia. The computer screen filled up, too, with the faces of new helpers, who would transform the lives of Kevin and Heather into a normalcy that included sleep and adult conversation. But the image that arrested me, that I stared at with enchantment, was of my grandchildren in their new preschool—three small white faces in a sea of Asian children, most dressed in batiks, silk shirts, and headdresses for Indonesian National Day. It looked like a scene from *The King and I*. I knew I had to see them in their new world.

In early January 2011, I arrived at that house in Jakarta. Tatum, shy but excited, had accompanied Heather to the airport. By the time we got home, she was chatty and full of stories, and excited about the trip she, her mother, and I would take to Bali. As always, she called me "Good News." But I had not been prepared for the transformation in the twins, who had just turned two, and called me "Good News," too.

They appeared as they had been, only on a bigger scale. Finn: big, rowdy, boisterous, running and laughing, and diving headlong into a plastic pool filled with rubber balls. Clara: reticent, quiet, playing for long stretches with one toy before getting up to chase with Finn. Finn would take my hand and say, "Come, Good News, find the monsters," and we would go to prowl the depth of my closet, where they lurked. I'd make a monster sound, and he'd shriek with delight. Clara was unmoved by monsters, but would sometimes bring a book or toy and watch me from the door and then run away.

In my new incarnation as a flying granny, I had no supporting role to play in a household with help, so my attention fell naturally on just being with the children in their new, exotic, and charmed lives. I drove with them through streets crowded with high-rise malls and districts where tropical flowers overgrew the pavement. I pulled them in their red wagon to the local park where neighborhood kids played on paint-chipped jungle gyms, and went to fancy indoor playgrounds where Indonesian children played with uniformed nannies. I ate, sang, and danced with them; visited their enchanting school; and watched them play in the pool with Kevin.

Interestingly, up close I could see in this second year there had been big changes. My perceptions of the twins reversed. If Clara wanted something, she took it. If somebody got in her way, she pushed him out of it. If Finn had something she wanted, which he frequently did in his grab-and-run method of teasing her, she howled and chased him until he relented. Then, just as quickly, she would hand it back, saying "Here, Finny." Heather said, "She wants to be in control. And she's tough. My toughest child." It was Clara who, upon finding a python curled up outside his cage at the zoo, had not only patted it, but also pinched it.

Finn, for all his bluster, was the generous one. He shared easily, even with perfect strangers. Hurt, he howled and sobbed melodramatically. "That's Finn," Heather said, "the drama queen." When we visited the home village of the family cook far south of the city, it was Finn who cried and Clara who decided to entertain the villagers by bursting into song and dance. One of my favorite pictures is of "shy" Clara grinning, surrounded by admiring village girls.

The twins' personalities seemed to have shifted with the trip to Indonesia, but the bond between them remained steadfast. They went to school, played, ate together, and slept in the same room. I remember

Clara standing in her crib cheerfully willing her brother awake with, "Finny, play?" and Finn putting his arm around her shoulder in protective big brother mode when she cried. They looked out for each other and rolled around together like puppies, with Tatum often in the fray.

It was in that mood that I had one of the most endearing moments of the day with the children. At night we'd gather on the mattress in Tatum's room, giggle, jump, and read stories. Each child got to choose stories. Every night Finn picked a book I had given them before they left called *Here Comes Grandma* by Janet Lord. In the story a very granny-looking gray-haired lady rides horses, trains, and planes until she reaches her grandson in his cozy house. Finn never tired of pointing with his chubby finger at the pictures and saying with amazement, "boat, car, airplane."

I loved that he had grasped a basic fact of our relationship. Now that I'm home again, once more connecting by Skype, I'm thrilled to have found a way to build on that story. I found another book called *The Amazing Journey to Grandma's House* by Cheryl Hawkinson and Mary Eakin. In this book a little boy rides a car, horse, helicopter, and magic bird until he reaches his grandma in her cozy house.

Late one recent afternoon, when it was morning in Jakarta, I dialed up Skype and found Finn eating breakfast. "I have a story to read you," I said, and read it through with emphasis on the special effects noises that went with each conveyance. Finn sat still, forgetting to eat.

"I like it," he pronounced at the end.

Similarly, I've read stories to the girls, and listened to Tatum tell me about her day. Then, amazingly, Clara even began to relay events to me. The day before I left Jakarta, we all visited a downtown mall celebration of Chinese New Year with Chinese dancers playing the role of two dragons who fight, jump around, and make a lot of noise until one eventually falls. The victor goes through the crowd and demands to "eat money," which kids obligingly feed him. Some children were frightened and fled, but not Clara. She boldly fed the dragon, and found me an ally in this.

The next day, she took me by the hand to go to their Bajay, a tiny, three-wheeled car, like a rickshaw, but boldly painted. "Please open. Go dragon," she said, somehow imagining our way back there. Now, on Skype she was telling me again. "Dragon, Good News," followed by "Clara jump," at which point she jumped out of sight.

It seems that, with Skype and the video chats, the twins and I really do know each other. And now that they can talk, we can really continue our connection through a kind of cyber call-and-response. I can tell them about their cousins and other people they know, and they can share with me what they are learning, doing, even eating. "Mango and pineapple," yells Clara, trying to share some on the screen. I can also tell them that I will be back to see them again and that Grand Doug is coming too.

What I won't be able to explain, but hope someday they will figure out, is that the flying grandparent arrangement is a thing of beauty, but has to keep adapting to meet our changing lives. I hope they will know we will try to meet them wherever they are—and that our lives would have been so boring and uncomplicated if they hadn't dropped into them one Christmas morning.

The Accidental Grandmother

....

KARINE SCHOMER

Surprises were in store for a globe-trotting French career woman who never intended to have children, much less grandchildren. Exposed to her second husband's grandchildren, Karine Schomer discovers a zany, imaginative side of herself and a knack with young people. Luck? Predestination? It worked out well.

WHEN I WAS GROWING UP in the 1950s, the one thing I knew I never wanted to be was a mother. Motherhood seemed to me a thankless job of household chores, cooking, and putting yourself in third place after your husband and the children. Later on, when I learned what a mother goes through to produce a child—nine months of bloated discomfort followed by an experience of excruciating pain—the notion of motherhood became even more unappealing to me. I set myself on a life path devoted to learning, work, accomplishment, and adventure. Marrying and raising a family were not on the horizon. The notion of someday becoming a grandmother was unthinkable.

I managed to make it through college, three years as a teacher in India, and six years of graduate school and into a tenure-track teaching job without meeting the "Mr. Right" who would have derailed my ambitions by starting a family with me. I did marry a fellow graduate student along the way, but our relationship was based more on the Jean-Paul Sartre and Simone de Beauvoir model of intellectual companionship than the *Leave It to Beaver* vision of family bliss. A second marriage later on was to a man as interested in adventure and unconventional undertakings as I was, and just as disinterested in having anything to do with producing and bringing up children.

Looking back on those days, I am struck by how this rejection of parenting made for a life filled with freedom and mobility, but lacking in a strong sense of rootedness, connection, and generational continuity. I was clumsy and uncomfortable around children, not knowing what to say to them, and felt inauthentic in my dutiful attempts to show interest in the young daughters my two brothers and their wives were raising at the time.

The historic times and my female peers encouraged this vision. We were the generation of the women's liberation movement. We were not going to be held back by the numbing duties of motherhood. We were meant for greater things. We were going to break glass ceilings (we did), forge new models of gender equality (we did), keep our last names from disappearing into conjugal oblivion (we did), and follow our personal dreams no matter where they took us (we did).

The years went by, but I continued to live with a twenty-eight-year-old graduate student mindset. Most of my friends were single or couples without children. I was thoroughly engaged in my teaching, writing, research trips to India, and the ongoing joy of a life fully devoted to the scholarly and creative work I loved. I felt mildly sorry for the peers I knew who were tied down by their families, and had to balance professional work with changing diapers and attending PTA meetings. No one I knew was a grandparent, and my own childhood experience of grandparents had been so limited that all I had was a photograph-induced memory of an elderly lady in a shapeless flowery dress and a bearded old man in a brown woolen bathrobe.

Then, in my forty-third year, divorced a second time, and somewhat chastened by the loss of my job as a professor, I sought to remake my life. After a few years of a giddy freelance existence that gave me all the autonomy and adventure I could have asked for, it was time to get serious about a new professional direction. At the same time, the rough-and-tumble of the singles scene, while certainly a fascinating learning experience, was wearing thin and starting to fill me with a gnawing sense of pathos and alienation.

It was then that I met Raphael, the man who became the love of my life. We were superbly matched in education, intellectual curiosity, humor, social ease, experience in academia, and international backgrounds, mine with France and India, his with South Africa and England. He was also at a point of self-reinvention, from former academic to full-time writer and photographer.

Raphael's first words of introduction to me, which I still remember as a thunderbolt, were: "I am the father of two wonderful grown-up daughters." Those words and the reality behind them changed my life. Suddenly, the perpetually free graduate student was being catapulted into adult life. Here I was getting involved with a man who had married and become a father at a young age, lived through all the phases of the father role, from bringing his newborn daughters back from the hospital to seeing these same daughters off to college and launched into their own life paths, and who along the way had also suffered the excruciating pain of a divorce involving young children.

He came to me with a depth of relational experience and an intensity of intimate feelings far richer than what I had known until then. He had a strong sense of family, with all its joys and strains. When we married, it was not a private affair between the two of us, as my previous marriages had been, but involved a real wedding, with my parents, my siblings and their families, and Raphael's daughters, Judy and Ruth, all present. Shortly thereafter, he persuaded my parents to move from the East Coast to be near us, which allowed me to be close to them during the last decade of their lives. Over time, I got to know and became friends with Judy and Ruth, in ways uncomplicated by the tensions of a parent-child relationship, but more like an aunt or a family friend. In short, I found myself closely enveloped in a family web for the first time since leaving home to go to college.

While I basked in this newfound sense of connection, I sometimes chafed at the need to deal with new emotional complications, new demands on my time, and the overall reduction in my personal freedom to do what I wanted whenever I wanted. It seemed I had successfully avoided the stress of being a mother and raising young kids, but I was finding an adult and family-entwined marriage to be in competition with the activities and ways of running my life I was accustomed to. The demands of my two new "encore" careers, first as a dean in higher education administration, then as an entrepreneurial corporate consultant and trainer, were pressure enough. Working with Raphael on joint writing and photography projects took time too. Later on, when he became afflicted by a series of life-threatening and energy-robbing health issues, the bulk of household responsibilities fell upon me as well.

So it was with mixed feelings that I heard the excited news one day that Ruth, married by then for a few years and living with her husband Jon in San Francisco, was pregnant with their first child. The first thought that crossed my mind was "Oh my God! There goes the rest of my freedom!" I envisioned myself having to hang around making "goo-goo gaa-gaa" noises at a speechless infant, being enlisted for babysitting and other jobs in which I had no interest, and having the small amount of free time I still possessed taken up with talking and worrying about the life of this new being. Naturally, I kept these thoughts to myself, and joined the family chorus of joyful celebration when my grandson David was born.

For Raphael and his ex-wife, this was a moment of historical significance, a positive coming-together of family. Their respective parents had fled from Nazi Germany and Lithuania to the safety of South Africa. Rafael and his ex-wife had left South Africa as a young couple to make a new life in the United States, and had later suffered the pain of divorce, as had their young daughters. All this seemed redeemed by the birth of this first grandchild, in the last year of the twentieth century. On the other side of the baby's family, the joy was equally profound.

Fast-forward a few years, past the millennium celebrations and the September 11 attacks. By then, I had become accustomed to the runs to Costco to pick up diapers, the San Francisco house with childproof everything, the countless photographs, emails, and phone calls about

David's antics and development. He had learned to crawl, walk, and talk and was exhibiting a lively, inquisitive, and forceful personality. Thanks to parents who avoided using baby talk with him, and no doubt by genetic predisposition, he was articulate from a very young age. A treat in store for us would be witnessing the evolution from the pre-school child's attempt at big words—"Duninditsu" or "San Fransikso" for San Francisco, "I was born in a hobstibble (hospital)," "Play minick (music)," "I want to gwirt (squirt) water," "There goes an amerlance (ambulance)," and "Merncy!" (Emergency!)—to his effortless fluency by age five with the polysyllabic words needed to share his cascades of ideas about mechanical engineering, space exploration, ballistic missiles, and prison reform.

David was doted on by child-centered parents who enveloped him in affection and were attentive to his every need. He gradually became aware that, courtesy of divorces and remarriages, he also had six loving older people who came around to visit him and take him to their homes. He learned to call them all Grandpa and Grandma. Except for me. I was always "Karine" or "Een-Queen." This was more than fine with me, because when I heard the word "grandma," I flashed back to the picture of the elderly lady in the shapeless flowery dress. I felt myself to be nothing like that. Whenever we went to visit, I wore my usual off-hours jeans and sweatshirt, and my instant reaction to the scene was to sit or lie on the floor with little David and play. I just couldn't do the "wise elder sitting in a chair" role of a real (and perhaps less limber) grandparent that I had seen with my own parents when they interacted with their three granddaughters.

To give David's parents some time alone and some respite from child care, Raphael and I got into a pattern of picking up David on Sunday mornings and keeping him at our place all day. Initially, I was lukewarm about the idea. What in the world would I *do* with a small child all day? Wouldn't it be extremely boring? How long would this go on? Given

Raphael's limited energy, would I end up having to do the bulk of the heavy lifting on this project? Would I never again be able to go on a hike, see an art exhibit, or visit friends on Sundays?

But then, something magical happened. The more time Raphael and I spent with this little squirt, the more I found myself developing a richly textured relationship with him that was filled with both emotional depth and intellectual delight. Increasingly, David displayed the qualities that had drawn me to his grandfather: imagination, curiosity, affection, sensitivity, articulateness, humor, and fun. He loved to talk and discuss, wanted to know about everything, liked to tease and be teased, was eager to try new things, from making hair for his bald grandpa out of shredded paper strips to mixing orange juice, cocoa, and yogurt as a special dessert. Discovering and relating to this lively little mind was a revelation to me. I had never imagined that interacting with a child could be so fascinating. I loved the energy David's presence brought into our home, and how the simplest of things took on a quality of wonder when seen with the freshness of his young eyes.

David was especially fond of stories. We were glad to oblige with tales from our own childhoods, Raphael's on the southern tip of Africa in Cape Town, mine in the small village of Le Chambon-sur-Lignon in central France, both exotic places and times from David's perspective as a twenty-first-century San Francisco child. I found that recounting the adventures and memorable moments of my childhood to this eager listener helped me reconnect to the continuity of my own life. It made me realize that the little village girl in pigtails who used to walk across a field of jonquils and through a copse of pine trees to reach the one-room schoolhouse was still alive and well inside me. My parents and siblings, too, came to life as I remembered them from those long-ago days. The weight of the present was lightened by the nostalgic recollection of a past filtered through loving memory.

It was inevitable that, at some point, I would try to recreate for David one of the story traditions from my own family: the "Cannonball" adventure tales, made up by my father, in which each of the characters was an alter ego for one of us kids. I invented Super Kid as a science fiction version of David, and amazed myself by finding that I was actually quite good at storytelling. Accustomed to stories from books, he would say "Read it again!" when he particularly liked an episode I had made up. Always the quick study, however, he soon took over the storytelling role himself, and Super Kid morphed into Super David, with a friend Untun on the planet Andracoola. Each episode ended with a huge battle scene with special weapons invented and stored in one of David's magic warehouses.

David's love of stories led me to share with him my favorite French childhood comic books: the adventures of Tintin, the boy detective, and the tales of Astérix, the brave little Gaul who successfully fought off the Romans. That, too, had the effect of collapsing the passage of time and bringing my past back to life. I went to the local public library to check out other children's classics I had loved, from Pinocchio to King Arthur, and thoroughly enjoyed the rediscovery of these long-forgotten treasures. My visits to the children's section of the library also introduced me to today's wealth of superb books for children, a literary genre I had never given much thought to before.

Our home had very few toys or other store-bought items specifically intended for the entertainment and edification of children. This was intentional on our part, because Raphael and I both remembered frugal childhoods in which a couple of cherished stuffed animals, a handful of simple toys, and a small treasure box were enough, and play was something that didn't require fancy equipment or gadgets. We were in fact somewhat put off by the cornucopia of store-bought toys David was surrounded with in his own home.

Consequently, when David came to our house, play often consisted of making things out of cardboard, cans, stationery supplies, string, aluminum foil, and other everyday household objects, with a large dose of fantasy. I had always loved making things as a child, and felt time fly as

David and I worked on various construction projects. I also encouraged him to make costumes out of old colored sheets and castaway clothes—another throwback to one of my childhood activities. We made a bow and arrow set out of a curved tree branch, string, and bamboo sticks. In the garden I taught David to rake, dig, plant, and weed, something he did with enthusiasm, even though he sometimes got distracted from the central purpose and preferred to dig channels for an imaginary Erie Canal and make mud to stomp around in. In contravention of the spirit of child labor laws, Raphael and I made play out of not only gardening chores, but also vacuuming, weeding, sweeping out the garage, and car washing, the latter always an opportunity to turn the hose on Grandpa.

We came to look forward to these Sundays, even though hosting David required that both of us be "on" for the whole day at our respective energy maximums. The three of us had a wonderful time doing things together. Raphael and I each had our independent relationship with David as well. Raphael's bond with his grandson was deeper and more intense, mine more playful and a relationship of "pals." (David once asked me, in genuine puzzlement, "Are you a teenager?")

It was all good. For one day a week, the parents got a break, and we had this wondrous creature in our lives. Instead of resenting the loss of my Sundays, I came to feel they were a privilege and a gift. I started looking differently at those of my friends who had no responsibility for children, feeling they were missing the joy of something special rather than envying them their freedom.

Being involved in the life of a child brought another unexpected benefit. I came to realize that connection to the place in which you live has a different and richer texture when you are part of the world of families and kids. I had heard from countless friends who had moved to the Bay Area that one can easily feel lonely in this best place on earth. I had experienced this loneliness myself, not only when single but also with the loneliness à deux of couple life unconnected to community. Now, thanks to Ruth and Jon's generosity about sharing their child's life with us, I found my sense of place deepen significantly. Places I had barely noticed before entered my consciousness: schools, city parks with jungle gyms, public swimming pools, the steam trains and old-style carousel in Tilden Park, the Scottish Games on the grounds of Dunsmuir House in Oakland, and the USS *Hornet*, where David walked across the flight deck on the painted "footsteps" of Neil Armstrong. Best of all, our immediate neighborhood took on a quality of enchantment, as we introduced David to neighbors who were glad to share with him their kids, dogs, cats, rabbits, fruit trees, tools, stories, and good cheer.

Having no preconceived notion of what a grandmother does, I simply followed my own sense of what would be delightful to do every week. I used my life-long proclivity to plan things in order to make them happen, and then settled into "special event" mode for the day. It was no doubt creative and generous on my part to go to all this effort (that's how others saw it), but it was also self-protective, as there is nothing I dislike more than aimless, unstructured days in which nothing happens but sitting around and the passage of time. David's father Jon sometimes referred to our house as "The El Cerrito Summer Camp," with me as the activities director. It was a good metaphor, not only for David, but for us too: Sundays were a complete break from the adult work-related concerns of the week, a neverland of imagination and play from which I emerged physically tired but mentally refreshed.

Indeed, imagination was at the heart of our Sundays with David in El Cerrito. The conversations, the stories, the crazy things we made, David's tying up the living room with string, the weird cooking experiments, the humor—all of it was about imagination. So were the tricks we pulled on one another. "Fooling Grandpa" and "tricking Karine" were always favorites. Raphael used Photoshop and other devices to try to convince David that he was related to the Queen of England, despite protests by Ruth that such "lying" would make David distrust grown-ups, and that David was now behaving like a little prince! But Raphael and I pulled off the most long-lasting hoax of all, by creating a character named Pirate

Jim, who interrupted his notorious adventures on distant seas to come by and secretly set up treasure hunts for kids. Because David was sharp and asked many questions, we were forced to add ever-new layers of fabrication, just managing to keep one step ahead of the little sleuth. If there is one thing I hope he will remember, it's the delight we all took in this weekly feast of the imagination.

When David was three and a half years old, a big change took place in his life: the birth of his sisters Hannah and Sophie. They were fraternal twins with very different looks (one brunette and one red-headed), and they developed distinctive personalities. From early on, Raphael and I referred to them as "the anthropologist" and "the actress." As they grew beyond infancy, we watched them evolve into the characters of our initial perception. Hannah was down-to-earth, task-oriented, assertive, and good at getting things done. Sophie was imaginative, creative, sensitive to other people's feelings, and good at appreciating and creating beauty.

Over the years, we would watch and sympathize with the whole family's struggle to deal with the complexities of the new configuration and the growing pains of the sibling relationships. But for David, the immediate result of the advent of the two newcomers was that he was no longer the only child at the center of everyone's attention. He had to share space, time, and his parents' now fragmented attention and affection. It was a very difficult transition for him. The other sets of grandparents stepped in to help with the infant care needs of the two girls, but Raphael and I preferred to do our part by concentrating on David. Despite my conversion to the wonder of kids, my willingness to be involved did not genuinely extend to infants and toddlers who could not yet converse with me. Also, both Raphael and I were better at hosting kids in our own home, in our own way, than at going over to the kids' home in San Francisco and making ourselves useful in the interstices of Ruth and Jon's household patterns.

Eventually, Hannah and Sophie grew old enough to come over on Sundays too. For the first few years, their babysitter Michelle drove the three kids over to us from San Francisco and became part of our Sundays in El Cerrito tradition. The extra cost was worth it to Ruth and Jon, who desperately needed one day a week without any kids around. By the time the girls were four, we switched to having me pick up and return the kids by public transportation (the underground BART system across the bay to San Francisco) as Raphael was not well enough to take on the two-way drive, and I was absolutely unwilling to be responsible for the safety of three children in a car speeding along a freeway.

Those Sundays in charge of three grandkids were among the most action-packed days of my already hyperbusy life. Every one of my creative, managerial, and communication skills was put into high gear. During the week, I plotted activities and food, selected new books at the public library, negotiated pick-up and drop-off times, and reshuffled the rest of my responsibilities so there would be nothing else but the kids on Sunday. There was also a need for contingency planning, as we were never one hundred percent sure until the last minute that the kids were actually going to come. Raphael's health issues also made things uncertain and required flexibility about changing plans at the last minute. Then the day unrolled, without a break, from 6 a.m. to 9 p.m.: get up, do yoga, fix breakfast, clean up, ready the house for kids, take BART to San Francisco, pick up kids, ride back on BART, prepare lunch, eat lunch, clean up, read books, do activities, eat afternoon snack, gather up for departure, BART back to San Francisco, deliver kids, BART back home, prepare dinner, clean up, put out garbage ... and then collapse! Bleary-eyed but contented, I would fall asleep at once, wondering how in the world parents manage this kind of pace day after day, instead of just as a weekend special.

Early on, Raphael and I both discovered that we needed to establish some rules of the house in order not to be overwhelmed by the energy of three lively beings pulling in different directions. One of the strangest behaviors we encountered at first was that they would all run into the kitchen, open the refrigerator, and each start making separate demands about what they wanted me to prepare for them to eat. I sat them all down: "Kids. Let me tell you something you may not realize. This is not a restaurant. I'm not a waitress. Here's how we're going to do things. We have a lunch planned. Each of you has a job: you're either Cooker, Setter, or Clearer." Since kids are teachable and responsive to rules when you set them with firm authority, the new pattern went into effect quickly. Each child took a turn at each job, and we were actually able to enjoy a sit-down meal. I was amused and gratified when, some time later, having come over to their home for a visit and offering to cook dinner there, I got an immediate chorus of "Who's the Cooker? Who's the Setter? Who's the Clearer?"

Sundays with the kids became a regular part of our life, reminiscent for me of the old French tradition of weekend family lunch at the grand-mother's house. We tried to endow the experience with as much ritual and formality as was possible with these freewheeling contemporary American kids. We did our best to reinforce Ruth's valiant efforts to teach her children social niceties by promoting "please," "thank you," and the idea that you pass dishes around rather than each person grab-bing food for themselves. The kids were all avid conversationalists, talking excitedly and simultaneously, each competing to be the center of attention. Our lunchtime discussions ranged widely, from details of their daily life to funny movies they had seen and shows they were put-ting on, to history, politics, science, music, and art.

A brief rest after lunch allowed us to read stories together, which inev-itably led to more discussions. Then came afternoon activities: bicycling to the park, planting vegetables in our garden, going swimming at the El Cerrito Swim Center, doing magic tricks, posing for or inventing pho-tographic images with Grandpa, or working with me on construction projects. The kids also liked to settle down into our home offices and see what they could make out of the materials and equipment we had there. Sometimes I led them on special adventures: coming to the East Bay by ferry instead of by BART, going to pick blackberries in a secret location in the hills, flying kites in the empty lot at the corner, taking a picnic lunch to the Berkeley Marina, canvassing the neighborhood for Barack Obama during the presidential election of 2008. Our time involved little or no time with media entertainment, of which they had plenty at home. I think we were trying to give them an experience of what childhood was like pre-TV, pre-iPods, and pre-video games.

Time has moved on. David is now in his twelfth year, and Hannah and Sophie have turned eight. Their lives are much more complex, and scheduled up like the lives of business executives. Ruth uses the Outlook function on her Palm Pilot to keep track of their school times, extracurricular activities, social engagements, appointments with doctors and tutors, and the "camps" that seem to take up most of their vacation time. The six grandparents, whose help was once vital to keeping the whole operation afloat, are now less needed in a practical sense, and become at times one more item to enter into the Outlook calendar.

While the kids are always glad to see their grandparents, they are becoming more involved in their own lives. We have learned from them the difference between a visit, a playdate, and "hanging out." What all three of them are most interested in now is "hanging out" with their friends, and the scene at our place (affectionately referred to by Jon as "Old Europe") is definitely a "visit" kind of event. In addition, as David nears adolescence, the gap between his interests and pace and those of his sisters is growing, and they don't really like all coming together.

On top of all this, the aging BART system makes riding the trains so noisy that the pleasant times we used to spend talking as we traveled across the bay have been replaced by a grim endurance of ear-splitting noise that forces everyone to shout in order to be heard. As a result, the kids are reluctant to come over and see us unless they get driven in both directions. Given that I won't drive them and that Raphael does not have the energy for round-trip chauffeuring from and to San Francisco, the regular Sundays in El Cerrito are no longer logistically feasible in the way they once were.

The weekly kid-free day Ruth and Jon had enjoyed for several years is being replaced for now by recreational activities as a family, ferrying kids to the homes of their various friends in San Francisco, or just plain "hanging out" at home as a family. We are meanwhile trying to figure out with master scheduler Ruth what new ways there may be for us to maintain regular face-to-face contact with the kids even though we can no longer see them as predictably as before. A golden era and its patterns are morphing into something as yet unknown. We're sure we will have a lifelong involvement with David, Hannah, and Sophie. But it will take some ingenuity to invent new patterns to fit new realities, as both the kids and their grandparents grow older, and the transportation problems of a congested urban area worsen. Calls and email are good, but they are not a satisfactory substitute for in-person experience. Perhaps David will have to invent one of his special imaginary space machines to spirit us instantly across the twenty miles between our homes.

This past decade of grandparenting the kids during the "golden years" of their childhood has gone by very fast for me. The experience has been so engrossing that I've had little leisure to reflect on how it has changed me. To my great surprise, I've learned how to relate to kids, and find myself gravitating toward children wherever I go. It feels sometimes as if kids spot me at once as a fan, and try to connect to me with their smiles. Family and friends say I'm very good with David, Hannah, and Sophie, who clearly love and like me, and I enjoy the idiosyncratic way I have been able to take on the grandparenting role on my own terms. But I still don't think of myself as a grandmother. It's not about being a step-grandparent rather than a "real" grandparent, but about never having been a parent. I feel I've been given the opportunity to play a wonderful and unexpected role, like a favorite friend of the family who has been taken along on a lovely ride.

I tend to get irked at the present-day fashion, well-meant though it is, of referring to grandchildren as "*our* grandchildren" when only one of the parties involved is truly the children's grandparent. I have a principled reticence about title inflation, and I'm keenly aware that my grandparent degree is purely honorary, that I did not earn it through all the hard work, struggles, and heartbreak of parenting first. This distinction makes little difference to any of us on a day-to-day basis or in terms of the bonds of affection, and I'm an integral part of the transgenerational family with its three kids, two parents, and six grandparents. For me, there are fewer of the deep tugs on the heartstrings, the grand hopes and anxious fears, and the capacity to be vulnerable and feel rejection. I love those kids dearly; I will do everything I can to support their happiness and development, but I am, and will always be, their loving older pal, not their ancestor. I'm in the grandparent role, but also a bemused observer with some distance on it all.

Do I look back now from my belated introduction to adult responsibility for children, and think that perhaps I should have become a mother after all? No, I think not. I may have regrets about some of the ways my life has unfolded and some of my major life decisions, but this is not one of them. Motherhood still feels to me like something I should have done "for the good of society"—contributing my health, temperament, education, and many life advantages to the propagation of the species— rather than something I would have chosen to do for personal pleasure and fulfillment. If I feel uncomfortable about anything, it's not at having missed out on something by not having children, but guilt at not having done my part.

Grandparenting has been a delightful experience, and, no doubt, as one of six grandparents, I will have contributed something of value to the upbringing of David, Hannah, and Sophie. But I have no illusions about where the real daily work of raising the children takes place: the real heroes of the enterprise are their parents, and the mothering role is absolutely key. The fact that I never took on that role and responsibility myself is a fundamental part of who I am. I made some choices about what I wanted to accomplish and experience in life, and am content with the path I took, because it was right for me. Being given the joys of grandparenting is just a piece of accidental good luck.

Part Three

GRANDPARENTS RAISING GRANDCHILDREN

A Heart's Perspective

Avery Bradford

This is the story of three people—a daughter, her parents who become the legal guardians of their grandchild, and the child they agree to raise. Grandparents who step up to the plate in this way have a generosity that is the soul of families and communities. To themselves, they are simply doing what's right. The emotional and practical complexities almost overwhelm. Kin support knits families across huge divides and holds communities together.

"Humor is a rare commodity—yet always economically affordable." This was a bit of wisdom offered to my son from his grandfather that has become a mantra for my husband and me as we navigate the uncharted territory laying before us as guardians and caregivers to our beautiful three-year-old granddaughter.

My father taught me the importance of tackling life's challenges with the right attitude—sprinkling a bit of humor to ease the discomfort. So my husband and I often laughed through our tears, as we embarked on this unanticipated journey. We had many questions. Would we have the physical and emotional stamina it takes? The financial stability? Could we *really* take care of Zoey?

My husband and I have been married for thirty-five years. We are both teachers, living in California's Central Valley with our granddaughter Zoey. A few years ago, we were successfully making the adjustment from a very busy family life with two careers and three fantastic kids to the freedom and independence of the empty nest. We had mixed emotions at this particular crossroads.

We were enjoying occasional day trips to Yosemite or to the Bay Area, and finally taking some of those well-deserved vacations together that we had been looking forward to for so many years.

Our daughter Mallory had been a wonderfully delightful, easygoing child. She enjoyed music, especially singing, and often performed for school and church events, often accompanied by her dad on his guitar. They made quite the duo, their voices and enthusiasm for music blended flawlessly. She displayed a level of confidence I had yearned for during my own childhood.

Mallory's teachers often spoke of her kindness and compassion toward other classmates. She was a bubbly, cheerful girl, who added a layer of joyfulness to the composition of our family. Simply put, she was a fun kid to have around the house!

The junior high volleyball team was fortunate to have the athletic and confident Mallory as a team member. Shortly before her junior year of high school, she made the bold decision to try out for the varsity cheerleading squad. Sitting outside the high school gymnasium, I anxiously awaited the news. She came running toward me and exclaimed, "Mom, I made the cut!" It was exhilarating to get the news that she had been chosen from a large number of talented girls! Life was busy and active around our house, with weekly trips throughout California's Central Valley, attending sporting events and proudly watching our daughter perform at every game. After graduating high school, Mallory made the decision to attend college out of state.

My husband and I received this news with some ambivalence. I was excited for her to embark on this new journey, but uncertain about her readiness for so much autonomy. We had some serious talks about *who* and what to avoid while she was living on her own. We warned her about the pitfalls, temptations, and snares that would be (not *could* be) waiting for her in the "real" world.

After she settled in at her college, we felt proud and relieved to hear that Mallory was responsibly juggling school and two part-time jobs, one of which was working as a job coach for disabled young adults. She was enthusiastic about that job and shared stories about the people she helped on a daily basis. I couldn't have felt prouder. It was no wonder that one of her aspirations was to eventually work in special education, like her dad. We were thrilled.

After about a year and a half of what appeared to be a fairly typical college experience, we began to notice changes in Mallory's lifestyle. She was frequenting "clubs" in the city nearby and hanging out with people who were nothing like her former friends. Tragedy struck our extended family when a cousin, who Mallory had been extremely close to, died unexpectedly at the age of twenty-three. A few short months later my father, Mallory's grandfather, passed away as well. While the family was naturally grieving the loss of these loved ones, Mallory seemed unable to get past it.

Things spiraled wildly downhill at this point. We began to receive phone calls from friends and family stating that Mallory was involved in an abusive relationship, drinking, and basically out of control. Our attempts to help her and discuss her situation were commonly met with "I hate you," or worse—words and phrases so foreign in or around our home that they were not even recognizable. Our daughter was unrecognizable at times, as well. This pattern continued for the next few years.

I felt a tremendous amount of guilt and confusion, as this child I had loved and nurtured for so long was now making horribly frightening and life-altering choices. I searched my heart for any sort of explanation, continually asking myself, "Where have I gone wrong?"

I can no longer afford my time or energy pondering the what-ifs and if-onlys. I know how unproductive and even destructive those questions can be. I've wasted time comparing myself to friends and relatives whose children didn't choose the same rocky path as my daughter. It's taken a long time to realize that Mallory has made her own choices, despite the way she was raised, and that she herself chose the treacherous path we tried to warn her about.

Toxic relationships, alcohol, drugs, and many clever cover-ups transparent to us took a firm hold on our once vibrant, talented girl.

She decided to move back home to heal her life and ended up living with us for a while. We were sure all she needed was a short stint in rehab and a leg up. As with most enabling parents, we had unwavering hope and determination that we could provide the guidance and emotional support Mallory needed during this healing period.

However, it was unbearable to witness what was happening to Mallory, and to endure the arrows of anger that she pointed in my direction. My questioning and pleadings were continually met with angry outbursts and harshness. My loving, supportive husband, as well as comforting friends and family members and our spiritual faith, were shields from the pain and heartbreak we experienced in those years.

Mallory checked into a rehab facility for a short while, which we hoped would be an answer. But as with most first-time rehab visits, the benefits were short-lived. She was unable to hold onto a job for more than a few weeks, her troubles compounded, and the confrontations between us escalated.

In the midst of this painful time, the atmosphere in our home was strained and tumultuous. Our teenage son was heartbroken over the choices his older sister was making. Our older son, living out of state, was devastated. He often commented that he hadn't "been there" to look out for his younger sister. We all blamed ourselves.

About four years ago, Mallory became involved in what we hoped and believed was a healthy relationship with someone who appeared, on the surface, to be responsible and who seemed to treat her well. During the winter of 2007, barely into the relationship, Mallory and her boyfriend moved in together. They began renting a small house not far from us.

It was near the end of the summer of 2007. We were preparing to return to our classrooms for the upcoming school year. We had just returned from a week in Hawaii and felt refreshed and hopeful at the prospect of a brighter future for our daughter. On our return, Mallory broke the news to us that she was pregnant. Unfortunately, within a few weeks, the relationship crumbled, and she moved back home again. It was surprising to us that, as distraught and disappointed as she was, her own health and the health of her baby seemed to be her top priority.

I was hopeful that Mallory could regain her old confidence, embrace motherhood, and rebuild her life. Our relationship was still strained, but we both acknowledged it as a work in progress. She and I looked for a small apartment for the baby and her to live in, close enough for me to visit and help out when necessary, but far enough to allow both of us our own space. We visited vocational colleges together in hopes of enrolling her, preparing her for a future with her daughter. Through all of these preparations, I was haunted by thoughts of "What'll we do if Mallory isn't a good mom?"

Many of our friends, now grandparents, often commented on how they loved every minute spent with their grandkids, but also liked the fact that they could go home and sleep in their own beds at the end of the day, and not have the child around—the perfect setup! We, too, thought this sounded ideal. We were optimistic that things would work out for Mallory and her new baby and we'd be grandparents who could occasionally babysit.

Witnessing Zoey's birth was amazing for my husband and me, not only because it was our first time experiencing the wonders of being grandparents, but also because of the pride we felt as Mallory bravely endured many hours of labor and we watched her joy at witnessing this miracle. This was the closest I had felt toward my daughter in a very long time. We held each other tight after the birth, contemplating what the future would now hold for each of us.

I was pleased with the attention and care Mallory was devoting toward her baby during the first few weeks. I held out hope that this child would be a positive force in her life, that Zoey would be the motivation Mallory needed to finally decide it was time to move forward.

Mallory relied on my help and advice with the baby, just as I had depended on the wisdom and experience of my own mother and mother-in-law during the first weeks of motherhood. I relished being needed by my daughter. My hope bounded along. I was proud of her, and knew it was not going to be easy to raise a child as a single mother. I was confident that she was making the necessary changes in her life to successfully grow into this new role.

About a month had passed when a few red flags surfaced. Some of Mallory's old bad-news friends started stopping by our home. We felt disturbed and alarmed by this new development. Within the next couple of weeks, Mallory would declare, "I need to go out for a little while, but I'll be right back. Could you watch the baby?"

I consented, since I knew it was just a little while. A little while, of course, turned into hours. No explanation upon her return; we kept trusting and hoping. "I'm going out for a few minutes" or "I'll be right back" became a more regular occurrence. These outings became Mallory being away from her baby for hours, sometimes even overnight. This was a nightmare for us as teachers, having to stay up worrying not only about our daughter and her whereabouts, but also wondering whether one of us would have to be calling for a substitute the next day to stay home to watch Zoey. I kept a log of what was happening, jotting down on a daily calendar exactly how long Mallory was gone. Her absences were excessive. We started to panic. This darling granddaughter of ours needed her mother. Again, we felt helpless about what to do to get through to Mallory.

On several occasions, I came into the house after work to find Mallory asleep in the recliner while the baby was lying on a quilt, kicking and cooing, waiting to be picked up and held. My husband and I had taken over providing for most of Zoey's physical needs, bathing and feeding her, while praying that Mallory would show up to care for her own child each day. In the months that followed, we realized we were becoming the sole caregivers for our darling Zoey. As hard as it was to, again, deal with the heartache and worries surrounding our daughter's situation, caring for Zoey became our first priority.

The first six months of Zoey's life were an emotional roller coaster. On one hand, we were elated to fully understand the depth of love a grandparent can feel for a grandchild, but on the other, we were in an awkward, uncomfortable place. We wanted to do what was best for Zoey, but were horrified to see what was happening with our daughter.

It became apparent that Mallory was not ready to accept responsibility for her child. She needed more help than we could give her. We knew we needed to seek legal advice so we could make decisions on behalf of Zoey, medically or otherwise. We felt this was in everyone's best interest. We were awarded legal guardianship by the time Zoey turned a year old.

The emotional toll that first year took on us was enormous. Thankfully, my husband and I grew closer than ever, probably because of our reliance on each other for the strength and stamina now necessary to keep up with a growing toddler. We were also fortunate to have friends who volunteered to care for Zoey while we worked until we were able to figure out our daycare dilemma. As Zoey grew, our love expanded, though our once closely held vision of the bliss of an empty nest waned.

Our daughter was now living outside our home, and there was a degree of unspoken acceptance of what needed to be. We kept hoping for her recovery. Always hoping.

With the first turbulent year behind us, we more fully enjoyed our once-again "full nest." (Full for two fifty-somethings!) Zoey was walking and running through the house, making amazing progress every day. By the time she was eighteen months old, we decided to take our first road-trip. We traveled in our car for eleven hours to visit family and friends and realized that for the first time we felt like a family unit. We felt confident and self-assured that we could actually manage parenthood again at our age.

Outings to the beach and Yosemite became favorite getaways. At two, when Zoey first glanced at Half Dome and Yosemite's awesome rock formations, we suddenly heard her first-uttered "Wowwwww!!" These firsts were the fuel that kept us progressing and advancing forward, despite the hectic physical schedule we were now adapting to. We wanted to make sure Zoey got the family experiences that she deserved and wanted to educate her about the world around her. We were learning about her, ourselves, and growing together.

When I feel like I'm barely keeping up with the middle-age droop, I am often revitalized by this two-and-a-half-year-old's unique perspective, which gives me a fresh outlook. After dragging myself out of bed one lazy Sunday morning, my hair hanging lankly, no makeup, in my worn blue, wraparound robe (which Zoey had never laid eyes on), she dramatically proclaimed, "Omma, you look like a princess!" I am so indebted to her!

This unexpected challenge of raising a grandchild has brought with it a complex set of emotions. We find a lot of joy from interacting with Zoey every day, laughing at her sayings and doings, and we feel excitement and pride from watching her progress.

Mallory visits Zoey three to four times a week for a few hours during the evenings. We haven't set any limits, and these visits are random and unpredictable. We don't yet see progress from our daughter on these visits. Sadly, yet realistically, we do not foresee changes in Mallory's lifestyle, despite regular conversations urging her to get help. Questioning looks appear on Zoey's face as she interacts with her mom. Eventually she will need honest and straightforward answers. We will never give up on our daughter. We hope that someday she will remember who she really is, at heart.

Until then, we keep hoping. Each day is an opportunity to learn more lessons of how love works: about enduring, and using humor wherever and whenever possible. We are smitten with interest and passion toward Zoey, and committed to the project of giving her a good life. There will be many peaks and valleys yet to come, but we're committed to this new journey, to each other, and feel honored to be entrusted—perhaps not forever—with this sweet creature named Zoey.

An Explosion of Love

·····················

JOANNE MAURITS

Joanne Maurits writes about how life changed when she and her husband took in their two grandchildren three years ago. "I love the challenge ... of going beyond into a place that is sometimes uncomfortable," Jo writes on her blog, describing the taking care of these children as "a raw, complicated endeavor." She is truly someone interested in the complex play of human emotion, not unlike her beloved Emily Dickinson.

HERE IN BEAUTIFUL KAMLOOPS, BRITISH Columbia, we are completely encircled by mountains. There is nowhere I can stand without being graced by their majesty. I have always wondered how much the geography of a place shapes the spirit of its people. Do prairie dwellers know a boundlessness that mountain people cannot understand? A friend once expressed that the constant presence of the mountains made her feel claustrophobic. I don't feel that way. In fact, I feel an excitement, an added dimension of intimacy with the cosmic. My heart and mind soar.

My younger son, Joshua, was just eighteen and his girlfriend sixteen when they came to my husband and me and announced their pregnancy. They lived with us for the first year of our grandson's life, and then decided they wanted to live on their own. With family help, they tried. However, with the birth of their second son, life at their household, already tenuous, started to deteriorate. The burdens of immaturity, lack of money, and unfulfilled dreams took their toll. Anger, resentment, and hopelessness seethed between them. Increasingly, my son and his girlfriend turned to unhealthy behaviors. My beautiful grandsons, Darian and Mattias, now seven and four, were three and seven months when they came to live with us full time.

At times during these past three years, I have felt like I was being swept away in the rapids, hoping not to be smashed into the rocks. It doesn't seem possible for such fear and extraordinary blessedness to coexist in my heart at the same time. I have been filled with uncertainty. I have battled guilt and shame. I have cried. I have laughed. I have panicked. I have felt so much love it has squeezed my entire body like a sponge.

I cut back my working hours as a nurse at our local hospital to two days a week. Those two days were at times the saving of my sanity. Sometimes I felt like a robot set to continuous play: hovering, leaping, singing on cue, filling sippy cups, dispensing Cheerios, building castles out of blocks, changing diapers, reading stories, trying to do whatever my grandsons needed me to do to keep them whole, to keep them nourished, inside and out. But I have been witness to the sound and sight of souls growing—theirs and mine.

When I was a child, I thought that my parents were finished growing, that they were complete because they were grown-up. I believed this to be true of all adults, that they had finished the voyage, and arrived at some mysterious place that I was heading toward. Now I realize that the journey never ends. My grandchildren and I are engaged in the same passage. We're just at different stages of it. They are teaching me to see and feel again the things I saw and felt in childhood.

If you ask two- to three-year-olds why they are screaming, kicking, crying, or what-have-you, they don't know. "Because and because," my son Josh once answered. During the years when my husband Gordon and I took on the role of parenting two of our grandsons, it gradually became clear to me that I was somewhat wiser than in days gone by. I didn't try to reason. I just made sure they couldn't hurt themselves, and went about my business. One day I accidentally found a little bit of magic that actually worked, at least with my grandsons. I put on Mika's "Lollypop" song and danced. Within a minute, my little tantrum-thrower was dancing too, his tear-flushed, angry face becoming wreathed in smiles.

Dancing together became an almost daily activity—two little boys and their fifty-something Nana engaged in an integral leap of physical and emotional joy.

The diversity of my grandsons' personalities as the world spills its treasures and trials is astonishing and interesting to me. The delightful, *I Love You, Stinky Face* by Lisa McCourt is one of my oldest grandson Darian's favorite books. For him, the idea of being loved even if you are a "big scary ape" or a "super smelly skunk" or a "Cyclops with just one big gigantic eye" is a reassuring, funny, and joyous prospect. Darian is incredibly determined, intelligent, athletic, energetic, responsible, and organized. Avid life burns into every molecule of his mind and heart. Darian, my morning sunshine boy, who springs out of bed eager for the activities of his day to begin. Darian, who would mow the lawn, paint the house, barbecue the steaks, and back the truck out of the driveway, if I would only let him. Darian, whose excitement when he started playing Mite hockey at the age of four knew no bounds. The night before his first session, I found him asleep in bed with his new skates, hockey jersey, and helmet.

Now, three years later, I am thrilled and amazed at his prowess on the ice. Darian has a wonderfully sophisticated palate and enjoys a huge array of food choices. At five he once requested a spicy shrimp sandwich on olive bread with carrot sticks and hummus for lunch. My Darian, who continually fuels me with his infectious enthusiasm and newly leaping skills.

Mattias, with his huge brown eyes, so like his daddy's, and those amazingly long lashes that gather adoring remarks everywhere. Mattias, who when asked by Darian's coach if he wanted to join his big brother in playing hockey next year, replied matter-of-factly, "No, I'm going to learn to sing!" Mattias, who at three years old startled me one day by belting out in perfect pitch, "Hey, hey somewhere ... you threw your fear in the sea of no cares," lyrics from one of my favorite bands, Great Big Sea. Mattias, who like Linus, uses his beloved blanky to enhance his world. Mattias, who spends hours blissfully lying on his belly playing with his beloved Thomas trains. Mattias, who enjoys creating private spaces and making tents of old blankets and chairs. Mattias, whose speculations are wise and quirky. "Animals think things, you know," he told me once in his inimitable way. My Mattias, whose endless wonder frees my own mind.

There were times when my other son and my daughter struggled with the amount of time and energy I spent with my grandsons as opposed to their own children. Their brains understood the necessity, but their hearts ached nevertheless. I was at a loss as to how to bridge the gap, and shed many tears at this seeming paradox. I only know my other grandchildren—my beautiful granddaughter Ariana and my beguiling grandson, Jesse—are no less beloved and precious to me. They too have given me many growing moments and unsolicited gifts of the soul.

Late last summer I was able to capture such a moment of sweetness with six-year-old Ariana. We were out for the afternoon, and at one point she lay down on the bench part of a picnic table with her eyes closed. I asked her if she was OK, and she replied, "I'm just dreaming, Nana." I was reminded anew that we all need places to accumulate the inexplicable dreaming notions of our minds, to relish the holy, secretive within us. My Ariana, whose imagination is the equivalent of music and poetry.

My five-year-old grandson Jesse draws in his breath in a delighted gasp whenever he is excited about anything. For him, everything is potent: rocks, hats, boxes, and sticks. He takes one thing and turns it into something else. Jesse already has an accomplished sense of humor, declaring while watching *The Princess and the Frog* with his Nana, Papa, and cousins, "Well, I won't be kissing any frogs, anytime soon!" My Jesse, who ignites me with his joy in life.

I know that children take what they need from us, and then one day roam away, like young elk, drifting south for the winter, leaving their summer meadows. It is the job of the adults in their lives to give the seeds they harbor within the space and light to bloom, to grow.

Darian at three and a half, once begged, "Can I ride my bike all the way to the end of the cul-de-sac by myself, please, Nana?" I stood, trying not to appear too anxious, at the end of the driveway, watching for his small figure to return. His smile when he completed his journey was beatific.

Precious grandchildren: at one with giggles and splashes in the bathtub, with grubby faces and hands, with sticky kisses, with seashells gathered at the shore and lovingly arranged in patterns, with endless stories read, with rocking small bodies, with new shoes, with tears of frustration, fatigue, and sorrow, with little hikes in the summer woods, with favorite pajamas outgrown, with damp, sweaty little necks ... with countless I love you's.

Raising them has been a raw, delicate endeavor complicated by worry about their parents. As the boys grew with us, they pulled with them the connection to the human beings who created them. Sometimes their parents rushed in like a gypsy wind, bearing gifts and hugs. At other times they bore only grievances and recriminations. I can't fully know my son and his ex-girlfriend's burdens or the sadness they bear. I can only know my own and that of my husband, my grandsons' dearly loved Papa, who has responded with magnificence. I know, too, that each of us has experienced fragility and tremendous pain.

Denial and courage are a complicated business, and there are many shades of each. Sometimes courage takes the form of simply admitting that you're afraid. In the end, perhaps the bravest thing we can do is simply go on however we can, finding grace in mercy. How true it is that so often we grow ourselves in the dark.

These past three years have taught me to know that sometimes abrasions and deprivations are to be blessed. I know now that when we allow ourselves to feel the hard edges of our world, we are participating in the metabolic dance that is fully life.

Saltwater and fresh ... parched, dry lips quenched by cold water on a hot day ... mouths moist and stained with strawberry kisses ... honey-sweetened tongues and tart lemon faces. Pooling heat on sun-reddened limbs ... chilling winds that cause delicious shivers. Cool mud oozing between fingers ... scalding sand beneath feet. Breath forced out in shrieks from a dip in glacial water. The rough rasp of bark ... the satin of moss. The pain of a broken heart, laughter and tears, the ordinary preciousness and fragility of human life. Life, like thunder, cracking open, pouring rain down to drench the heart.

Each of us, my husband and I, our son and his ex-girlfriend, our other two children and their families, and our grandsons themselves, holds an accumulation of these past years, the tangy explosion of our reconfigured family creating itself, communicating its essential belonging.

Three years of milestones passed, some with more grace than others, but passed nonetheless. I discovered reserves of strength, humor, and bravery I didn't know I possessed. I became more fully aware of the infinite preciousness of children—of how vulnerable they are, and how ultimately, it is our job to send them away whole.

Just over a year ago, after much counseling and hard work, my son and his ex-girlfriend turned their lives around. Each has a new partner in their lives. My son's new girlfriend, a strong, intelligent, gentle, lovely woman who saw the beauty beneath his brokenness, has helped him find the way back ... to himself, to us, and to his sons. We have seen the return of our Joshua—the fire, joy, sense of purpose, humor, and zest for life. He has become a man.

My grandsons spend weekdays with their mother, who has been on her own journey of growth, and weekends with their father. They live the largest part of their lives away from me now, in another rhythm. However, I am reassured our bond is unbreakable, our closeness something I need never question, like the rising sun. I returned my grandsons to the care of their parents gradually, but I feel a powerful grief that lingers. I miss them. I feel myself folding endurance like a blanket, around love. I have learned to know for sure that grief will not define me. Love will. Graceful or clumsy, this is my soul's contract. Blessing, loving, and forgiving as my heart breaks open. This is the labor of parenting.

The Grampy Diaries

JOHN LUNN

Many parents are enjoying an empty nest when they become grand-parents, which may include being able to work unencumbered by the demands of children at home. So imagine the surprise when a son arrived home for good with his three children. Writer and master flute maker John Lunn captures real time at Grampy's Little Acres in New Hampshire.

GRAMMY GETS UP EVERY DAY at the crack of morn to let her dog out, get some coffee, and browse her morning emails. I've only been in bed a couple of hours. As soon as she goes, the other three dogs scramble around the bed to fill the hole she left. No one said, "Seat saved."

An hour later the grandsons get up and get ready for school. It wakes me up again. I think about what I need to get done, whether I'll get any more sleep, and if everyone is going to have a good day. Our son Darren and his three boys have been living with us for nine months now, and life for my wife and me as we knew it before has flown away.

Michael was gibbering in the kitchen below me. "Where's Daddy? Where's Daddy? What time is it? Can I have eggs? I don't want that. Where's Daddy?" He still had separation anxieties over this new world he's in. He was barely five.

"He's getting up, Michael," Grammy said calmly. "Eat your bagel."

"All done!" he announced. I know all the way from upstairs he barely took a bite.

I heard Alex next. "Can I have a bagel? I want mine with butter not cream cheese. Where's my magazine? Hey! Gimme that. It's not yours." I could only hope he wasn't going to start a fight with his father this morning. He was nine and would rather live with his mom, or at least, that's what he said.

"You can't wear that to school," Grammy told him. It was final.

"But I like it. Grampy said I could wear it!" His voice went up in pitch, ready for battle. Alex had his own ideas about fashion. I could just imagine the homemade ensemble that he'd concocted, and I doubt I said any such thing.

"I don't have anything else," he insisted.

Grammy was firm. "It isn't appropriate for school." Or anything else, I could imagine her thinking. "And for the umpteenth time, will you leave that dog alone! Maddie! Get down."

"Grammy. Grammy. Grammy," Michael repeated relentlessly. "Grammy. Grammy. Grammy."

"Yes, Michael? What is it?" she replied through a sigh. We both knew what he was going to say. I could see her sitting at the table, white laptop open next to coffee, a big red dog at her feet on a leash. Her eyes on her screen while talking to the boys.

"Where's Daddy?" Bing-o.

"Go get your clothes on. Both of you," she said. "See if your dad is up and tell Brandon to get out of bed."

"But I haven't eaten my baaaayyygellill!" Alex whined, always the performer.

"It'll be here when you get back."

"I wanna eat it nooooowwwwww."

It was his daily dance. He could never decide what he wanted so everything was wrong. Wrong food, wrong school, wrong parent, wrong life.

Zoe, our fourteen-year-old blue Aussie bitch, slipped off the bed like a seal into water and started pacing and panting around the bedroom. It meant only one thing: if I didn't let her out, she'd pee on the floor. She was too old to wait long. I slipped out of bed like a brick off a windowsill and opened the door. All three dogs ran downstairs barking and yapping for Grammy to let them out. Brandon appeared at the bottom of the stairs, a solid kid in boxers and T-shirt. He's twelve and knows everything that's worth knowing.

"Good morning, Grampy," he said. "Can I go to the rec center this afternoon? I made my bed and emptied the trash."

"Mornin'," I replied. "Sure thing. Go to math club first."

That inspired a grim expression. Too bad. "Thinking's as important as sports."

Alex poked his head in view. "Hi, Grampy!" he sang out pleasantly. He always wanted to please me. "My bed was dry. Are you coming down?"

"Alright! Four days in a row. Good stuff," I yawned. "I'll see you at three. Remember: listen to your teacher today. Don't come home with a bad report."

"I will," he laughed. "I mean, I won't. I mean, I will."

"Who's on first?" I said and headed back into my room.

Michael's turn. "Grampy, grampy, grampy. Um ..."

I stopped to hear the inevitable. "What time is it?" He needed to know where his dad was at all times and he needed to know the time, as though he had some pressing appointment or somewhere else to be.

"Time for school, little one," I said. "Learn things."

After much fuss and confusion, all three of the boys tromped down to the bus stop with their dad. I could hear Alex berate his father all the way down the street. Alex was angry about the divorce and about moving, and his dad took it all on the chin, some of it deserved, some of it way over the top. The two of them were going to be locked in battle as long as neither turned the page.

I woke up again around eleven. Time for my day to really start. Meredith, that's Grammy, had taken Maddie with her to work, leaving the other three dogs with me. Darren went to work soon after. I had three hours to do laundry, pick up around the house, work on a bit of writing, get a short nap, and think about supper.

Our little slice of tourtière was a New England cape on a couple of semirural acres in western New Hampshire—nice open space with a view of some very pretty hills. We moved here with our son and daughter twenty years ago. Seven years passed, and Darren had a child at twenty-one. Another twelve years, two other sons with a different mom, a bad marriage, moving around so much that even the post office couldn't keep up, and an ugly divorce later, he got custody of the boys when child services removed all three from his ex-wife's home for neglect and abuse. We built them three bedrooms and a living room in our cellar, leaving a tiny area for laundry and my workshop, and turned overnight from a household of two to an extended family of six—ten if you count the four dogs.

When the kids moved in, it was obvious that I'd be the primary caregiver and homemaker. I had been a young Grampy when the boys were small and had lots of energy to build rockets and tree forts, ford rivers, and conquer alien worlds with Alex and Brandon. The three of us grew as close as vines wrapped on a pole. I taught them writing, reading, bike riding, and dreaming. We made videos and made up stories, all mixed in with a whole wad of other stuff. Michael was born during their parent's umpteenth separation so I didn't get the jump on that relationship, but we're catching up fast. My wonderful relationship with them gave me a trusting foundation to be the homebody, and my already working at home supplied the time. Meredith worked at a humane society as a canine behavior specialist and Darren sold shoes at a local clothing chain. Both of their schedules changed on any given week, leaving me to fill the gaps.

After reading some emails on the sofa with the dogs, I finished my coffee along with the chores, got through a sink full of dishes, and managed to find a half hour to catch a quick nap cuddled up with Bunnie before all three dogs started barking like the hounds of hell.

"I get it," I said with a yawn. "The boys are home. Now shut up." Bunnie and Gully jumped at the door to get the first licks in while Zoe disappeared upstairs to stay out of their way. I started boiling water for mac and cheese and some more coffee.

"Where's Daddy?" were the first words out of Michael's mouth.

"He's at work," I assured him. "He'll be home before bedtime. Did you like school today?"

"Tyler wasn't on the bus," he said. Any change bothered Michael. He noticed everything.

"I only got one card," Alex admitted. Cards were reprimands for not paying attention. Not good. He was getting them almost every day.

"Better than yesterday," I said. I really wished there were something I could do to get him to pay attention in class. I'd tried offering rewards, withholding privileges, offering help, whatever I could think of, but it was tough.

"Can I help make subber?" Michael asked. Along with still being in diapers at four and a half when he came to us, he was speech delayed. Nobody had been helping him learn to talk, and he struggled with it every day. We started right away insisting that he enunciate his words and worked with the school in hopes of having him up to speed by grade one.

"You sure can," I said while I slid a gate across the kitchen doorway to keep the dogs out. "We need a … a … a carrot smoother," I improvised. There's always a job you can give a five-year-old. "You take this big old carrot and smooth it out with the back of this spoon like this. It's an important job. Can you handle it?"

He bit his lip and sang out in hardly contained glee, "I getta smoo da carross!"

"Carraw-Ts. Ts."

"CarroTs," he repeated.

"Perfect." I set him up over the sink so the smoothin's could drop in just so.

Alex asked, "Can I smooth carrots, too?"

I winked. "Work with me, Alex." It was our code for "I'm messing with Michael."

He peered in the sink at Mike rubbing a spoon over a carrot and said, "Oh. Never mind."

"So what do we do about your fidgeting?" I asked Alex. "You're falling way behind." It was the middle of fourth grade, and he still couldn't master the basic times tables. "When your teacher says to stop fiddling around, you have to stop."

"I do!" he remonstrated a bit too hastily. "I was just telling my friend to stop calling me names."

"It's always an 'I was just,' isn't it? You have to accept that you start some of this."

That was a toughie. He clammed up. I knew he could get past this if he really wanted to. I just needed to find the right incentive. A mix of stick and carrot—without the smoothing.

After they ate the mac and cheese we struggled for a half hour on his math, mainly because he hadn't heard a word the teacher had said during the lesson. I could see the struggle in his eyes. He didn't understand why he didn't understand, and that was the hardest part. We started knocking heads over the definition of the word *vertical*. It was time to take a break.

"Let's go to McDonald's and get a soda," I suggested. "We can come back to this when we're not feeling so itchy."

"Yaaaaaaa!" Michael dropped whatever he was doing. The word *McDonald's* has that effect on little kids. "I wanna toy!"

Alex whined his insistence, "I wanna finish!"

"I know you do. But it'll wait and we can't go to …" I whispered, as though Michael hadn't already heard it, "McDonald's later."

The local McDonald's had a play area for the kids, and I could get a decent cup of coffee. There were other families there, and all the kids got along crawling through tunnels and chasing each other around. Watching them playing with others, learning to get along, I thought about how different I was from them.

I was a desperately shy daydreamer. I never interacted with strangers in public, and I daydreamed my way through twelve years of school, wasting a perfectly good public education. All of my boys were outgoing.

But both Brandon and Alex hummed and sang aloud all day without even noticing. I never thought much about this when I only saw them for a few hours each week, but it became a problem since we lived together. I could handle noisy, messy kids who were underfoot all day long. But when they weren't talking, they were singing over each other, with each other, and at each other. It drove me out of my wits so thoroughly that I couldn't think. I had to ban them from the upstairs saying, "You have to sing downstairs, outside, or in your own head, just not here." Wanting to stay upstairs and hang out with me they tried but failed to stop. It was a real struggle for us all summer.

It occurred to me that humming, like daydreaming, was an avoidance mechanism. Growing up, I desperately wanted to avoid the troubles in my family, my fears at school, and a world too large for me. Daydreaming about being a superhero or a spy gave me sanctuary. They found that with their singing. It filled their brains with something easier than the frightening thoughts and feelings of their world. I'd say to Brandon, "Tell me stuff, ask questions, whatever." Without his songs the silence was an ipecac that churned ugly and frightening thoughts up from his subconscious.

He'd divulge horror stories of his former life. In his twelve years, he'd lived in a dozen different places, been abandoned by two mothers, witnessed alcohol- and drug-induced adult misbehavior the whole time and knew he had only himself to count on. I hid from different monsters but always knew, like him, there was no one in the world to fall back on but me. I've spent a lifetime learning to trust and wished so hard there was something I could do to just suck the troubles from his mind and heart. I guess we weren't that different after all.

Perhaps that's why I knew that for the next twelve years the focus of my heart, mind, and creative energy would be getting these three boys through their troubled childhood as best I could. There was no one else. Meredith started raising kids when she was a teenager because her mother dumped two baby brothers in her lap. This would be the third time around for her, and she didn't have the patience. I couldn't blame her for that. Darren didn't have the know-how or the concentration to manage more than basic coping. He'd probably improve as life calmed down for him, but in the meantime, these small, needy voices were calling. If I didn't step up, no one would. Do you walk away from a drowning man, a car crash, or someone in a burning building? This was my family in need, and whether I was ready for it, here I was.

This road was fraught with as much danger for me as for them. Even though the water was ice cold, I still had to plunge in to save them. I'd known these boys since birth and their troubles ran deep. But what of my own needs, issues, and life? Would I be able to survive this? Mine has been an anxiety-ridden life that I've only recently gained control of. I thought I was in control all along, but I was wrong. I survived a dysfunctional family, raised a troubled family of my own, ran a business, and tried to fit into a world I never felt I belonged in. All through the kaleidoscope of obsessive anxiety, fear, and self-doubt. At the end of that road I've found peace of mind, and taking this turn in life could well reverse it all.

Within weeks of their moving in, I was already cycling the kids' needs round and round my head like a double Ferris wheel gone wild: who's got what homework, how are they getting along and progressing at school, how to resolve today's issues, how to maintain social skills, and how to keep on top of diet, bedtimes, bed wetting, laundry, cooking, and social interactions with their friends and family. Each day presented a new challenge, and teaching children is not math. I love the challenge and have a knack for reading problems and personal issues to find effective and peaceful resolutions. But at what price? I needed to learn how to find peace of mind and some sanctuary during the day-to-day struggles we faced. I didn't do that as a parent. I went full out and took it all as it came with all the health issues and emotional baggage dragging along behind. I knew it would kill me if I did that this time around.

I gathered up a reluctant Alex and Michael and left the restaurant. We picked up Brandon on our way home. Brandon's a real boy's boy.

All sports, big talk, and competition. He's good at everything he tries, good-looking, outgoing, and an honor roll student all bundled into one. He couldn't be more different from Alex, who spent his entire childhood wishing he could be a girl, playing with Barbies, cueing into all the female fashions, sensitivities, and needs. He's a good-looking boy too; they all were. But as half brothers, all they shared was a troubled past. They've fought all their lives, and they fought all the way home. I had to stop the car and pretend to take a nap until they were willing to lay off and we could drive on.

"What's for supper?" Michael asked for the millionth time while I fed the dogs and got dinner on the table.

"Chicken fingers, mashed potatoes, and a salad," I said. "Come on, sit down. Pour some milk. It's just the four of us tonight. Grammy and Dad are still at work."

"I don't like chickie figgers and tadoes!" he insisted. "I want MaDonal's."

"Mic-Don-Ald's," I corrected.

This was his usual patter. Control over food is one of the few things a five-year-old has—other than his poop.

"Don't worry. I got you covered." I said while I fetched the chicken from the oven. Before I took it to the table I separated a few pieces from the rest on one corner of the platter.

"I know you don't like this chicken, Michael," I said in a gentle "how-I-understand-you-so-well" voice. "That's why I picked up these chicken fingers just for you while we were at McDonald's." I shoveled the special pile onto his plate and passed the rest of the nuggets to the other boys.

Michael's eyes lit up like he was King Tut looking over a hoard of gold.

Brandon looked from the platter to Michael's plate and said, "Dude!" His parlance for "nicely done."

I'd been pulling this kind of sleight of hand on all of them for years. Like carrot polishing there was always a way to help them feel good about something while keeping them safe, or eating properly, or doing whatever needed getting done. Brandon picked it up fast. At the age of seven he could see me pulling it over on Alex. Alex on the other hand still hadn't caught on.

"Hey! That's not fair. Didn't you get us McDonald's, too!" he whined.

That made the treat even sweeter for Michael. "Ha ha, you don't get any!"

"No ha ha's, Mickey," Brandon reminded him. It was a family rule not to laugh at each other.

"Work with me, Alex," I said. "Work with me."

He looked at me, back at the plate, at Michael, and so on while the wheels went round and round. His eyes narrowed and his outrage turned to indulgence. "Oh! Lucky you, Michael. I wish we could have McDonald's, too."

Michael savored every bite.

I hated being the bad guy. I can handle being a tough parent when it's called for, but I always tried to find ways to mediate that didn't require a heavy hand. But I'm Grampy—not Dad. I liked being the one who gives out candy and then sends them home with a measure of good advice and an extra buck lining their pocket. I'd rather be the grampy who goes bike riding and has adventures in the woods, the one they confide in and trust. That role was no longer an option for me. First, I don't have the energy for it anymore, and with all three needing other more pressing things, I don't have the time. Now I had to be disciplinarian, as well as confidante, teacher, and the guy who makes them eat their peas.

After supper, Brandon did his homework and then scooted down to his bedroom for his hour of video games. The other boys watched TV with me and the dogs, all rolled up on the sofa together until Grammy and Dad got home. As soon as it was dark, the mutts jumped and barked at whatever lights went up the road until Meredith actually got home. She brought Maddie in, and all four dogs milled around and jumped all over everyone until their pecking order was reestablished for the evening. I made Meredith some tea and supper and got Alex to do his reading. It was another subject he struggled with.

Seven o'clock was coming up. Darren texted that he was on his way. Time to get Michael in his pull-up and ready for bed. They liked to read bedtime stories together. Unlike the two older boys, Michael had no baggage that prevented him from loving his dad openly.

I tucked Alex in bed an hour later and we talked quietly for a few minutes. It never mattered what we talk about. He just needed to know I was listening. He was struggling with reconciling the stable world he lived in with the troubled one he was yanked out of.

He adored his mother and couldn't understand her behavior. It was always hard to watch. I didn't sugarcoat his mom's inappropriate and often contradictory behavior, but I didn't rub his nose in it either. I tried very hard not to show anger toward what I felt were serious wrongs. It's a tough line. I was one of only two people that Alex confided in. The other was his mom. I didn't betray that trust. She was trouble, but he didn't need to know why.

"I'll be back in two hours to wake you for your pee," I said. "Good night, Sweetie."

"You're my best friend, Grampy," he said, as he often does. I knew it was true, and I also knew that we were headed for a collision one day. As with Brandon and Michael, we had some serious bumps ahead, bumps that a grampy shouldn't have to take, bumps that should be for a dad and a mom. We'd survive them. I'd done it before, but it was going to be tough on me to feel them slip from this place of absolute trust and into teenage suspicion.

I spent what was left of the evening with Meredith curled up with some dogs in front of the tube, sharing stories of our day. Even if we only grabbed a few minutes, it was important to our well-being. She told me about a couple of dogs she was hoping would get adopted.

"I've been working with them for weeks. They'd be perfect for a couple without kids. One came in as a turn-in from someone who can't afford her. There's a lot of that these days." She had so much compassion and affection for dogs that it was always a pleasure to watch her interact with them. Sure, they were noisy smelly beasts with mile-long tongues and a habit for treating us like furniture. But that's only half the story. Cuddling up with them, taking them on walks, and watching them interact with their environment was as interesting as watching the kids. Each one an individual with needs and traits that interacts with the world.

All I had to share were a couple of kid stories. A joke one of them had, a problem we encountered, nothing special. Just being with Meredith reenergized my batteries. There wasn't enough "us" time lately, and our relationship was going through some adjusting. We'd survive it; we always did. We'd been through plenty in our life together. There would be more to weather and to enjoy.

I said goodnight to her and let the dogs out for a leak before going to work. Bunnie and I headed down to my workshop where I spent a few hours forming and shaping silver into pieces of art and flutes. All things in my life may change and swirl around like a tornado, but for the thirty-five years that I've been making silver and gold flutes, it's the one thing I count on to be the same. From my tools and benches, the feel of the metal under my hand, opti-visors perched on my head, to the movies I listen to on DVD like favorite tunes over and over, my flute shop is my personal sanctuary. Behind that door I really am in control of my environment, unlike the behavior of children or the uncertainty of business and social life.

I work until 3 a.m. The house is still when I emerge with my dog. I hang a last bit of laundry, look through the boy's backpacks to find out if there's anything going on in school that they aren't saying, make sure they're sleeping well, turn off any lights, and let the older dogs out for a pee and a snack. When the weather is clear, I step out onto our deck to watch the night—the stars and the moon lighting the hills in white—for a couple of minutes. Perhaps a planet might be gracing the sky along with the constellations that are as familiar to me as the streets I drive by day.

The town is quiet. New England is quiet. No one is calling me. I can't make appointments or do errands. Children around town are all in bed. The night shift clicks by at its own pace. We live on an amazing little wet rock in a universe so huge that I take comfort in being so insignificantly small that nothing will change when I leave it. I can't screw that up, whatever else I may do.

In a lifetime of struggling as an artist, living outside the conformities of typical expectations, I realize that a life's work is a series of successes and attempted success. Failure, after all, really is a reach for success. I've written novels and created beautiful flutes, raised children, and volunteered in my community to make life better for my neighbors. I've had my share of disappointments and regrets. All of these things are part of the puzzle that makes up who I am. None of it came without hard work, commitment, and years of skill development.

Here I stand on the brink of another challenge that will take all the will and courage I have. I am in the unique position to help these three boys and their father have a better life. All four of them need me. I can't turn away. I don't mean that as a metaphor. I literally cannot turn away. That would be against my nature. I must put everything I have into this. Meredith and I are investing our retirement fund, our home, our peace of mind, our marriage, all of it on their lives being better, whatever may become of ours. I guess I am trying to change the universe in some small way.

"Time for bed, Bunnie. "

We curl up next to Meredith and let sleep find us.

Grammy will be up in a couple of hours to start the day.

A Legacy of Parenting
LENORA MADISON POE

Lenora Poe's work has primarily been helping black children and their families in private practice and group settings. In this piece she describes the training and experience that led to her twenty-two-year leadership of the Grandparents As Parents support group in Berkeley. She has achieved national prominence for bringing the needs of grandparents parenting grandchildren to the attention of federal and state government.

I BEGAN MY PROFESSIONAL CAREER as an elementary school teacher, first in Alabama and later in California. After earning a master of science in educational psychology in 1972, I became a guidance counselor in the Berkeley Unified School District, where I worked primarily with at-risk students and their families. That position, which I held for ten years, was very exciting and challenging for me, since I have a tremendous passion for working with children and families.

In 1980, I earned a master of arts in clinical counseling, and began my internship training. First, I worked with inmates at the Federal Correctional Institute in Dublin, California, which was then an all-female institution. Many of those women were mothers who had their children taken from them during their incarceration and placed in foster homes. At Berkeley Mental Health, where I interned next, I worked with adults, none of whom were parents. It was in my final internship position, at the West Coast Children's Center (WCCC), in Albany, California, that I first came into contact with the kind of work I do today.

At WCCC, I dealt primarily with children of all ages and their parents or grandparents. It was during this assignment that I became aware that an increasing number of grandparents were bringing their grandchildren to the center for psychotherapeutic services. I also noted that many, if not all, of these grandparents did not acknowledge that they had, in fact, taken over most or all of the parenting responsibilities for their grandchildren. These grandparents often appeared tense and depressed and were reluctant to offer much information about their family issues. In particular, they denied that their children—the parents of their grandchildren—were living outside the home. In most cases, the grandchildren also confirmed this denial.

When I became a licensed marriage and family therapist in 1985, I began to research the number of children in foster placements, how these children were adjusting to out-of-home placements, the major reasons they were being placed in out-of-home care, the connections these children had with their birth families, and what percentage of siblings were placed together in foster homes. I intensified this research when I entered the doctoral program in clinical psychology at the Center for Psychological Studies in Albany, California, in September 1986. It was in the course of this research that I learned how *many* grandparents were parenting their grandchildren, especially in the African American community. I discovered that there was virtually *no* research on the subject.

I called various departments of social services in different states and counties in search of helpful information, and quickly learned that they were overwhelmed by the number of children in the system who needed placement, and were focused on that task. All they knew about the grandparents was that most of them provided a safe and caring home for the children. I then contacted churches, schools, hospitals, television and radio stations, magazines, and newspapers, but no one seemed to know very much about what life was like for these caring grandparents.

My first break came in November 1988, when a child care referral agency in Oakland, California, called Bananas, noted that an increasing number of grandparents were bringing their grandchildren in for child care while the grandparents themselves went to work. Bananas sent flyers out to churches, child care centers, family courts, social service departments, pediatricians' offices, and the Children's Hospital in Oakland, inviting grandparents to attend a meeting to discuss their concerns as well as the services they needed for child care. As luck would have it, I spotted a small announcement about this in the *Oakland Tribune,* and called Bananas director Betty Cohen, told her about my interest in the subject, and asked if I could attend the meeting. She said she would be delighted to have me there.

When I arrived at that meeting to sign in, I met Betty Cohen and chatted with her for a while. There were already TV cameras, as well as newspaper reporters, in the room. When Betty opened the meeting, she introduced me to the group and told them about my work in the field. The applause of the group made me feel really welcome. During the meeting, I observed that none of the twenty grandparents (all grand-*mothers,* by the way) said a word about parenting their grandchildren. Instead, they talked about health issues, work experiences, financial concerns, and, in a few instances, their relationships with their own children—usually their daughters, but in a few cases their sons.

A week after this meeting, Betty called me to ask if I would consider organizing a Grandparents As Parents support group. If so, she said, I could have a room at Bananas for the group and a second one for child care. She didn't have to ask twice. Before the month was over, I had my plans in place to facilitate a support group for parenting grandparents, which would also be open to other relatives, including great-grandparents, aunts, uncles, and teenage children. The idea was to provide a comfortable, safe, and confidential environment for parenting grandparents to express and share their feelings, concerns, and challenges. The group would also seek to provide resources, services, and tools to assist these grandparents in adjusting to their new parenting roles. For the first two months or so, these every other week meetings were attended by only two or three grandparents, even though child care was provided for anyone who brought her grandchildren with her.

At this stage, the children ranged in age from two months to five years. One problem was that, although the group was designed to provide a safe environment for sharing feelings, some grandparents were afraid that their own adult children would be opposed to them airing their concerns in public. This was because most of these adult children were drug addicts, who showed up once a month to pick up their welfare checks and then spent the money on their drug of choice—mostly crack cocaine then. The grandmothers feared that their addicted daughters might harm them physically or run off with the children—or both.

By early 1989, four months into the program, the issue of grandparents parenting their grandchildren was beginning to receive increased attention from the media, and more and more grandmothers began coming to my support group. It soon became apparent that, in addition to the drug addiction problem of the children's mothers, there were other reasons why these grandmothers were parenting their grandchildren. As well as parents who had neglected or abandoned their children, there were parents who were away on military deployment, were incarcerated, were immature teenagers, had physically or sexually abused their children, were mentally ill, and even parents who had died, either from illness, accident, suicide, or homicide. In the mix of problems were poverty and disease, at a time when HIV/AIDS was raging through the nation.

The children of these absent mothers most often had special medical and emotional needs. Many of them were experiencing abandonment issues and post-traumatic stress disorder (PTSD), which usually led to severe anger, rage, and depression, along with asthma, attention deficit/hyperactivity disorder (ADHD), and learning and speech disabilities.

One day in the fall of 1989, I received a call from Wendy Tokuda, a newscaster from Channel 5, the CBS affiliate in San Francisco, inviting me to appear on a segment of the national program *48-Hour Crack*. The idea was that I would be interviewed, along with some grandparents from my support group, to address issues of grandparents parenting their grandchildren. When I presented the offer to the group members, five of them volunteered to come with me—four grandmothers and one grandfather. On the night of the program, all the grandparents showed up in their finest clothes (as did I) for their exposure on prime-time national television. I got to describe the support group, and the grandparents were interviewed in turn about their stories. This media exposure encouraged even more grandparents to attend my support group.

At the meetings the grandparents indicated that they were beginning to receive positive recognition as parenting grandparents from their friends and neighbors. Fewer were being blamed for the inappropriate behaviors or choices of their adult children. Although the grandparents acknowledged that parenting young children was challenging for them at their age, none of them spoke of this challenge as a burden. They had taken on these responsibilities, they said, for two primary reasons: because they loved their grandchildren and wanted to keep their families together, and not to have their grandchildren placed in foster homes with nonrelatives.

One Sunday afternoon in June 1990, I got a phone call from a staff member of NBC's *Today Show,* asking if they could film one of my support group meetings. In fact, they wanted to film the very next day! I told them we met every two weeks, and had just met on the previous Monday, so I asked if they could wait a week. No, it had to be tomorrow or not at all, because they had the schedule all set up. I said I would do my best to round up some members of the support group. When I got on the phone, every grandparent wanted to come, so I called NBC with the good news.

The next day, a camera crew came to my office, led by a woman named Ann, who asked me a lot of questions about the support group— some of my answers actually got on air later. Then the crew followed as I drove to Bananas to meet with the grandparents. Three grandfathers and twenty-two grandmothers showed up that night, all dressed TV-ready with gloves, hats, and suits. Fifteen grandchildren were in the next room, also dressed to the hilt. Bananas had to give us a larger room to accommodate all these people.

As at all our meetings, we sat in a circle, but this time with the TV crew wandering around on the outside. There were bookcases on the walls, and Ann had placed boxes of tissues around the room. From time to time during the meeting, she would ask the group a question, but otherwise the session went like every other, with people speaking freely about their feelings and needs.

After the meeting, Ann came up to me and said, "I'm amazed! Nobody cried. And here I brought all these tissues."

One of the grandmothers named Geneva, said, "We came to talk, not to cry. We've already done our crying."

Everyone laughed.

The taping aired the following Monday and Tuesday in two segments, the first one showing the interview in my office, the second showing the meeting.

After our appearance on *The Today Show,* so many grandparents began to come to our group that we had to find a larger meeting space. I called my pastor, who offered me two rooms at The Church by the Side of the Road in Berkeley, one for the grandparents and a second for the grandchildren. Since some of the kids were getting to be of school age, we added tutoring services to the child care. That is the model we have followed to this day in the same location.

By 1991, many of the members of the support group were becoming advocates for their cause by speaking to community meetings and conferences. In 1992, I broadened my audience and the public awareness of the issue by converting my doctoral dissertation into a book, *Black Grandparents As Parents.* In that same year, a group of concerned supporters organized a California Coalition of Grandparents/Relatives Caregivers. The members included religious leaders, doctors and nurses, judges and attorneys, educators, social workers, politicians, and media personalities. This coalition was organized to spread awareness of the issues and provide networking and outreach services for parenting relatives across the state. I later served as the cochair and then as chair of this organization.

In August 1992, Barbara Rodgers, the hostess of *The Barbara Rodgers Show* on Channel 5, began taping a number of our support group meetings. For one of her broadcasts, she and her crew followed Esther Jones, a grand-mother in our group, around in her home, from 6:30 in the morning. The day began with Esther getting her three preschool-age grandsons out of bed, dressed, and fed. The boys were called The Three T's because their names were Thomas, Timothy, and Terence. After breakfast, Esther dropped her grandsons off at child care and went to work. At the end of the day, Barbara and her crew returned to film Esther arriving home with the boys, feeding and bathing them, putting them to bed, and read-ing them stories.

In September 1992, my grandparents' support group celebrated Na-tional Grandparents Day for the first time. In those days, the celebration was very modest, consisting mostly of my telling the congregation at The Church by the Side of the Road the history of the day, which President Jimmy Carter proclaimed in 1978. Then I introduced the grandparents and their grandchildren to the congregation and described some of our work together. Over the years, the ceremony has become more elab-orate. Now we have the grandchildren pay tribute to their parenting grandparents with prayers, praise dancing, poetry, songs, and stories. We also print a program booklet, in which we announce any achievements earned by the grandchildren in the past year, as well as proclamations by local, state, and national politicians about National Grandparents Day. In 2010, we had a proclamation from President Barack Obama in the booklet. During the 2010 celebration, we honored Nancy Davis, the old-est grandparent we have ever had in our group, who turned ninety-three the week before and is currently parenting her eighteen-year-old great-grandson, Lennard Davis.

We now have a guest speaker at every year's celebration. In 2010, our speaker was a birth mother whose five children were parented in the 1990s by *her* mother. Back then, this mother, whom I will call "Susan," was addicted to crack cocaine and abandoned her children. Periodically, she told us, she would clean up her act, get sober, and actually go to col-lege. But then she would hear the drug literally calling to her, and back she would go. Finally, in 2002, she gave up the drug for good, finished college, and got a decent-paying job. She also started to coparent her children with her mother, and she is now a grandmother. Ironically, Susan is also helping two of her daughters parent their children.

Today, in these difficult economic times, the biggest challenge for survival of the Grandparents As Parents support group is finding sufficient financial support and resources. We have primarily been operating from small grants, in-kind donations, and private contributions. Despite our limited funds, we've been able to provide exciting and meaningful respite activities for our families. For example, we have taken Amtrak on several tours to Sacramento to visit the capitol and the California State Railroad Museum, have lunch, and tour the old city. We have also used charter tour buses to take families on several trips to Colonel Allensworth National Historical Park, in Tulare County, the only California town to be founded, financed, and governed by African Americans.

On these trips, the families have enjoyed full days of activities, including picnics, touring, various outdoor games, and just hanging out. On trips to a farm in Arbuckle, California, in Colusa County, the families have been able to observe and pet animals, go on hikes, enjoy picnics, catch fish, and play games. Closer to home, we have also taken a cruise on the Oakland Estuary sponsored by the City of Oakland, followed by a luncheon at Nellie's Restaurant.

In 2004, we made a king-size grandparents and grandchildren quilt under the supervision of an angelic woman named Alisa, who knew everything about making quilts. The grandparents brought in poetry, handprints, or photographs of themselves and their grandchildren. They selected an eight-inch fabric square provided by Alisa, onto which she later transferred these images. The completed quilt, which we named The Quilt of Unity, was uniquely beautiful and compelling. I have taken it with me and hung it at numerous grandparenting conferences all across the nation, and we display it during every National Grandparents Day celebration.

My Grandparents As Parents support group in Berkeley is one of many national groups in cities and rural areas around the country. There are parallel organizations elsewhere in the San Francisco Bay Area and the United States, all of them performing noble services to assist the grandparenting *she*roes and *he*roes of their communities.

My Grandkids Keep Me Young

JoAnn Wynn

This single grandmother stepped up to take guardianship of her grandson as a baby, then three years later, her granddaughter. JoAnn's story shows a rocky initial road, later moments of being overwhelmed and despairing, then gradual stability, hope, and joy. Helped by her faith, JoAnn grows wiser, and periods without major difficulties last longer.

FIRST, THE BASICS: I LIVE in Richmond, California, and have custody of my grandchildren Rondez Jr. and Destiny, who are nine and seven. I make my living as an IT technician for IBM. I've been with IBM since 1984, first in customer service in the Bay Area and Texas, and more recently in tech back in the Bay Area. The IBM work is interesting. There was a lot of work in the beginning. It's slowed down a good bit. I might be working one week, not the next—which is good because I can be available for my grandchildren, but it gives me so little income that I'll be exploring something else.

I was born in Arkansas as one of twelve siblings. I'm the sixth child, the middle one. Four are in Texas, one's in Arkansas, the rest are in Sacramento and the Bay Area. My eldest brother Daniel just died at sixty earlier this summer—he's the first of all of us to die. I'm close to all my siblings. I spend the most time with my sister Betty, whose children and grandchildren are older than mine, because she lives near me in Richmond—she's a very talented, good-natured woman.

It's quite a story, how I inherited my grandkids.

I was living in Dallas, Texas, where I'd been transferred by IBM from the Bay Area. I was doing fine—enjoying life: I'd bought a house; I could imagine retirement later on.

177

One day a girl my son, Rondez, had been seeing who lived in Beaumont called me out of the blue. I barely remembered her; I had met her briefly just in passing.

"I'm pregnant by your son," she said. Susan was six to eight months along—so far! She called me first, before telling him. Initially I thought this girl was a nice person. I didn't know there was anything wrong with her. She said she didn't know if she was going to keep the baby and that she needed money. I said I'd help as much as I could.

My son was twenty-four and living with me, working as a bill collector. He had finished high school and gone to two years of community college in Marin. I was trying to get him to go back to school and finish. When I told him about Susan's call, he denied any part in it.

"She's a big liar," he said. "No, that's not my kid."

I never ruled out that he might be lying, but I couldn't tell for quite a while. I didn't hear from her for some time. A few months after Rondez Jr. was born, an adoption agency called me to see if my son or I would take the child. They couldn't give the baby up without his consent. Susan had obviously decided she didn't want the responsibility and was willing to give him away. It began to enter my mind that this baby could come to me. "A baby?" I thought, "Oh, my God." It was the furthest thing from my mind. I began to picture how my life would change with this baby in it. I began to imagine how it might be to take care of him.

It was a very confused time. More months went by. Susan kept changing her mind about giving him up or keeping him, and Rondez Sr. delayed on giving his consent. The baby was with Susan, but my son wasn't involved with him consistently until after the birth. He didn't feel equipped to raise him and was still saying he wasn't sure if it was really his. The months went by quickly until baby Dez was seven or eight months old. Then the adoption agency got more serious. They wanted to send papers for us to sign, saying the child would be adopted if a family member couldn't take him. Rondez kept saying no, so they couldn't do anything without his consent.

Along about this time, he got in trouble with the law and he faced going to jail. We were dealing with lawyers and court dates. He was running with various girls and had a different girlfriend than Susan, Dez's mother. I didn't know who to believe, her or him. He said the baby could be anyone's. Gradually, after a while, he began to say that it was a possibility, and talked like he wanted the baby. He said he would never give up his child to strangers. He didn't completely admit it, but said it was a possibility. Suddenly Susan came to Dallas from Beaumont with the baby and wanted to stay with us. She was on the list for Section 8 housing, she said, and stayed with us.

It was very hard from the beginning. The first couple nights the baby was crying wildly. He was downstairs, and Rondez and Susan weren't doing anything with him. I had to go downstairs, get him, and take him into my bed with me. The first day Susan was with us she said she wanted to go for a walk. I thought, that's strange, she doesn't know anyone in Dallas—she was gone for quite a while. This happened more and more—going out for what she said would be a short while, and then being gone for hours. She left the child with Rondez, but he had to go to work.

And so did I! I was having to take vacation days from work to take care of the baby. Finally I told her, after a month of this, that she'd have to leave. I found out later she was on drugs (I didn't know which ones), and she was in trouble with the law herself. She started doing more crazy stuff—dressing like a prostitute, leaving all the time. She and my son started arguing.

She would leave for six months and come back and want to be mommy again, take the baby away all together for say, three months, and put him with the other child she had by a different father. But finally she left Rondez's baby at day care without picking him up so often that Child Protective Services (CPS) intervened. Rondez did the same thing: he'd go out, take my car, and not come back, and not pick up the baby at day care either. I'd fall for it so many times. It was always me who was stuck with the baby. Rondez didn't take any more responsibility than she did. He learned how to feed him a little, but he just couldn't do the day in, day out care a baby really needs.

I worried that I'd lose my job. At about this time CPS found out that Susan was in jail. They came over and asked me to take temporary custody of baby Dez.

Three years later Rondez got involved with Susan again, and Destiny was born. Susan was bragging, "I'm pregnant by your son again!" With Destiny, who I named myself (she had named Rondez Jr.), she started right off with her old behavior of not coming to pick her up at day care. Once I kept Destiny for what I thought was going to be a few hours, and she never returned.

Things began to seriously fall apart. I got carpal tunnel syndrome, lost my house, IBM wanted me to retire, and I got care of Destiny when she was three months old. The company offered a large number of people early retirement after twenty years, so they wouldn't have to pay out the larger pension at twenty-five years. CPS recommended a restraining order that Susan wasn't to go within one hundred feet of either of her children and advised me to move much farther away from her, the mother of my grandchildren. So I moved to the Bay Area, where I had family. I was offered a job at IBM as a supplemental tech.

Rondez Sr. went to jail in 2006. He calls every Sunday—the kids tell him what they're doing and what they have planned. He's pretty good about communicating with them. He was on five-year probation and came up for parole last year, but it didn't work out. Overall, he's done all right in prison. He's taken courses and gotten certificates in carpentry, plumbing, parenting, and anger management. He'd like to do carpentry when he gets out.

After we moved to the Bay Area in 2008 I found Dr. Poe's Grandparents As Parents monthly support group. In the first years I went I was so embarrassed by my problems that I couldn't say a thing there. The older grandmothers seemed so experienced. I didn't want anyone to know what was going on with me and my grandchildren, as I struggled to keep things together. But as time went on and I listened to them talk, I realized they'd all been through the things I've had to struggle with, and it's helped a huge amount to talk about things.

Dr. Poe has us keep a diary so we can see how things change, and she makes up an annual little book of them for us and the children. The point of the diary is to focus on our feelings and become better at talking about them to others. Here's an excerpt written in 2008 after we'd just arrived. We were staying with my sister, Rebecca, and I was looking for our own place. Destiny was four then, and Dez was six.

When I read it over, I do see that things have gotten better.

4/17/08 9:30 p.m.

Dear Diary:

Today I decided to write to you, because I am at the end of my rope. Every day I'm so angry and frustrated. I try so hard to control my emotions, but they come thru anyways. A lot of times I take it out on the children because they always seem to mess with me when I'm like this. I never want to let them see my tears, afraid of what they might think.

I feel like giving up so many times, I pray and pray asking God to help me, then I feel so guilty because God has done so much for me already. I can never seem to stop crying. I'm crying right now as I write this letter to you. I never really tell anyone just how I really feel, because I'm afraid they may think I'm weak. And really I am. I used to be a strong person—what has happened to me? What's going to become of my life?

I can't stand to look at myself in the mirror anymore. I hate what I've become. I feel so mean sometimes. I'm always screaming at my kids. I worry they will break something in my sister's house or do something to upset them—she and her husband and my brother. I love my grandkids very much, but sometimes I feel like I can't cope. I feel embarrassed about everything. I don't know what to do. I don't know whether I should keep staying with my sister Rebecca or go to a shelter. It's not my sister's fault I feel this way. I just don't want to make her angry. I try so hard to make sure the house stays clean to the point where I'm late almost everywhere I go. I get up early and then end up being late. Destiny, my granddaughter, always at the last minute manages to get upset about something. She's four—she cries, cries, until she gets her way. No matter what, she'll manipulate me into something I don't want to do by crying all the time.

Rondez is having digestive problems, and trouble being dry at night, which happens in big transitions when everything's unsure. We're all sleeping in the same bed. I can't remember when I last had a good night's sleep, because I sleep on the edge of the bed. Destiny is either kicking or slapping me in the face. Rondez snores and will not move over. Betty is my God-sent sister; she is the only one who seems to care about me and my feelings. I love her so dearly. Thank you, Lord, for her. She is so special to me and a lot of others. I wish I could be like her in so many ways. She's the only one I feel truly comfortable around. She always makes you feel so special, even when she's not feeling well herself.

Well, I guess I need to get some sleep, I've been up since 2:30 this morning.

4/18/08

Dear Diary:

Today was a much better day for me. I got up and prayed to God and declared his favor for my life and my children. I started expecting good things in my life, and I started my day.

I took the kids to school and came back home to get ready for work. I went back to look at the apartment where I'd put down a deposit to hold it for me, but they wanted a letter stating I make $3,300 a month. At first I thought it would be fine. I had always called a friend for this kind of thing. She agreed, but I could tell she wasn't happy about it. That day and all through the night I thought about my decision and felt bad because I was fudging things again. I was not trusting in God's word; I was fixing things yet again MYSELF. I knew in my heart it was not going to go well.

So I decided to go back and tell the lady I'd changed my mind, that I needed a two bedroom apartment, and I know I can't afford that right now. I told her I'd wait till the Good Lord blessed me to be able to stay in the right place. But the lady said she had a two bedroom with everything I wanted. She showed me the place and I was shocked: it was just what I wanted, the price and all. So the deposit I had on the one bedroom I put on the two bedroom. I was so excited! The children are finally going to get their own bedroom. I got to work and found out I would be assigned to the Fireman's Fund in Novato for a month, 40 hours a week at $21 an hour. That really just completed my day. All because I declared God's favor in my day and looked forward to it. This really works. Thank you, Lord, for all you've done. I love you, Heavenly Father, with all my heart. Amen!

Things have improved since then, but we still have really rough spells. Dez has a great third-grade teacher, and I like the school they're going to. A few months ago he was suspended from the after-school program. He was looking through other kids' backpacks, which is very wrong. But to suspend him? It doesn't seem right—how is being kicked out of the after-school program going to help him? But I guess it's the right punishment—that is pretty awful, they have to nip it in the bud. So now he's coming home after school every day. If he's done well in school that day, I let him go to the PALs basketball, which he likes so much. I'm lucky I'm not working very much, because I can pick him up and am home for him. Although that means we have less income, when I'm not called to work. I'm on the Internet every day, looking for help for some kind of counseling for both him and me.

I'm still the newest member of Dr. Poe's group, since we came here just three years ago. I haven't wanted to open up to anyone because I've felt like maybe I've been doing something wrong. But now I'm talking more to my sister and relatives. They lecture Dez, and tell me to dole out the punishments, but there can be just so many lectures and punishments before a kid tunes you out. It'll all work out. I just pray to God to make it work out.

Dez saw Dr. Poe as a therapist for a year. Medicare doesn't cover him now because she's in Alameda County and we're in Contra Costa. He was in counseling in Richmond for a year, but they stopped paying for it. When things come up, people say "get him in counseling," but it's expensive. With me, he listens, then goes right ahead and does dumb things. I punish him, take the television away. I can't take him on outings more because he's always in his room from previous punishments.

Recently Dez slammed something and was disruptive in the classroom. One day he crawled on his belly up the aisles through the desks, saying he was a snake, while the lesson was going on! He got punished by the school for that. His third-grade teacher has patience with him and I can talk to her easily. I'm trying to work with the school—we're having trouble making him understand that he's not in control, that he can't change the way things are there. He's beginning to make some progress working with the counselor at school on his tremendous anger.

Destiny doesn't seem to have such severe problems—she just wasn't damaged as much in the early years as Dez was. My household was more organized, and I had it more together by the time she came to me. We haven't heard a word from their mother since we've been here, and that's fine.

This spring I took Dez to a doctor because the same bowel incontinence problem he had in 2008 returned. It turned out he was constipated, maybe too anxious to be having normal bowel movements. He was given some medicine to regulate this—*and* was diagnosed as ADHD and given medication. I cried initially when he had to start taking it, because I didn't want him to be on any powerful drugs, but gradually it's taken hold and helped a lot. He's more in control of his moods now and doesn't have such trouble focusing. I also bought him a computer, as a reward for doing his homework carefully each night, which he's very excited about. He and Destiny mainly play games on it.

Summer 2011: The main thing I'm struggling with now is that my eldest brother Daniel died in June. Daniel, Betty, and I had gone to my hometown in Arkansas for a visit. I went into Daniel's room in the morning and found him facedown on the floor, dead of either a heart attack or a stroke. My sister Betty and I had to turn him over and call 911—it was just awful. I made all the arrangements, called the coroner's office, and arranged for shipping of the body and burial, which was so hard. He's the oldest of us all, and the first of us twelve siblings to die. I adored him. He was just sixty.

I've had anxiety attacks since then, crying very easily. I'm going to a grief counselor now in Richmond. Daniel was my dearest brother; I was very close to him. He lived with my sister, Betty, right around the corner from us. I often dropped Dez and Destiny at Daniel's, and he picked them up from the after school program when I was working out of town, in Sacramento or the South Bay. He was a good father figure to them and they've been very shaken up by his death—the first person close to them to die.

I guess that's how life will be—hard times and better times. Yesterday I brought the kids to Keller Beach in Pt. Richmond, and they had a great time. Dez rode his bike around, and Destiny was on her scooter—it's just so beautiful there, and we were happy. The kids are in the summer PALs program, taking a lot of classes in good things (boxing, computers, and sports). They'll go to summer camp up near Boonville for a week, a camp for the children of incarcerated parents.

I'm spearheading a reunion August 5 and 6 in Alabama for our family, who are scattered all over—we're chipping in to help the folks that'll find the plane fare hard to afford. More than one hundred people have been invited. I'm looking forward to it. People have been slow paying their money, and the deadline is the end of July. But somehow it'll all work out. I have faith.

I've gotten a lot out of making sure my grandkids have a loving home, where they feel safe. Even though I've had a very hard time some years, it's all been worth it.

Being There for a Child Forever

KAREN BEST WRIGHT

One of the most well-known grandparents who have raised grand-children is Karen Best Wright, who took her three granddaughters, all younger than four, when her daughter couldn't care for them. With a teenager also still at home, Karen made a stable home for them for six and a half years, and then faced the heartbreak of giving them back. Her grandparenting blog speaks to many.

FOR GRANDPARENTS RAISING GRANDCHILDREN, LURKING beneath the surface is the fear of *not* raising the children.

In summer 2002, with only the youngest of my eight children still at home, I called my mother. The conversation went something like this: "Mother, I am so glad I still have Angela at home. I'm just not ready to not have children." Life was easy with one lovely fifteen-year-old daughter at home. I loved being a mother, and now I had the time and energy to be the "perfect" mother. Angela was just starting high school, so I had three years before facing the empty-nest syndrome, which I dreaded.

In autumn 2002 the simplicity of being a mother to one child was about to change. A phone call from my oldest daughter Heather changed the course of my life for the next several years. Because of some unforeseen challenges, she needed my help. I immediately left home and drove from Virginia to Texas, bringing back with me three little granddaughters: premature infant Faith on a heart monitor, two-year-old Marlie, and four-year-old Lauren. I wasn't sure how I was going to manage everything, but like other grandparents who faced the same situation, I did not hesitate. Heather had been conscientious about providing me with a power of attorney, the children's birth certificates, and their social security cards. She wanted to make sure I had everything I needed to properly care for the children and to get any possible services that might be available for them.

The first year was the most difficult for everyone. There were frequent visits to the neonatologist with an infant carrier in my right hand and the heart monitor in my left. Feeding the baby every three hours 24/7 for a year took its toll, as I was going through menopause at the same time. Many nights I woke up to the *screaming* of the heart monitor. I would get up, make sure the baby was breathing properly, reset the monitor, and go back to sleep—that is, until I needed to feed her again. Often I strapped Faith to me in an infant sling and carried the monitor on my left shoulder as I took care of Marlie and Lauren. For obvious reasons, I was not sleeping well. When I did sleep, I had nightmares. I dreamt I was missing my plane, riding backward on a bus, or simply lost. I was exhausted. I had a hard time keeping up with my home-based business, which consisted of extensive computer use, and the normal responsibilities of caring for a home and family, as well as helping the little ones adjust to a new life without their mother, which proved particularly difficult for Lauren.

By the second year, the girls changed from calling me Nana to Mama, then to simply Mom. This hurt my daughter's feelings tremendously. She felt as though I was shoving her out of her children's lives. However, my intention with letting the children call me Mom was to help them not feel different from their peers. Angela called me Mom, and their friends lived with Moms. They did understand that I was really their grandmother, but they preferred calling me Mom, and I admit that it was comforting to me as well. When they eventually returned to live with their mother, I reverted to Nana.

During the early years, Angela, my youngest daughter still at home, was a busy teenager with school, musical performances, and church activities. She was wonderfully helpful with the children. Once when I asked her, "What's going on? I thought you had play practice today?" she responded, "I dropped out of the musical. You're under so much pressure, Mom. I don't want you to have to worry about driving me back and forth to practice." I broke down and cried. Being the "perfect" mother to my *own baby* wasn't happening.

I eventually found a good day care for Marlie and Lauren, but Faith stayed home with me until she was four because of a weak immune system. Becoming a full-time "mommy" to babies and toddlers, in and of itself, had been natural the first time for me, but I had never been a fifty-year-old menopausal woman with babies. Regardless of the difficulties, I loved raising my grandchildren. I did a lot of rocking and singing, which was heaven to me, building an unbreakable bond between us. It did not take long for the girls to quickly choose their favorite bedtime songs—usually the longest ones.

Over the next few years, we managed. As I could afford it, the girls participated in various activities such as music and dance. We took advantage of low-cost activities—outdoor concerts and any free event I could find, especially hiking and long walks in state parks, county day events, and church activities. The girls loved attending bluegrass concerts, and we laughed and danced to the merriment of the bands. I knew the importance of family traditions, so as the girls grew, they learned all of the "family songs" that I had taught my own children. Kids can't fight if they are singing, so we sang lots of songs.

Along with singing, they learned other family traditions, like our "um bite." I learned while raising my own children that children will compete to see who gets dessert first. So early on, we solved the problem by requiring no eating until everyone was served, and the first dessert bite was taken together with a very dramatic "um-m-m-m-m" being verbalized in unison. The tradition stuck and continues to this day as my children pass the "um bite" requirement on to their children. These little girls not only enjoyed our "um bite" tradition but started a new tradition as well. If we were having a dessert, we would light an antique oil lamp, turn the lights down very low, and pretend we lived in the "olden days" while we ate our dessert. This tradition soon became their favorite.

As time went on, Heather was able to become an important part of her children's lives again and visited them as often as she could. While

I welcomed her, there was always the nagging, horrifying feeling (that I consistently pushed to the back of my mind) that she would actually be in a position to take them back someday. I wanted her to have a good life and have healthy relationships, but I did not want to lose the children. In my heart, they were my children. The bond I felt with the girls was as strong as if I had given birth to them myself. I was living life as a mother, not grandmother, and I did not want that to change. This disturbed Heather: she never intended my help to extend from months into years.

In summer 2008, as my daughter's situation changed, she understandably wanted to raise her own children. An ugly, angry battle between two women over three little girls began. For two years, we fought. We both had lawyers. Our entire family seemed to be splitting apart, as family members took sides. Legal fights such as this always bring pain, especially for the children. I wanted to go into court and show in a positive way why the children should stay with me. She wanted to show why they should be with her. What resulted was a battle emphasizing who was the worst mother, not the best.

Unfortunately, we both had plenty of ammunition to fire at each other, encouraged by our lawyers. After two years of fighting, the judge ruled in my favor. The next year, 2009, a different judge ruled in my daughter's favor.

She was elated. I was devastated. I did not request visitation with the children because I believed that if Heather was to have sole custody, she should decide how to raise her children. Because of the animosity between us, I began to believe Heather might never allow the children to even see me. My relationship with them was put on hold. I cried daily for months, barely functioning.

In summer 2010, I knew I needed to pull myself together and move forward. I convinced myself that even if I had to wait for ten years to see the children, they would eventually someday be back in my life. I feared that they would forget their time with me, the songs we had sung, the games we played, and how deeply I loved them and that they might think I'd abandoned them. I reminded myself, "God knew all along you would only raise the children for six and a half years. You just didn't know that. It was always meant to be this way."

Since my life had changed, I needed it to change completely. I understood that this was my chance to focus on my other passion, healthy living from a mind, body, and spiritual perspective. This was my chance to put into action my deeply held beliefs about holistic healthy living. I moved to a new location, closer to all five of my daughters. I went back to school to earn my master's degree in psychology, specializing in health and wellness. I began to make new friends. I had a new life to create, no longer centered around being a mother to little children but being a mother to grown children, a grandmother to my other grandchildren, and establishing my new career. I tried not to focus on the deep loss I felt at losing these little girls. I still sang to them, alone, and prayed that, through some manner I did not fully understand, our souls would connect. I believe it worked.

My daughter truly loves her children, and she knew they needed to keep their relationship with me. She did not want them to feel that either of us had abandoned them. After several months and with much hesitation, she invited me to become active in their lives once again in spring 2011. At first, I could sense the unspoken fearful emotions between us. Eventually, her resentment and fear softened, and trust began to grow again. One day as I related how I'd been thinking I might have to wait until the girls were grown to reestablish my relationship with them, she responded, "Gee, Mom. You sure don't give me much credit." I was actually relieved by her response.

We are all making the necessary adjustments for me to be the grandmother. I am now just Nana, as with my other grandchildren. As often as I can, at least every month or two, I travel from Richmond, Virginia, to

Maryland and stay a few days, being Nana. I have even acquired a really nice son-in-law and two terrific step-grandsons in the process.

Mending the hurts and anger that engulfed us has required effort from my daughter and me. Our desire to put our family back together and help the children heal motivated us to work together, put past hurts behind us, and move forward. Heather needed to learn to trust that I wasn't going to pick her apart and criticize her anymore. I have learned to focus on all of the good things she has done and is still doing.

The children and I cherish our visits. Sometimes I bring crystal beads to make bracelets and necklaces, ingredients to make something tasty, a new game to play, or new dance steps to teach. The first thing the girls usually say with great excitement is, "Polly! Polly is here!" Polly is my pug. I might be greeted with "Did you bring your crystals?" or "Do we get to make fudge?" or even "Will you sing our songs to us?" On one visit, I surprised them at the bus stop. Faith smiled and said, "Mommy told me there would be a surprise after school that I would like. I knew it was you."

Even though I'm Nana now and not Mom, the very special bond we built is still there. We sing songs together, record them, and end up laughing so hard at our mess-ups that we can't see straight, or we curl up and rock in the large overstuffed rocking chair. One evening while we were shopping, I slipped up and said, "This is just like old times." I quickly added, "But these are new times." Marlie replied, "New times are better than just memories." Our good memories are invaluable, but yes, the new times are definitely better than just memories.

Sometimes even between planned visits, my daughter will text me when someone is ill, "Can you possibly come up here and help us?" Currently most of my work and school is done online, so my Nana motto is: "Have laptop, cell phone, and dog. Will travel." I usually text back, "I'll be there in a few hours."

Part Four

GRANDCHILDREN REMEMBER

Hark, the Moaning Pond
A Grandmother's Tale

• • • • • • • • • • • • • • • •

TISSA ABEYSEKARA

*This moving piece from the Sri Lankan film director Tissa Abeysek-
ara's collection* Bringing Tony Home *portrays a soothing grandmother in a stern household where secrets and strict caste codes rule
behavior. The excerpt captures in filmic images the world of Tissa as
a boy, and the grandmother he loved.*

GRANDMOTHER'S FACE IS ONE OF my earliest memories. She died when I was
five, in 1944, a year before the war ended. There is a story around her
death too.

She had returned from a pilgrimage to the Holy Peak—the same place
she went purporting to be a pilgrim when she eloped with the Buddhist
monk who covered his shaven head for two weeks to hide himself—and
on the day after her return came to see me. Whenever this story is told
it is stressed that she came to see me. Once a week she would come,
Mother used to say, mainly to see me. She lived with her son in the north
end of the city, which was fifteen miles from where we lived.

To see me she had to come by two trains. The first one brought her to
the Central Station in Colombo. From there she would board the south-
east-bound narrow gauge train, which moved along the Kelani Valley all
the way up to a terminal on the western slopes of the country—the same
slopes along which my grandfather descended with his sixteen-year-old
girl from the hills—near the Holy Peak. From Central Station Grandmother traveled twelve miles on this train to a station half a mile from
our house. From there she would walk to our place, and sometimes on
hot days, she would hire Thomas's buggy cart, which was always there by
the railroad for passengers.

195

I can remember the day she came to see me on her return from the pilgrimage to the Holy Peak. I can't remember her arriving, but I can remember her seated by the bay window on the upper level of our house where there was an easy chair. I was seated on her lap, and looking out of the window I could see over and beyond the treetops in our back compound to the sun on the rice paddies. I was trying to tell Grandmother that I could, on some days, see the Holy Peak in the sky, beyond the rice paddies from here. It was pleasant on Grandmother's lap. Her sari, white with purple flowers—or was it blue?—and worn in the style of hill-country women, was crisp and clean of freshly laundered starch, and there was about her the smell of perfumed oil and betel with areca nut and cardamom. I remember the warmth of her face against mine.

The next thing I see in my memory is Grandmother near the front gate—the blue wooden gate with the grill of the rising sun and always closed except when Father's people came in their big cars—and Carolis, the servant boy, trying to open it. I was in the veranda with Mother looking across the porch and through the palm tree. I had never seen Grandmother come or go through that gate. Her people—my mother's people—always came from the gate of zinc sheets at the back. But this day it was different. Perhaps that's why I remember it.

The story is that Grandmother went away offended by something I had said. I had walked up to her with a discarded leather bag and offered it to her saying, "Good for Grandma to carry beef in." I can't remember doing that, but I must have. Grandmother had alleged my mother put me up to do that. I don't remember Mother doing that either. Now there's a point to all this. Grandmother would observe Sil regularly on the day of the full moon. But she had a partiality to beef. A pious temple-going woman eating beef! It was an inside joke in her family.

If I did what I was supposed to have done, it was natural Grandmother was offended, especially when she had just returned from a pilgrimage to the Holy Peak. I can't remember any of this now, but having heard it repeatedly over the years, it is taken for granted that I said what I was supposed to have said, and Grandmother went away offended. But I distinctly remember her at the gate. I can still see her moving out of the gate, turning left, and walking past the scaly trunks of the fir trees that stood along the parapet wall between our garden and the gray asphalt road. I hear the sound of children coming from the school on the other side of the road—a continuing buzz like bees humming. It would have been late in the morning on a weekday.

I never saw Grandmother again.

A few days after she went through that wooden gate, painted blue and with a grill of the rising sun, a man was at the same gate calling.

"Is someone home?" That's how anyone would call when they came to that gate, and they had to call loud to be heard across the large front garden and through the veranda, the drawing room, and the dining room. Anyone who came to that gate and called from there also had to be someone coming for the first time and therefore didn't know it would not be opened unless under special circumstances. But that day it was opened. When Carolis, who had gone to see who it was at the gate, came running back looking frightened and told Mother there was a message from Kelaniya—now that was where Grandmother lived with her only son, the one who wore a red shawl and gave me a wooden car with a pedal—Mother wanted him to open the gate and let the man come. She stood on the edge of the veranda holding my hand.

The man came walking slowly along the left crescent of the driveway and stood under the portico.

Grandmother had died.

The day she left our place because she was offended by my giving her a bag to carry beef in, she had arrived home—meaning at her son's place where she lived—a couple of hours after high noon and, complaining of a headache, had gone to bed. She may have not had anything to eat since morning, because, according to Mother, she didn't stay long enough at our place even to have a cup of tea. She had woken up after dark and taken a cold bath. Her daughter-in-law had warned her not to bathe at that time, but Grandmother never listened to anyone, least of all to her daughter-in-law. In the night she had a blazing temperature, and by morning she was in a delirium.

Over the years something about this whole affair has nagged me. Had she been starving the whole day? Did anyone ask her whether she had had anything to eat? If she had been starving, why didn't she ask for something to eat? I have not been able to find this out, and there is this feeling within me that she starved herself to death. No one speaks about this, and it is like they want to avoid something. If she deliberately didn't eat anything, did it have something to do with what happened at our place, that stupid thing about my giving her a bag to carry beef in? I can't help but think that simple incident would have sparked off something that lay smoldering, something far more serious. I remember Mother telling Father, the night of the day Grandmother went through that front gate, that she insisted the gate be opened.

"I am not some vagrant to come and go through the back door. Why should I? I have a pedigree. My people were from the Maha Wasala. I am not a mixed-up half-caste." (By Maha Wasala, she meant the royal court of the Kandyan kings where Grandmother claimed her ancestors served; I don't know Grandmother's complete name, but she and her relatives—I have traced some of them now—lay claim to a family name that is of an illustrious highland clan, but I can't substantiate this. The reference to "half-caste" implies the hybridity of my father's side, whose ancestry can be traced through their family name to Kerala, and they also have a Portuguese surname.)

As usual, Father had come home late in the night, and I was pretending to be fast asleep listening to Mother reporting the incident.

Now Grandmother was dead. The day after she developed a high fever and became delirious, she was taken to hospital. She had died there sometime toward midnight, never once regaining consciousness. No final word, no dying wish.

But I knew nothing of all this until four years later.

The day the messenger came and Mother allowed him to come through the front gate, and he came slowly along the driveway, I was told that Grandmother was very ill. Mother kept crying because, I thought, she couldn't go see Grandmother, and that was because Father was not at home, and Mother couldn't leave without informing him, even if her mother was very ill. Father came home, as usual, late in the night.

[Tissa is taken by his father to his maternal aunt's huge house, where he has never been without his mother, and where he has never slept alone.]

Lunch was like being at a prayer. Aunt sat at the head of the table and I sat on her right and there was total silence. Barnis the freak hovered in the background. I began to hate him. I felt my aunt's eyes on me, which made me uneasy, and I kept looking away from the food. The walls reached very high to a carved wooden ceiling. On the walls were large portraits of men and women in elaborate ceremonial dress, and the frames were very ornate, and some had gilt edges. In front of me, and kept against the wall, was a large chiffonier, and its mirror was framed by a grapevine with bunches at regular intervals carved into the ebony wood. I saw myself reflected in the mirror, and just behind me, standing like an evil spirit, was Barnis.

That monstrous sound like the bellowing of a dying beast rolled over everything once again, and I woke up and wanted to scream. It was like not being able to open my eyes, and I was shaking all over. Slowly I realized it was night, and that I was somewhere in that big house with those high walls going up to the carved ceiling. I had sat up in bed, and now I could see a faint glow through the open door of the room I was in. It was a dim light in the dining hall, and I was in a room opening out into that hall, and I could see the mirror of the chiffonier there, a rectangle of muted reflection. I laid back on the bed, where the bedsheet and the pillowcase felt like crisp paper and smelled of laundry starch.

I now remembered Aunt preparing this bed, and the fear I had of having to sleep there all alone because I had never slept alone, and Aunt not even asking me whether it would be all right by me if I was to sleep alone. At the time she left me there and disappeared, the lights were still on in the house, and Uncle Eugene was playing the piano, and it was a beautiful sound, rather sad, and I felt good. I heard cars on the lane going by the side of the house, and all the cars seemed like they were coming home. Dogs barked, some far away and some not so far away, but they never barked altogether like they did in the village where my home was, and the sounds were different. These were deep pedigreed barks, arrogant and full of assurance, not sounds of fear, pain, or appeal.

The piano had stopped. It may have stopped when I was listening to the dogs. I first heard the silence like some emptiness. Then the lights began to go out one by one. I heard the click of the switches putting out the lights. It must have been Barnis the freak. Once all the lights were off and the clicking of the switches stopped, it was dark except for a vague light that fell across the dining room. From the bed on which I lay, I could see that light through an open door. That's when I began getting frightened. I did not know where that light was coming from, and it cast shadows on the wall. The mirror of the chiffonier reflected a corner of the dining room, and there were certain dark shapes there. I shut my eyes and began crying into the pillow. I tried to cry softly without making a sound, and that gave me a pain inside me like my chest was going to burst.

Waves crashed on the beach and seagulls squawked and Grandmother was with me but constantly running away, and her face was a blank, and I couldn't run, and there was a pain in my chest like I couldn't breathe. It was then that the dying monster howled, and I woke up and sat on bed shaking all over and then saw the vague light in the hall beyond the open door and the muted reflection of the mirror on the chiffonier in the dining room and realized I was at the big house where my aunt and that freak Barnis lived, and the sound like a dying monster's was really the siren at the mill. As I lay back in bed, there was a huge silence, as if the sound of the siren had created a vacuum. As I shut my eyes again, I was listening to that silence, wanting to hear some sound, and through that dark and the awesome stillness I began to hear something. At first it was like part of the silence, and the sound I thought I heard was like the humming you hear in your ears when you cup them with your hands. It rose and fell, and then I recognized it, and it was like someone held your hand and you were not frightened anymore. It was the sound of the sea. The sea was about a mile away from the big house I was now in, but you never heard it during the day. Now in the still of the night, and after the siren seemed to have blown away everything and cleared the air, you heard the waves crashing on the beach. I knew that sound well by then.

I first heard it when I was with Grandmother in a house somewhere off the south coast where Father had a rubber plantation, and once he took us there to stay for some time. That was the only time that Grandmother was with us like part of the family, and Mother made me sleep with Grandmother in another room, and I liked it because she—Grandmother—told me wonderful stories and held me close when we slept, and it was nice and warm and pleasant holding on to her and sleeping.

We arrived at the rubber plantation one morning—I remember it was morning because I woke up in the car where I would have been put while still in my sleep, feeling hungry, and Mother said we were going to have breakfast at the estate bungalow, and sure enough there was a feast of hoppers, the best I have eaten so far, awaiting us, and immediately after breakfast I went for a walk with Grandmother. Mother wanted us to go until she arranged things at the bungalow. We walked under the rubber trees, and it was cool, and the thick carpet of dead leaves was still wet with overnight dew, and there was a strong smell of latex mixed with decaying leaves, and Grandmother picked rubber seeds on the ground—brown-shelled and brittle, enclosed in two ear-shaped clasps. Grandmother showed me how to separate the clasps and reconnect them in a different way, and when you blew on one, it made a whirring sound as it spun like a bobbin. There were women collecting latex in galvanized buckets, and they paused to look at us, smiling diffidently at first, and when Grandmother spoke with them they grinned from ear to ear, and some of them touched me on the head. We kept walking, me blowing at those bobbins until my mouth was dry, and the ground began to rise, and then we were clear of the rubber trees and above them on an open expanse of flat rock, and suddenly I heard Grandmother's voice, excited like a child's.

"There's the sea."

I looked, and it took some time for me to see what Grandmother saw. It was a sheer expanse of emerald green touching the blue dome of the sky at the far end in a wide crescent, and on the land side, where the green tops of coconut trees ended on a gold-colored strip, there were what looked like white plumes forever appearing and disappearing. There were boats all over on the green water, and they were bobbing with their sails bright in the eastern sun. A strong wind was blowing from the sea, and it was heavy, unlike the winds that blew across the paddy fields at home.

Grandmother kept explaining all of this to me, and I can still hear the sense of wonder in her voice. She called what we were looking at— that great big spread of green water touching the blue sky with those milky-white plumes at the land's edge—the Moaning Pond. That's what her people up in the hills called the sea. Because, she said, the sea always keeps making that sound—here she imitated the sea sound—like a woman is moaning. When she was a little girl, very few people up there in her village had seen the Moaning Pond, and those who had were held in great respect. She herself had never seen it until she came down to the lowlands with her husband.

However, once when she was a little girl she had gone on a pilgrimage to the Holy Peak, and there at the summit at daybreak, when the sun rose from the east and cast the peak's shadow across the land, people with her had pointed in the distance and said if you keep looking hard you will see the Moaning Pond. She kept looking hard and for a long time, she said, and thought she saw something shimmering at a faraway point where the shadow of the peak seemed to end. But she was not sure.

Ever since that day, she wanted to see the Moaning Pond and dip her feet in its salty wash, which was almost a necessary ritual for those who come there for the first time. They called it "walking the waves." Waves were those things like white plumes, and they keep dashing on the beach. The beach is that strip of gold-colored ground. That's all sand. Fine white sand. There are shells of various colors to be picked up in the sand. Bathing in the sea was good. It cured you of many ailments and made you healthy. The sea, in the way Grandmother described it, was a marvel, something that began nowhere and ended nowhere. A great big mysterious pond, which kept moaning eternally, like a woman in anguish. She dashes herself on the shore all the time. I have always carried with me, associated with the waves breaking on the shore, this image of a woman throwing herself on the ground weeping, because that's how Grandmother first described it to me. She didn't say it directly, but her choice of words implied that image. For her, waves did not break on the shore, they threw themselves, and the word she used is a verb in our language that connotes an act of penance, and when she first said that on that rock above the rubber trees looking toward the sea, her voice, as I have always remembered, was very sad.

That night, when I slept with Grandmother, snuggled comfortably to her warmth, we listened to the sound of the sea, now coming from far away. I drifted away to sleep listening to that sound, but before that, until sleep came, Grandmother told me the first of many stories connected with the sea I was to hear in the days to come.

The next morning, Father took us to the beach. It would have been the monsoon season because the sea was rough and tall waves crashed on the shore—wailing women throwing themselves in penance—and my mind was full of concern for that beautiful princess who was put out to sea as a sacrifice. In my mind it was like she was still out there tossing perilously on those angry waves in her golden boat. Mother wouldn't let me go near the waves, but Grandmother was at the water's edge "walking the waves," and she seemed as happy as a child. That's another memory of Grandmother that I carry with me—dressed in white playing like a child by the sea, the white foam of the waves rising up to her, and she not running back but standing there, very still, as if in some secret communion.

That's the image of Grandmother that came back to me when I heard the sound of the sea coming from far away on that lonely night in the big house where Father had left me with his sister, my aunt, and I had woken in the night to the fearful cry of a dying monster. Now with the sound of the sea floating gently up to me from somewhere, it was like being with Grandmother, and I almost felt her warmth, and the room filled with the strong-sweet smell of betel, cardamom, and perfumed oil, and I was not frightened anymore.

I began speaking with Grandmother. I told her I was sorry she was ill, that I hoped she would be all right soon and that she would come to see me; maybe Father would take us to that bungalow in the rubber estate again and we would—Grandmother and I—walk under those rubber trees on the dead leaves wet with dew, blowing that bobbin made of those ear-shaped clasps until my mouth was all dry, and that we would walk all the way up to that rock from where we would watch the Moaning Pond in the distance. I also told her I was sorry if I hurt her with that fool talk of the leather bag for her to carry beef in, that I didn't intend to hurt her because I loved her more than anything else in the world.

"How's Grandmother?"

"She's all right."

Mother wasn't looking at me straight.

"Can I go see her?"

"No, you can't."

"Why?"

"She's gone away to the hills."

"Why?"

"Because it's cool up there and she would get better soon."

"Can't we go up there to see her?"

"Not yet."

"How long will she be up there?"

"Until she gets completely well."

"Then will she come back?"

"Yes."

"And then will she come to see me?"

"Yes."

"If she doesn't come can we go see her?"

"Yes."

Three years pass, and I am still waiting for Grandmother to return from the hills, when Doreen and Felicia came to stay with us. They were sisters, and their mother had died—or so I was told, but I think it was something else—and their father, who was a friend of my father's, wanted them to stay with us until he made some other permanent arrangements. Doreen and Felicia were older than I—I was going on eight—and I knew they were older because they had boobs. Not big ones, but boobs nevertheless. We soon became very friendly, and among the things I told them about myself was that I had a grandmother and that she was up in the hills where it was cool and where she had gone to get well and that she would be coming back one day soon. Doreen and Felicia looked at each other and didn't say anything.

After Doreen and Felicia left, there was something I wanted to ask Mother. They left in the morning, and I spent a long time making up my mind about what I wanted to ask Mother. It was late in the afternoon, and through the bay windows in the upper level I could see the light dying on the rice paddies beyond the treetops. The blue hills in the distance had vanished in a gray sky, and there was a hint of rain in the wind that blew over the trees right inside the house. Seated on that easy chair where long ago Grandmother sat on the day she went through the front gate never to return, Mother was reading a book. She always sat there when she read something, because at those windows the light was there long after it had gone from the rest of the house.

"Mother!"

She didn't look up from the book she was reading but made a sound like she heard me.

"Is Grandmother dead?"

Now she looked up. She seemed surprised. I am sure she would have detected the complaint in my voice. I had waited for this moment, since Doreen and Felicia told me that Grandmother was dead and that this story about her being in the hills was a big lie. But they swore me to say I wouldn't say that they told me so. Now that Doreen and Felicia were gone, I was free to ask.

"Who told you?"

"Tell me, is she dead?"

Mother took a long time—or it seemed to me—to answer. She looked down at the book then looked away through the window to the dark coming under the trees in the back garden down below. I heard the whistle of the Little Train before I heard Mother answer me at last.

"Yes."

For a moment I was silent. I felt something building up within me, slowly. At first I began sobbing, and Mother reached out like she wanted to touch me. I screamed as loud as I had ever done. Mother stood up like she was struck by something. I tore into her, screaming all the time. By the time the servants came running, I had sunk my teeth into Mother's hand. I wouldn't let anyone touch me, and I rolled on the ground and then stood up again screaming still, looking around for things to throw at those who kept reaching for me. I now remember that there came a point when I couldn't stop myself thrashing around. I wasn't doing it only because I had not been told that Grandmother was dead. That was only one reason. I felt cheated like you're getting hurt when you are made a fool of. There was something more. I think it had much to do with Mother bursting into the room when I was playing "doctor" with Felicia, the "patient," lying in bed with her frock raised and the knickers down.

At that moment, something stopped within me, and I became still and stood where I stood when Mother took me by the hand and led me out of the room. She didn't say a word, and for two days something was choked up within me. What made it worse was that everyone was behaving strangely with me. Alice, the servant woman who would bathe me and dress me, had a funny look when she changed my clothes, and I was feeling uneasy. There was a silence whenever people moved past me or they were in my presence. It was like some horrible thing had happened, something that should not be spoken about. What was choked within me perhaps was shame.

During those two days between Mother bursting into the room and Doreen and Felicia going away, I didn't want to talk to anyone. Guilt was a feeling unknown to me then, I suppose. But death, I was vaguely aware of. People who die never come back.

When Doreen—and Felicia too was there—first told me that Grandmother was dead, and that she would never come back—that was many days before they had to go from our house—I was not sad immediately. I was angry. First I was angry with the two girls because I thought they were lying. Then over the next few days when I began to realize that maybe it was true, I was angry with Mother. Then when I went to sleep in the night, and lying in bed next to the bed where Mother was sleeping, I began to think of Grandmother. I listened to the night, and I thought I heard the sound of the Moaning Pond come from far away, and then the room would be filled with the sweet-strong smell of betel and cardamom and perfumed oil, and tears would come. I cried softly not to wake up Mother, because if she woke up I would have to explain why I was crying and that would be bad because I had promised Doreen and Felicia I wouldn't tell Mother that they told me Grandmother was dead.

However, when Doreen and Felicia went away, and I asked Mother whether Grandmother was really dead, and she said, "Yes," and I screamed and yelled and thrashed on the floor, it was not only that I was sad Grandmother was dead.

I had been doing something horrible with Doreen and Felicia inside their room.

Everyone's looking at me in a funny sort of way because of that.

Doreen and Felicia have been sent away.

There's something choking inside me.

Grandmother isn't in the hills getting well.

They have lied to me all these years.

I have been cheated.

Grandmother was dead.

Really dead.

Dead.

All of this was there in my scream, in the way I tore into Mother, thrashed on the floor and looked for things to throw at those who were trying to reach out and calm me.

I screamed all those things and many other things I couldn't say with words.

It was also the end of something. The screaming and the rolling on the floor and the biting of Mother's hand and the rushing at people who tried to touch me like a yapping, snarling dog were the death throes of something that died that day. Whatever it was, it died hard like a grievously wounded animal struggling and thrashing around until the last breath was drawn.

After the coming and going of Doreen and Felicia, life somehow became different. A new shame had entered me, and I had things to hide, things I would see that I had not seen before and I would not talk about.

There were also other things that changed. A year after Doreen and Felicia left, we moved from the split-level house with the bay windows to a smaller one in the same neighborhood. The servants left one by one, and only Carolis remained. The red car with the long bonnet was gone. Father came and went in a small Bug Fiat, and one day he kept it behind in the portico—small though the house was, it had a portico with an un-paved floor that was full of dust—and it remained there for a long time until someone came and towed it away and it never came back. Things were going away never to come back like Grandmother. Only Tony, my roly-poly, fluffy pup, now grown lean and tall with his puppy fat gone, remained, and it was fun going around with him under the rubber trees across the paddy field at the edge of the compound and collecting fish from the little streams into empty Horlicks bottles. Grandmother was dead, and when I went to sleep alone in my room next to my parents' room with a communicating door, I did not hear the Moaning Pond anymore, and I didn't seem to care.

When I began going to the movies, the Moaning Pond was always there behind the Savoy theater, and very near the Majestic, and not so near yet visible in the distance from the front of the Liberty. Sometimes after a show I would walk with my friend Wicky along the rail tracks that went just above the beach where, on the rocks, couples would be huddled under black umbrellas and the waves thrashed on the shore—the wailing women—and Grandmother was never there in my thoughts.

And so a little girl in the mountains inherited this longing from her ancestors. From the time she could climb the hill in her village, where there was a temple and from where people believed you could see the Moaning Pond if you have done enough merit in your previous birth, she would come to gaze into the distance beyond the mountains of home to the edge of the land where everything was what you thought you saw. She never thought she saw the Moaning Pond from there. Like a migrant bird flying back along the route of some ancestral memory, she reached the sea to "walk the waves" that brought her ancestors to a copper-colored shore and also carried a beautiful princess on its cradle to safety and motherhood.

I see the little girl on that rock where the temple is, gazing toward the west with the rising sun at her back. I see Grandmother, a vision in white standing against the rising waves almost to receive them, un-moved, unafraid. I also see in between, Grandmother leaving the front gate of that split-level house, turning left and moving slowly past the line of fir trees along the asphalt road, looking ahead with head held high, never to return.

And then I am a child once more, of eight going on nine, waiting for her to return from the hills where she has gone to get well.

Calling Clotilde

LAUREN ACZON

*Lauren's beloved grandmother died while she was away at college,
and memories of this stern Filipino matriarch and her wry sense of
humor flooded through Lauren as she remembered the Clotilde of her
childhood, and recent conversations with her on the phone. We feel
her fierce love for this Filipino grandmother who wanted all things
Filipino to be forgotten.*

CLOTILDE ALBANO ACZON, OR MRS. Benjamin Aczon, was the matriarch of
the Aczon family. Even though she and my grandfather lived together,
she linguistically represented both of them. "Grandma's house" referred
to the house they shared. "Don't forget to bring your report card to
show Grandma" implicitly meant Grandpa, too. She and my grandfather spoke with heavy northern Filipino accents, in broken English to
us and in Ilocano to each other. He sang Frank Sinatra hits while chop-
ping up the chicken for dinner; she watched *All My Children* every noon
and *Jeopardy* every night.

She rejected the Filipino part, or at least blocked it out from us. They
kept Tagalog, Ilocano, and stories of home between themselves and
away from us. We were too young to want it. As an adult I've found the
Filipino-est parts of me to be my industriousness, adaptability, sense of
humor, and sense of honor. I didn't get much of a sense of "how to be
Filipino" from my grandparents, as they seemed ready to leave that behind for American culture. They pushed us to go to school and pursue
extracurricular activities and gave us money to do so, usually a twenty-
dollar bill in a white envelope.

Their house in South San Francisco was every living Aczon's pre-
kindergarten day care. None of the seven cousins, including me, can
count how many times we rode in the backseat of our parents' Hondas

over the Bay Bridge from the East Bay. Big steps led up to the front door of their house. There were plenty of toys in the playroom (what was probably once a dining room, a central carpeted room with a rich, dark built-in breakfront where spare sets of dishes lived), including plastic cars, building blocks, and stuffed animals. When I graduated from playthings to reading everything I possibly could, I read *Better Homes & Gardens* (subscription dutifully bought from one of the grandkid's elementary school magazine sales), the *Encyclopedia Britannica* circa 1968, discarded paperbacks from my older cousin, and the Sunday comics.

My younger brother Evan, our cousins, and I had distinctly American things for lunch, like Cup o' Noodles, Spam, Campbell's chicken soup, and sandwiches of Best Foods mayo, Foster Farms ham, Kraft cheese, and iceberg lettuce. Traditional Filipino foods (*lumpia* and *pansit* and seaweed soup) were prepared only for holiday dinners, simmered all day long, and served up with gallons of white rice. Grandma made me eat until I couldn't eat anymore, pressed us for seconds and thirds. She wasn't going to let anyone be hungry, ever.

We grandkids laugh about it now, but in our earliest years our grandma unapologetically terrified us into good behavior. If I ran in the street, she would yank me back by the arm and bark, "When you fall down, the car won't see you because you are too small. You will get run over." If I was too shy to ask the bus driver for a return ticket, she told me she would leave me on the sidewalk unless I spoke up for myself. If I was sassy, she pulled a pair of red-and-white plastic Hello Kitty scissors from a drawer and threatened to cut off my tongue. She was stern, but never missed the routine hug and "I love you" when we went home in the evening, waving in the doorway until we were out of sight. At the dinner table we always got to choose from three juices: grape, apple, or orange. There was always the trifecta of neapolitan ice cream or Chips Ahoy cookies for dessert. She loved us hard, harder than anyone.

Grandma Aczon was discipline. When she said, "Pick up your plate," you picked up your plate … and knife, fork, and cup. And brought them to the sink, washed them, then dried them. I guess we got this from my dad and his brothers, who respected her to the utmost, delivering swift smacks to the backside of whoever dared talk back to their tiny mom.

Devoutly Catholic until the very end, she brought us along to church on Sundays and sometimes during the week—kerchief on head, sturdy (if ill-fitting) black shoes, nylons, and rosary. She curled her own hair every night with water, parting it carefully in halves, quarters, and six-teenths, and pinning up her curls with black bobby pins—the poster girl for economy and thrift. She held us firmly by the hand when we walked to the grocery store or to the bus stop, always to buy food. I liked to poke the plastic-encased meat in the refrigerated section, and she'd slap my little hand with a stern look. *Behave yourself.* The calendar on the wall was from All Hallow's parish and named every saint day. I received Hallmark cards on Christmas, Easter, Valentine's Day, and birthdays, my name scrawled in meticulous cursive at the top and her name scrawled on the bottom.

My grandfather didn't speak with us as much as she did—his voice was limited to "Make good your art" and the pre-dinner blessing, "Bless us, our Lord, for these thy gifts, which we are about to receive from thy bounty, through Christ, our Lord. Amen."

She did the Jumble in the paper every morning, with a cup of black coffee and a Bic pen, and usually still in her polyester robe. My dad tells me that this is how she learned much of her English, thumbing through a black pocket Webster's dictionary to find words. When she died I asked specifically for this dictionary, but to this day haven't found the courage to hold it in my hands.

My parents both worked full time in San Francisco, so we spent a lot of summers at my grandparents' house—playtime, too much TV, home-work, and falling asleep on the sofa until Mom and Dad came to pick us up. When I was able, I read a lot, everything. The big outing of the day was usually a bus ride to San Bruno Avenue, and a long morning of stopping into stores that smelled like fish. Often she spoke Tagalog to the man behind the counter or to other people she recognized. Then I became a prize. "Look how tall my granddaughter is," she would say as she pushed me in front of her so another old lady could inspect me from behind her cataracts.

I remember singing loudly from my seat in a shopping cart, with Grandma smiling proudly when other shoppers complimented my rendition of "Somewhere Over the Rainbow."

I liked chipping and then peeling paint from the bathroom wall. I thought the shape of the hole looked like a continent. My favorite hide-and-seek spot was the hall closet, among cases of paper towels and Top Ramen. Evan and I laughed when my grandpa snored from his seat in the corner, until Grandma smacked one or both of us, that severe disapproving look. We sometimes helped to water the potted spider plants all over the house and to set the table for dinner. Grandpa often ate dinner with his fingers, chewing loudly, but Grandpa was Grandpa. We kids were required to put our napkins in our laps and hold the knife in our dominant hand. Poking holes in the side of our Styrofoam Cup o' Noodle so that the broth ran out in arcs wasn't exactly funny. I drew and drew and drew at the kitchen table, while she played solitaire at the other end. My grandpa taught me the fancy way to shuffle a deck of cards. They were poor.

When I consider all the years my brother and I spent at my grandparents' house before we began school, all the evenings and weekends my grandma played babysitter to us, it surprises me that the sweetest part of our relationship came after I left the state for college. When I consider how remote the concept of technology was for her, a slight brown gnarled immigrant wife content to play solitaire in the half dark or flip through the latest *Better Homes & Gardens,* it surprises me that our most meaningful conversations took place over the phone. Nearly two decades of Cup o' Noodles, *Wheel of Fortune,* horse-racing radio programs, and getting whacked on the backside with a slipper for sassy back talk, simmered down to a delicate paper-doll chain of phone conversations between grandmother and granddaughter. Military wife and liberal arts undergraduate. Matriarch and young, graceless knight.

Nearly all of my college classes let out at noon, and the trek across campus to the mail center lasted just long enough for me to check in. Every couple of weeks, I would call. I switch on my phone as I leave the classroom, letting it ring while I pack *Robinson Crusoe* and notes into my bag. Her landline rings in San Francisco as I clump down the front stairs of Armstrong Hall in Colorado Springs.

She shuffles through the shadows of her empty house.

Squinting at the afternoon, I join the student march from lecture to lunch. In one ear the phone rings and rings, but I know this and have other conversations in the meantime—"John! Do you wanna get dinner before rehearsal?"—because I've learned what the few of us who love her know: that a good nine or ten rings' wait precedes any conversation. Her brittle energy can hardly stand to be wasted on people she doesn't know. Telemarketers are met with a politely disconnected line, and I imagine she pants faintly after setting the phone down with such control as to not offend the caller. Whenever the grandkids are at her house, she makes us answer the phone, cultivating in even my youngest cousin's voice the authority of a homeowner.

"Yeah, and then they went in the backyard—oh, hold on," I point to my busy ear and silently mouth, "My grandma."

There is the opposite of a hang-up click. A line being opened, timidly and suspiciously.

"'Ello-o?," in a thick Filipino accent, afraid it might, after all those rings, be someone she doesn't know or want to talk to.

"Hi, Grandma!" I sing loudly into her hearing aid.

"Who is this?"

"Lauren, Grandma," I assure her, stepping out of the noise and rush to pace an unhurried circle on the grass while we talk. She speaks low; I can hear her age.

"Who?"

"*Lauren,* Grandma," a little louder, "your granddaughter. Michael's daughter."

Relief curls the edges of the phone line upward like tulip petals in a drawing, and I can feel her grip loosen on the receiver. I wonder if it is heavy for her. We celebrated when she gained back some of the weight that chemo had ungraciously snatched right off her slight Asian frame. With the help of an uncomfortable daily intake of whole milk, she crept back up to ninety-eight pounds. Hands like chicken claws, thin cloud hair. When I approached puberty, those chicken claws used to scritch through the back of my blouse for straps and little hooks, and I was mortified to receive a three-pack of Hanes bras for Christmas (along with matching underwear), not as a joke. This is my grandma.

"Oh, 'allo."

"How are you doing?"

"Oh, pine." The easiest part of the Filipino accent for non-Filipinos to imitate is pronouncing Fs as Ps, like adding "uh" to the end of every word to sound Italian or stretching lips over young teeth to sound like an old geezer. "You?"

"Good, I just got out of class. The teacher brought his dog to class today, it was so weird. I have a lot homework."

"That's good."

"How do you feel? Are you tired?"

"Pine, thank you."

"Did you go to church today?"

"Yes."

"With who?"

It's quiet in San Francisco. She might be fiddling with her hearing aid, which I know she doesn't really like because she doesn't really understand how it works and therefore doesn't trust it.

"Hey, Dad told me that he took you to see Evan's baseball game. I heard it was superhot."

Nothing.

"Was it hot?"

"Oh, yes."

I laugh because I remember what Dad told me. "Did you really get sunburned? He said you forgot to wear a hat!"

"Oh, yes."

"Does it hurt?"

It's quiet again. She is confused. These paper doll conversations are largely identical: school, health, church, grandkids, I love you, so when I go off script she has to fumble for notes. I have no problem waiting; these calls acquainted me with a reserve of patience I had never known despite my years of child care. The patience used with the elderly is ever so much gentler than that required by children: one is condescending and didactic, while the other is laced with mercy.

"Eh?"

"I was just wondering if your sunburn hurts."

"Oh, yes," I can hear her uncertainty, "it was hot there."

"Was Evan good? Did he play well?"

"Oh, pine."

I hope she can hear me smiling at her. "Good. I bet it was good to see him play. Was his girlfriend there? I think she comes to a lot of his games. I wish I could see him play. I won't be home until the season is over, so you have to cheer for me, OK?"

"OK."

"OK, now I'm going to have lunch with my friends. What are you doing today?"

In the short pause, I visualize her telephone with its comical keypad, each number more than an inch square, and the kind of thick, rubbery coil I haven't fingered for years in my wireless, mobile world.

"Oh, yes."

Easier to stick to what's familiar.

"OK, I love you, Grandma," I sing into the corner of her living room that houses the phone. She might be sitting down, in which case she looks impossibly small, especially around the eyes. I want to open the windows, to wipe all the grime away from the doorframes she clutches to stand. She's weak, but she's stubborn, and is much more content to knead the hall carpet with her slow slippers than to deign to use a walker or cane. For years I sought her hand to cross the street; for a time we walked upright side by side; now I would offer her the crook of my arm to cross her own kitchen, but I live in Colorado and can only offer this long-distance phone call.

"I lob you, too, 'oney."

"Talk to you soon, OK?"

"OK."

"Bye," I call, waving to her figure in the front doorway as we drive away.

When we are together, in the summer months or winter weeks that out-of-state studies afford, actions speak louder. I play recordings of my a cappella group performances, sift through photographs, eat her food, and protest loudly when she tries to slip uncreased twenties into my jacket pocket—she loves that banter, takes great satisfaction in triumphing at the last with a phone conversation citation, "Now you can pix your bicycle like you said."

One of the last things I will ever do for her is file and buff her yellowed fingernails before polishing them a rosy brown that almost matches the lipstick she wore to our graduations. It's the only manicure I'll ever give her, and I'm not even sure why I did it because I don't think she kept her nails painted.

"Hi, Grandma."

"Who's there?"

"It's Lauren, Grandma."

"Oh, hi!"

"How are you?"

"Good. You?"

"Fine, just kind of stressed." I try to direct my cough away from the receiver, but she's still sharp on occasion.

"You 'ave a cold," she accused, scolding me. "Don't porget to eat, sleep." When she felt strong, she commanded. I hung my head.

"I know, Grandma. I'm fine. How was church yesterday?"

"Pine." She wheezes a little, and her dry cough is more distressing than my young, rumbly, healable one.

"Are you OK? That doesn't sound good. Do you have a cold too?"

"Oh, I'm OK. OK, lob you, 'oney." Sometimes she ended our conversations abruptly like this, a mystery for me.

"Love you, too."

I won't remember our last phone conversation, because I won't know that it's the last one. I will, however, remember the last time we were on the same phone line: when my dad interrupted a class session to let me know that the priest was at our house giving her last rites. A Thursday afternoon in January, nowhere close to our usual noon. Everyone in my family was gathered around her deathbed in California while I knelt, weeping, in a nondenominational Colorado chapel. My dad murmured a string of Hail Marys for his mother, and I heard my uncles, cousins, mother, and brother in chorus around her. I pressed the cell phone to my ear—my only way into that room. I wanted to sing into her ear, to help. For weeks after her peaceful death I let the phone with the oversized numbers ring thirteen or fourteen times before remembering that no one hovered, suspicious, on the other end.

I'll write about the experience in my student feature journal on the Colorado College website, and continue to receive comments on the vignette for years after. *Sounds like your grandma was a pretty special lady.* Except she wasn't really; only a small devout spoiler of grandchildren who trusted the crook of my arm. And all she needed from me to be there in the room with her, every couple of weeks, was a familiar conversation whose words need not even appear in the correct order to conjure the same plush velvet knowledge that we were loved.

The Collapse

....

DAVID JACKSON COOK

Part of having a grandfather you treasure is losing him. In this piece David Cook reflects on his grandfather's life and the experience of dying. It is difficult and scary, even for a grown man, the father of children. The passage of the generations is so palpable as the author sits by his dying grandfather's bedside. He realizes what a wonderful life this man had, that his father will die—and that he will too.

MY GRANDFATHER IS DYING.

Outside, snow is falling. The forecasters on yesterday's six o'clock news predicted rain, but a few hours ago large flakes began gently falling from the white sky to earth. My city in the Deep South endures winter after winter without any snowfall, so today felt unusual—as our streets turned white, schools were closed, snow rebels built tiny snowmen with thin crooked sticks for arms, and hardware stores sold out of those circular plastic sleds by lunchtime.

It is so strange the difference a day makes.

Today, we are in the hospital, on the floor of the intensive care unit. Unconscious, my grandfather lies in a bed, a white sheet pulled up to his chin. My mother, his youngest daughter, sits near the door, as if on guard. My grandmother stands at his side, the fingers of one hand fiddling with the corner of the white sheet, tucking it in and out from under his chin, while her other hand's long fingers—she has played piano for years—stroke his thin arm. They have been married for sixty-eight years. I am in the corner of the room, facing the window, looking past my grandfather, looking anywhere but there, watching the snow outside.

Yesterday he was at home, doing things he has done for so long: walking and talking, answering the telephone, watching television, noticing the birds that come and go. Did he think, "This may be the last time I ever see a crow? This may be the last day I ever eat scrambled eggs? This may be the last day I hear the sound of my wife laughing?" Does anyone ever think these things before they happen?

It is so hard for me to look at him. His face does not look like his own face. I am aware of this, aware that I can only seem to stand looking at him for a few seconds before having to turn away. I am aware that this moment is so unlike any other, so foreign; it feels like I am being asked to speak a language I have never heard before, to interpret the words someone is telling me, except they keep speaking with a tongue from a mouth that is alien. Otherworldly. I am used to English. I am used to speaking about life.

Outside, the snow just keeps falling. Even if I wanted to, I could not stop it. Even if I were to wage war on the snow, to commit myself whole-heartedly to its ruin, to try to prevent it from falling with every resource available to me, it would continue to come. Quietly and slowly, its presence changing the entire day of everyone in the whole city. It seems to fall unconditionally, even benevolently, regardless of folks in the hospital giving birth or dying, regardless of this or that, it just does what it does. Fall to earth. Cover the ground. Melt. Disappear.

My grandfather is dying. Several years ago, we took a pilgrimage of sorts to his boyhood home in South Carolina. It was ungodly hot during our trip, and he developed a rash. He would scratch until his arms bled, and keep scratching after that, as if something was underneath the skin and just would not surface, no matter what. My mother, who came with us, helped him undress at night, and rubbed lotion onto his arms and back, where he could not reach, where the rash was its worst. We were in the hotel room, which had a wide-plank balcony and a wobbly ceiling fan. I stood by, watching.

He grew up in the town of Abbeville. Cherokee Indians lived there for many moons, until British colonists arrived in the seventeenth century. A treaty was established between the Cherokees and white men, and like every other treaty written between these two groups, it was eventually broken, violated by white men. Two centuries later, legend has it that rebel leaders met among the tall pines of Secession Hill one night under a half moon, shaking hands and signing the first writ of secession that removed South Carolina from the Lincoln-led Union, beginning the Civil War. Years later, when my grandfather was a boy, he would play Dixie on his fiddle to veterans of the Civil War as they gathered in the Abbeville Opera House. The Opera House still stands, as do the alleyway metal stairs leading up to the balcony, the only way in and out of the building for black folks when it was open.

His father was a railroad conductor on the Union-Pacific line, which ran up and down the eastern shore. His mother was named Septima and walked with a wooden leg, hobbled after gangrene infected a long-ago wound. When he was a boy, they would walk to town together, down the straight sidewalk running like a long arm into the town square. One hot afternoon, a horde of wild dogs emerged from the thick red woods. My grandfather heard them howling before he saw them. The howling got closer and closer, and Septima told her son to run and take cover in the neighbor's house. Ignoring his mother's pleas, my grandfather carried her down the street, the hounds literally on his heels, taking refuge in the first house that opened its door.

At night, when I lie down with my two young children as they fall asleep, I like to tell them this story. Their eyes grow huge, and I imagine the way this story takes form in their young minds. The teeth on the dogs large like knives. Their paws huge like a bear's. The wooden leg clomping and clomping on the stone sidewalk. My grandfather sweating and pounding on the neighbor's door. How close do the dogs get in their minds? How fast does the door swing open? How much do they learn about loyalty and courage in this story about their great-grandfather?

He was eating dinner when it happened. Sitting there on the couch, then falling over. His heart stopped beating—no one is sure how long. When the EMTs arrived, coming so fast into the room that they knocked over an antique table my grandmother adored, which fell to the ground next to my grandfather, they cut off his plaid button-down shirt and khaki pants—which he called "trousers"—and revived his heartbeat through the electric paddles so popular on emergency room television.

He has not woken up since.

A few years ago, around the time he turned ninety, my grandfather asked me to help write his obituary. It would be a sort of gathering up of his life, a recollecting of the jobs and awards and accomplishments that, when placed together, make up the story of one's life. In doing so, we spent many hours talking, and I began to see him like a bridge—this time capsule or topographic map of another time and place so unlike the one we inhabit today.

His childhood home had no indoor plumbing. Years later, when toilets became common, his grandfather refused to have one, unable to imagine the foolishness of using the bathroom inside one's home. He said, "Some things were meant to be done outside." In the winter, the only heat source was a wood-burning fireplace. As a boy, my grandfather delivered newspapers every morning, riding his bicycle through town with the papers in a bag strapped over his shoulder. On special occasions, his father climbed pecan trees and shook the limbs, the nuts falling to the ground and scooped up by the kids like some arbor piñata. As a teenager he rode the train to Atlanta to see Christmas displays at the Rich's Department Store window.

Today, no one lives like this anymore. What has been lost? I know that every day more than one hundred species go extinct from this world of ours. I feel like my grandfather is going extinct, the stories and memories and molecules that make up this very long life of his are dying out. Yet contained in this so-small body are memories that are alive, still. The sound of those chasing hounds is still rattling around somewhere in him. The touch of the cold train window glass against his cheek riding to Atlanta in December is still cold somewhere inside his soul. The feel of her splintered wooden leg, the sound of newspapers hitting the front porch at dawn, the moment the pecans began to fall—all these moments must still be there, somewhere, as if hiding out deep in the corners, perhaps together, sitting around the flame that gets dimmer and dimmer, smaller now than it has ever been.

What happens to those moments? Are they eternal? Do they now reside in me? Is this how stories remain alive?

My grandfather is dying, and nothing can replace him. There is no other him.

And of course while I write this I am not writing about my grandfather only. He is not alone. He does not lie here in the hospital bed by himself. My own father, who is now a grandfather to my young children, is here. My mother, grandmother to my young children, is here too. My wife and I, even my own children, are lying dying in that hospital bed. It is a symbol—a gate we all pass through. My dying grandfather is once again my teacher, allowing me to practice for the tomorrow when it is my father who is dying or myself who is dying. We die every day. Every breath—in and out—is a death, as is every sunrise and sunset. Every moment of our lives holds hands with death. Yet I feel so inadequate, so unprepared, for his death and my own.

I am very afraid of dying.

I keep thinking of ladders. With the collapse of my grandfather, all of us have moved one rung higher on a ladder in my conscious mind. When he dies, I will be one step closer to being a grandparent myself. The loss of this exquisitely unique grandfather means that hole in our family ground will soon be filled by my own father, who is now learning how to become a wonderful grandparent to my young children. And one day—now it is even closer than ever—I will become a grandfather to my children's children. One day each of us will climb all the rungs, from child to parent to grandparent to great-grandparent, as the passing of one elder before us vacates another rung above us. We who are alive must climb higher. In doing so, we find ourselves closer to the elementary rawness of life and death.

Climbing this ladder, I feel cold and naked and unprotected, the way I do when I am alone in a foreign place, a stranger to a new land. As a child, I was near the bottom of this ladder, protected by so many people above me: my parents, uncles and aunts, grandparents, and even great-grandparents. Life is about saying goodbye to so many people, and finding yourself now in their place. I have heard from friends who have lost their parents that there is always an emptiness when they are gone, in the same way many amputees confess to feeling a ghost limb. This thing that was here is no more, a wound that takes too long to heal.

As I see my grandfather lying there, I also see his father and his father's father nearby. My grandfather is a thread, connecting to his people, who have gone before and are watching and waiting. I feel the thread inside me, faint, but stronger than ever. I wonder if, as the body grows old and thin, the thread grows stronger, becoming like mighty tendons, stretched and pulled between two worlds, unbreakable, like the wood on some eternal ladder upon which we climb and from which we never fall. When our first son was born, we named him after my grandfather.

What a life. What a life! Jackson Emelius Gilleland is ninety-two years old, and has lived through so many happy days. A family, meaningful career, warm home, and even a vacation cabin on the lake. A resilient faith and several grandchildren and great-grandchildren he has seen crawl, walk, and run. Many friends and service awards and medals from World War II. Strong memories from so long ago kept alive by his sharp, precise engineer mind.

As the days of his dying go by, I understand that perhaps gratitude and happiness should begin to crowd grief out of the room. Grief has a magnitude about it, a loud immediacy. When I walk into the intensive care unit, it jumps to my side with a loyalty and stubbornness hard to shake. But when I look a little longer, I feel gratitude and happiness too, waiting quietly, patiently, as if they had all the time in the world. And they should, for his life was wonderful. It was rich and full and touched by kindness, grace, and meaning. As our tears fall, my prayer is that they may fall on a face that also carries a touch of joy and thankfulness.

Along with gratitude, fear has arrived. What happens when that evening sun goes down one final time? Where does that door lead? Where is the dawn? Is my grandfather thinking these things? After so many years, do these questions fade away, collect dust, and cease to raise their heads any longer? Are they ever-present, raging in from all the corners at every moment? I don't ask him, for I'm afraid of the answer, and afraid I would have nothing to offer, nothing to give as comfort to whatever answer he gave.

My grandmother has been staying every night at his bedside, refusing to go back home. In the last seven days since his collapse, he has regained consciousness and is even able to speak, so she waits with an urgency of sorts, as if his improving condition could suddenly turn and he could fall down into unconsciousness, into death, once again. As if he could collapse all over again. So she does not leave his side. I think about this and will always remember this as a gift for my own marriage. *No matter what, do not leave her side.*

I told my grandmother I would sit up with him, and let her get some sleep, so tonight, I am my grandfather's keeper. Over the next few hours, I move closer and closer to him. Instead of the corner of the room, I stand at his bedside. Instead of tucking my hands in my coat pockets, I place them on the bed railing. And then, instead of the bed railing, his leg. And then his arm. And then his hand. I begin to look at him deeply, even though I want to turn away. His back is hunched, and his skin so thin, like a leaf found late in the winter. He has forgotten so much. I have been secretly worried he would even forget my name. But he does not. He recognizes me, speaks my name. Quietly, softly, but instantly.

One of the strongest memories I have: I am ten years old, and he is in his sixties, but still very young in my mind. It is summer; the green grass is tall and needs to be mowed. My father is grilling hamburgers, and we are all outside. I am jumping on a pogo stick, or at least trying to. The sky is blue, the pogo stick is painted red, and our black dog is chasing a brown squirrel up a big oak tree near the forgotten sandbox. That's when my grandfather asks if he can try the pogo stick. Sure, I say, handing it over. Everyone turns to watch. He is agile, active, and alert, and everyone is expecting this moment to go well, to add to the pleasantness of this late afternoon. And it does, at first. He bounces a few times, puts his feet down, smiles, steadies himself, and then begins bouncing again. Our driveway is sloped, and it may have been a rock or even an acorn, but somehow the pogo stick slid out from under him. It kicked him up into the air and then hard to the asphalt. He landed pretty hard on his side. Everyone rushed over. He got up, a little dazed and bruised, but was fine.

He was fine. But at that moment, things changed for me. He had fallen. With his fall, my view of the adult world collapsed as well. All my childhood beliefs—that there is no death, there is no weakness, *there is no collapse*—fell to the ground too and did not get back up. All the adults there knew: it was just a pogo stick, people fall all the time. But to me, the world shifted. When he fell, part of me fell too. He—my invincible grandfather—had fallen, and this suddenly meant that the ground was stronger than the adults in my life.

In the intensive care unit, the white sheet tucked around his neck, I relive this memory again. My feelings now are similar—the curtain of my illusions are pulled back. Reality asks me to look long and hard at the man dying before me. As I look, I am asked to understand that this moment is also part of life. This moment of dying can't be removed. Dying and the time of dying are woven as intricately into the fabric of our lives as the times when I was hugged and cherished, the moments when our conversations cut straight to the heart of my grandfather and his grandson, the days when we are surrounded by sunlight and love.

I am learning from my grandfather's collapse how integral dying is to life. These moments are the painful, yet proper order of things. Dying *belongs* here. I am being asked to make friends with dying, to honor my grandfather and his dying, by being present as the fire dims. Somewhere else the pecans still fall, the newspaper still hits the doorstep, the wild dogs bark, and the long train whistle blows and will continue to blow and will always blow.

Outside, it has stopped snowing.

Grandmother's Lap

NANCY HATHAWAY

Without a mother who listened to her, or a grandmother who would turn off the TV, Nancy Hathaway grew up looking for warm guidance. In this piece a Native American spirit guide becomes the grandmother figure who not only impels her to begin valuing her Native American Maine roots, but gives her an image of the grandmother she would like to be.

GRANDMOTHER IS AN OLDER, BUT not elderly, woman with a soft, round face. It is leathery and brown from sun and open fire over the years, with deep wrinkles around the lines of her eyes and a slight twinkly smile. She peers closely at me and then off into the distance. Dressed in a white chamois dress with long sleeves, she sits on a chair made of deer and moose antlers. She is my grandmother—my long sought-after lap. She is truer than true, as my son described a story when asked if it was real. Grandmother is truer than true, a Spirit Guide for me.

It is her grandmother energy that is of ultimate importance. Her riches do show in her dress and overall appearance, but deeper riches hide beneath her particular cultural dress. Out of this grandmother's pores breath wisdom, love, and compassion. Her in-breath draws me in with welcoming words, "Bring me your truth, your joys, and even your problems. Come sit with me awhile. I'll hold you."

Nothing is too big for her lap to hold. She is subtle and playful; she knows this world, and she knows its suffering. After experiencing the phases of girlhood and the full life of being a woman—young, middle-aged, and older—she has touched many layers of this human condition and is now an immigrant in her own culture. She is on her way to passing elsewhere but is still here, in body, spirit, and mind, with feet dancing softly on the earth. Even though this body has some difficulty walking, she can dance. You should see her whirl, with yellow ribbons flying, feathers spread, and deerskin dress closely clad to her round frame.

This strong vision of grandmother came to me while staying in a log cabin in the north Maine woods with a dear friend I have known since young adulthood. Now we are alone again, our hair gray. Our children are the ages we were when we first met. We take quiet breaths in each other's company and meditate. We reach into our pasts and share our heart-most presence, for an hour each. We are silent, except for the words we say when we explore our inner depths, while the other listens.

As the fire in the woodstove warms us, we're absorbed in our own thoughts. I intended to think about the cold, dark winter months ahead and what my life alone on the coast of Maine will bring if I pay attention to a deeper place within me.

But the moment has another plan. This vision of grandmother dancing appears instead. A surprise! She comes from deep in my soul and bones. A sense of comfort and ease, of fullness, cradles me like the feeling I might have had when I was first born—before separation between comfort and discomfort occurred; being cared for as part of the whole, and separate from others. Forgotten.

In those days it wasn't nursing that fed a newborn but a bottle on schedule. When I was hungry, comfort and nourishment often didn't come. Here now, is a soft, full feeling, and yet a spaciousness. It feels safe. As an eighth generation Mainer, Native American roots on my father's side, this grandmother I have been looking for since early childhood appears to me in *my* native indigenous Maine culture … not Chinese, Korean, Japanese, or Middle Eastern.

My mother was busy cooking, cleaning, changing my brothers' diapers, and having more babies. Memories of special attention from her are rare. She gave me tea parties, helped me learn the alphabet, made Valentine's Day lunches with schoolmates, and planted pansies, her favorite flowers. When these memories appear, I do feel cared for. But memories of Mother don't include quiet holding. She was always moving, standing, stirring soup, ironing, working, doing more ironing, making more suppers, washing dishes, doing something. I don't remember sitting in her lap, as she moved quickly about from one task to another. I longed for her to stop.

Laps appear when one sits still, I have learned through these many years of sitting meditation. I would have enjoyed being held in another's lap when I was very young. Mom was occupied. I longed for the wisdom eye. Dad was at work; my maternal grandmother died years before my birth.

My grandmother on my father's side had many children and grandchildren. She lived across the Kennebec River, four far away miles. She didn't drive, and my mother didn't either in the early years. Grandmother Nana was pretty unavailable, but I kept her in my mind's eye. When I grew old enough to walk across the bridge by myself or with cousins, I began to visit her. She was kind, slow, and sat a lot. When we visited, she was often occupied with a TV show. She did have a lap, but I was too big for it. She didn't invite me to talk and tell her anything of my world. The TV was amusing her. There seemed little room for stories that might have made a meaningful connection between the generations.

I longed for empty full space, when adults would sit down and "do nothing," making room for a twelve-year-old to ask questions about family stories of ancestors and share her own stories.

Once we three girl cousins were told the story of Nana's father—how he came from Northern Ireland, sailed up the Kennebec River on a three-masted wooden schooner, then jumped ship and hid in the icehouse on the river.

"In that big old empty wooden building on the side of the river?"

I was delighted. Finally! Something important ... stories of Great-Grandfather.

Nana told more of her own—"Always remember," she would say now and then, "Croc-na-Mac, Port Rush, County Antrim, Northern Ireland." This small bit of oral history was so much richer than if it had been in a textbook. I loved it. She showed me how it was to get old. I cut her long, curly, hard toenails, kneeling at her feet.

"I hope someone will do this for you," she said. The words penetrated, but I said nothing because I couldn't imagine myself old. Years later I remember her words. When I climbed to the top of her kitchen cupboard to get a bowl for her, she was so appreciative that I asked what else I could do for her. Her crisp fresh-from-the-bank one-dollar bills on my birthdays, even at the age of eighteen, bring tears to my eyes now. These one-dollar gifts showed me the meaning of giving coming from love. They touched my heart more than receiving a twenty-dollar bill.

Once Nana almost wet her pants. She came to visit and couldn't make it to the house, so we found her a tree. I loved it. A tree! Who in my family pees on a tree?

Childhood passed. Even though Nana was still alive, I went elsewhere looking for more wisdom. As she sat in a nursing home at the age of ninety-six, I think wistfully of what she might have said, "This is what getting old looks like, dear one." Now I call up my Spirit Guide grandmother, who does this for me now.

In my twenties I took a spiritual journey to the East. In the Himalayas I spent a month in a Gompa, a Tibetan temple where I met and studied with two Tibetan Lamas, Lama Yeshe and Lama Zopa. Wisdom and compassion were so new that I lost my balance when I returned home to my mother and father's. After this journey to the heart, with eyes cleared, when I got home I felt alone in a sea of attachment to the physical world. Holding the world of desire and attachment by myself in my parents' home was too big.

I found a Zen teacher, Dae Soen Sa Nim, direct from Asia with broken English difficult to understand. I moved to a Zen temple and studied there for six years. My teacher said, "Bring me your problems," which I had never heard anyone say. He introduced me to the Buddhist goddess Kwan Seum, who is Kwan Yi in Chinese. She was a being disguised under layers of Asian culture and thinking, desiring mind. Over many years my connection with her has deepened, as I've developed wisdom and compassionate energy. I had been looking for her—a traveling companion who supports me in going deeper into wisdom and compassion.

Studying, practicing, and teaching Buddhism for thirty-six years, I began to recognize this sought-after grandmother as an archetype in Asian and Buddhist cultures.

It appears that I am transposing this longing for a supportive grandmother figure, which has been partially fulfilled in my Zen practices, to my own culture, as I meet my Native grandmother. Just as Buddhism came to America in the twentieth and twenty-first centuries and took root, I am curious also about inhabiting my own Native American background, which is what the Dalai Lama encourages westerners to do. "Don't leave your culture. Do both."

My Native American grandmother wears animal skins of my native land on my grandfather's side. Her spirit is the same as Kwan Seum. This grandmother archetype is deep in the human condition. She is similar to the Virgin Mary, who wasn't a big enough part of my life when I was a young girl attending catechism, taking communion, and being confirmed in order to link me to her energy. Mother Mary represents the female force or polarity for the western world; to Muslims she is Maryam, or Mariam.

How will we nurture our equanimity as grandparents to find the balance that can welcome and handle discomforts skillfully? Grandmothers know that life has pain: we don't get what we want when we want it. Grandmothers have learned the Second Truth of being human, that we suffer when we want something other than what we've got. A grandmother's mind understands that the way out of suffering is the Third Noble Truth. A wise grandmother mind knows that living life with awareness and acceptance relieves suffering and brings true happiness.

Grandparents must have a lap and the possibility of offering a sense of spaciousness for our grandchildren so big that it can hold their world.

This lap should be made of attention, receptivity, loving presence, and sympathy. Nourishing mindfulness and empathy will help us as we hold still in our relationship with the newest generation.

The Russian Album

·················

MICHAEL IGNATIEFF

If we don't take the opportunity to speak truth to our parents and children when they are alive, these truths will slip into the grave, Michael Ignatieff says in this first chapter of The Russian Album, *his memoir of his family's life in nineteenth-century Russia. As a statement about working to understand the people you come from,* The Russian Album *is inspiring.*

MY GRANDMOTHER WAS BORN PRINCESS Natasha Mestchersky on an estate near Smolensk bequeathed to her mother's family by Empress Catherine the Great in the late eighteenth century. In her family she counted a chancellor of Russia, a general who put down the peasant rebellion of Pugachev, and the first modern historian of her country, Nicholas Karamzin.

When my Russian grandfather was nineteen and choosing a career, the tramlines of his past ran straight into the future; he would enter a Guards regiment like his father, grandfather, and great-grandfather before him. He could then make a career in the army or return to the family estates and live as a gentleman farmer. At some point in his life he would be expected to leave the estate and serve the Tsar, as his grandfather and father had. He would "shoulder the chains of service." It is in these precise senses—a destiny inherited and shouldered without questioning—that his identity is irrevocably different from my own. My identity—my belonging to the past he bequeathed me—is a matter of choosing the words I put on a page. I am glad that this is so: his is not a fate or an identity that I would wish as my own. But it is a difference that makes full understanding between us impossible.

My grandmother's self was made within a frame of choices even narrower than those of her husband: to be a dutiful daughter and then a faithful wife. The fulcrum of her life, the one moment when fate could

235

be heaved this way or that, was marriage. There would be some choosing for her to do, among the young officers with wasp-waisted uniforms who were allowed to dance with her at the Petersburg debutante balls. But she was Princess Mestchersky, and once her eyes had fallen on a man, his particulars "back to Adam and Eve" would be investigated. If they were found wanting, she would have to choose again.

Both of them were born into a time when their past was also their future. Life had a necessity to it: it was not a tissue of their own making. They grew up in a time measured by a protocol of family decorum. They ended their lives in the formless time of exile, a time with no future and a past suspended out of reach. When they landed in England in the summer of 1919, they were already too old to start again, too old to feel the emancipating energies of exile. My grandparents could only remember; they could no longer invent the present.

Between my two pasts, the Canadian and the Russian, I felt I had to choose. The exotic always exerts a stronger lure than the familiar, and I was always my father's son. I chose the vanished past, the past lost behind the revolution. I could count on my mother's inheritance: it was always there. It was my father's past that mattered to me, because it was one I had to recover, to make my own.

My earliest memories are not memories of myself, but of my father talking about his ancestors. I recall being on board the *Queen Mary* during a crossing between New York and Southampton in 1953 when I was six and hearing my father tell the story of how his grandfather Nicholas rode from Peking to Petersburg in six weeks to bring the Tsar the news of the treaty he had signed with the Chinese Emperor; and how, when a blizzard struck on the Siberian plains, Nicholas had formed his Cossack horsemen into a circle, bivouacked in the center, and warmed themselves through the blizzard by the breath from the horses.

Since my father was a diplomat who moved every eighteen months of my childhood, the things I came to count on as icons of stability were not the houses we lived in, since they changed all the time, but the very few Russian objects we carried with us from one posting to the next. There was a silver ewer and basin that stood on a succession of dining tables in a succession of official apartments, which had once been used by my maternal great-grandmother to wash her hands when she awoke at her country estate in the mornings during the 1880s. Objects like the silver ewer and basin, like the Sultan's diamond star that my mother wore on family occasions, were vital emblems of continuity in a childhood without fixed landmarks.

Few of these were still left: some embossed volumes of Nicholas Karamzin's history of Russia and an icon or two on the wall above my parents' bed. Sometimes these objects turned up in family photographs. I still remember the pleasure I got as a child from discovering that a piece of jewelry my mother wore was to be seen in a photograph of my grandmother Natasha taken seventy years before. It was as if the little pearl and diamond brooch had flown free of its amber imprisonment in the photograph, vaulting all the time between me and her.

I heard very little Russian as a child: my father did not speak it at home. I went with him to the Russian church in the cities where I grew up—New York, Toronto, Ottawa, Belgrade, Paris, Geneva, and London—and I was moved by the service because I did not understand it. Standing beside him in the church, watching him light his candles, say his prayers, and sing in his deep vibrating voice, I always felt that he had slipped away through some invisible door in the air. Yet he kept his distance from the Russian émigré community, from their factional intrigues and antediluvian politics. He presented himself to the world throughout my childhood as the model of an assimilated Canadian professional. And to this day he is a much more patriotic and sentimental Canadian than I am. For him Canada was the country that gave him a new start. For me, being a Canadian was just one of those privileges I took for granted.

Father often met Soviet diplomats in his work, and they always spoke Russian together. Yet the meetings were edgy. I remember one Soviet diplomat, dressed like a Zurich banker with a large black onyx ring on his finger, being introduced to both of us in a lobby of the United Nations building in New York. He doffed his astrakhan and in a great sweeping gesture said in English, "As the son of a peasant I salute you." Other Soviets treated the family past with the same mixture of respect and irony. In 1955, my father returned to the Soviet Union as part of an official Canadian delegation led by Foreign Minister Mike Pearson. The Soviet officials, led by Nikita Khrushchev himself, called my father *Graf* (Count) and took him aside and asked in all sincerity why he didn't come "home" again and continue the diplomatic work of his grandfather instead of serving the diplomacy of a small satellite state of the Americans. But my father didn't feel at home at all in the Soviet Union of the Tsars. Even the moments of remembered connection were brief, as when he was shown into his room at the Hotel Astoria in Leningrad, frozen in its prerevolutionary decor, and saw on the writing desk two silver bears exactly like two little bears that had once stood on his father's desk in the same city forty years before. On that visit, he also realized how archaic his Russian sounded to Soviet citizens and how rusty it had become. He found himself stumbling in his native tongue.

Back home, family feelings on the Russian side were as intense, but there were few actual occasions when we came together. Throughout my childhood, the Russian half of the family was scattered abroad. My father's eldest brother Nicholas had died in my childhood, and the remaining four were thousands of miles apart. When the brothers did come together for the wedding of my cousin Mika, we all made a little space for them apart, and they sat on the couch, balding giants each over six feet tall, talking in Russian, while none of us understood a word. They had all married outside the Russian circle, and so none of their children grew up with the Russian tongue. I never learned the language.

In my inability to learn Russian, I can now see the extent of my resistance to a past I was at the same time choosing as my own. The myths were never forced upon me, so my resistance was directed, not at my father or my uncles, but rather at my own inner craving for these stories, at what seemed a weak desire on my part to build my little life upon the authority of their own. I wasn't sure I had the right to the authority of the past, and even if I did have the right, I didn't want to avail myself of the privilege. Yet as one of my friends wryly says when I talk like this, no one ever gives up his privileges. So I used the past whenever I needed to, but with a guilty conscience. My friends had suburban pasts or pasts they would rather not talk about. I had a past of Tsarist adventurers, survivors of revolutions, and heroic exiles. Yet the stronger my need for them, the stronger too became my need to disavow them, to strike out on my own. To choose my past meant to define the width of its impingement upon me.

My father always said that I was more Mestchersky than Ignatieff, more like his mother than his father. Since he was more Ignatieff than Mestchersky, the statement underlined how complicated the ties of filiation really were between us. Inheritance is always as much a matter of anxiety as pride. If I were a Mestchersky, what could I possibly make of myself? How could I ever master my temperament, that tightly strung bundle of fears and anxieties that seemed to have me locked in its grasp? From the beginning, the project of finding out about my past was connected to a struggle to master the anxiety of its influence.

I also found myself face-to-face with what I liked least about myself. My grandfather's favorite phrase was: "Life is not a game; life is not a joke. It is only by putting on the chains of service that man is able to accomplish his destiny on earth." When Paul talked like this, my grandmother Natasha always used to mutter, "The Ignatieffs would make hell out of Paradise."

Early on I learned that both my father and my uncle Nicholas had wanted to write a history of the family. My father had even been to Bulgaria to research the story of his grandfather's role in the creation of Bulgaria after the Russian defeat of the Turks in the war of 1877–78. Nicholas had had similar ideas, but he was dead and his manuscripts lay in his widow's basement. My father was a busy man, and his project languished. So the idea of a history of the family had germinated: it was an idea I could bring to fruition if I wanted to. But I held back.

I was in my teens when I first read my grandparents' memoirs. Beginning in September 1940 in a cottage in Upper Melbourne, Quebec, my grandmother Natasha typed out a stream of free associations, beginning with childhood on the estate, her marriage to my grandfather Paul Ignatieff, life in Petersburg, revolution, civil war, and escape. She wrote in the English that she had learned from her governess, in the English that she knew her grandchildren would grow up speaking. When she got to 1919—when she got to the moment they left Russia—she stopped. Everything became harder then, harder to say, and all the period in exile she left in silence. By then there were more than 250 pages, a jumble that my Aunt Florence sorted and retyped after her death.

My grandfather Paul had written his memoirs in Sussex and in Paris during the 1920s. He wrote in Russian and only much later translated them into English with the help of a Canadian friend. My grandmother's recollections are a frank and faithful echo of the woman she was, put down just as she spoke in every meandering turn of phrase, but his dry, orderly, and restrained prose was, or so I felt, an exercise in discretion and concealment. He confined himself to his official career, as gentleman farmer, governor of Kiev province, deputy Minister of Agriculture and Minister of Education in the final cabinet of the Tsar. It is a restrained public document. Emotion cracks through the shell of measured phrases just once, when he describes his last meeting with Nicholas II in the final days of the regime.

Their memoirs were unpublishable, hers because what made them so alive also made them unreadable, his because they so meticulously excluded the personal and because the events he described had been so exhaustively retold in the deluge of Tsarist memoirs. I decided, nearly ten years ago now, to retell their story in my own words. As a historian,

I thought my first task would be to locate them in their historical setting, to distance myself from them as members of my family and to treat them instead as historical specimens, as objects of study. It took me some time to realize the unintended consequences of this strategy.

I can remember a moment during the early days of my research when I was reading the proceedings of a Russian land-reform commission of 1902, searching for a mention of the family estates through spools of faint microfilm. Since my grandfather was a local marshal of nobility, he had to write a report for the commission. It was the first time I had read something by him that was not addressed to his family: the memoirs, the letters I had read before all had us as their intended audience. In this little report he was suddenly a tiny figure in a historical setting. The irony was that the process of tracking him in his historical context did not make the contours of his character come into sharper relief. The reverse occurred.

The more I came to know about him as a historical being—as a quite typical member of the liberal service gentry, as a non-party constitutional monarchist—the more he began to slip out of reach. The sharper I drew his definition as a historical being, the more blurred he became as my grandfather. As an object of historical knowledge he could only be grasped in the plural; as an object of desire, I sought him in his singularity. In the process of finding him as an exemplary imperial character, I lost him as my grandfather. The historical way of knowing the past is to place a figure in the background of serial time; I wanted the opposite, to make him present in simultaneous time with me. Yet I always knew that this was an impossible desire and that even a history of their lives was doomed to failure. I could never recreate the past as my uncles remembered it or hope to conciliate the quarrels between contending memories. Even today the brothers still argue heatedly about some things, and I could not hope to establish who was right.

Most of all, I could not hope to bring back Paul and Natasha. Even the simplest physical detail about them, how she moved the hair off her face, how he used to snap a book shut when he had read it, required acts of painstaking reconstitution for me; for my father these details were such simple primary memories he scarcely bothered to mention them. It soon became apparent that the only portrait I could hope to paint of Paul and Natasha would always be a crude sketch, a study in the unbridgeable distances between first and second generations.

For a long time I thought that if a history was doomed to failure anyway, I should abandon history and turn my grandparents' life into fiction. It was a tempting idea: my characters would be sufficiently grounded in a real past to be authentic, and yet they would do my bidding. They would wear my clothes, speak my lines, live out my dramas, and fulfill my ambitions. In creating them I would create myself. In the end the idea of fiction foundered on the realization that such a novel would be peopled by characters neither real in themselves nor faithful to their originals.

It was years before I began to see Paul and Natasha apart from my needs for them. I learned that their lives were not an adventure that existed so that I could quarry them for meanings of my own. There were too many silences, too many things I could not know about them for me to ransack their experience for my purposes. Very slowly, it dawned on me that instead of them owing *me* the secret of my life, I owed *them* fidelity to the truth of the lives they had led. Fiction would have been a betrayal. I had to return and stay close to the initial shock of my encounter with their photographs: that sense that they were both present to me in all their dense physical actuality and as distant as stars. In recreating them as truthfully as I could, I had to respect the distance between us. I had to pay close attention to what they left unsaid; I had to put down a marker at the spots that had not been reclaimed by memory. I could not elide these silences by the artifice of fiction.

I went twice with my father to the Soviet Union to find their traces. There was a lot to find: until the fall of Khrushchev the folk drama of socialist reconstruction justified the leveling of palaces and the conversion of

churches to printing plants or lumberyards. Only poverty and backward-
ness saved old buildings. A country too poor to replace them lived out the
drama of the new in the tattered stage sets of the old. In the late 1960s and
1970s, the vandalism of Khrushchevian modernism produced a counter-
reaction that reached back to national traditions untarnished by Commu-
nism. Now not just the great palaces and monasteries were regilded, but
anything with a patina of age began to reacquire authority. A new national
past uniting pre- and post-1917 was constructed by artful elision of the
revolution's destructive work. As a result of this ironic and uneasy attempt
to recuperate the Tsarist past, in some ways it is easier to find traces of a
Tsarist family past in the Soviet Union than it is in the West.

In the leafy shade of the cemetery of Novodevichy convent in Moscow,
near the graves of Khrushchev and Stalin's wife, we found the grave of the
family renegade, Uncle Alyosha, who began his career as a Tsarist officer
and ended it as a Red general. In Leningrad, we found the family house
on Fourstatskaya street where my father had watched the first demonstra-
tions of the February Revolution in 1917. It is now the Leningrad Palace
of Marriages. In the ballroom where my grandmother once served tea,
young couples were being married, one pair every ten minutes, by an
imposing woman in a red ball gown and a sash of office. Downstairs in
the schoolroom where my uncles used to take their lessons from their
French tutor, Monsieur Darier, mothers with pins in their mouths were
making last-minute adjustments to their daughters' wedding dresses.
And down a small back hallway with dim portraits of Lenin on the wall
and an Intourist calendar of scenes from a Crimean resort, my father
found the room that had been his nursery.

In Kislovodsk, a south Caucasus spa town between the Black and Cas-
pian Seas, one September afternoon, my father and I found the green gate
of the garden in which stood the house he had lived in with his family
during the civil war in 1917 and 1918. Several houses had been crammed
into the garden since the family's wretched years there, but there were
still apple trees and poplars at the back, just as there were in 1918.

Yet the apparent ease with which we picked up the traces of the family past inside the Soviet Union proved deceptive. I remember suddenly feeling the unseen distances separating me from my past while standing in front of the Matisse paintings in the Pushkin Museum in Moscow, all collected by Tsarist merchants before the First World War. For Russian visitors to the museum, the Matisses are a strange and discordant departure from the realism of Russian nineteenth-century genre painting; they are equally alien to the socialist realism that was to carry this tradition forward in the Soviet period. For Russians, the Matisses are thus fragments of modernism suspended out of reach of the European tradition that nurtured them. For us the Matisse paintings are the founding canvases of our very way of seeing.

As I looked at the sunlit ateliers, the bright deck chair, the bowl of flowers, and the woman in the lustrous blue dress and looked at the dates of their composition, 1910, 1911, and 1912, I realized that they were collected by my grandparents' generation. This generation was the first to have successfully resolved the old dilemma of whether Russians were a European or an Asian people. Natasha spoke and thought in German and English; her dentist was an American who lived in Dresden; she bought her lingerie in Nice; she had Lyle's Golden Syrup for tea in her nursery. Paul was raised by French tutors and grew up thinking and speaking in French. Yet both were passionately attached to the religions, customs, smells, architecture, curses, and chaos of their native land.

They travelled across an open frontier to countries whose painting, food, and landscape they regarded as their own. Matisse's Mediterranean light was as much their own as the eternal summer light of Petersburg. They were the first generation to reconcile their European and their Russian identities, and they were the last. A border of barbed wire, searchlights, and gun emplacements has been sawed across a Europe they once believed stretched from Moscow to the Atlantic, and when I try to follow their footsteps across that frontier I am aware that I am entering a country that now seems more a strange new Asian empire than an old heartland of European culture. The distance that I now must try to cross between them and me is much more than the distance of time. It is the chasm marked by the no man's land of barbed wire that divides European culture into two armed camps.

My Soviet guides were often unsettled by my estrangement from their native land. They wanted to help my search for connections, phoning local history museums to find the new names of streets we knew only from their original names in the 1914 edition of Baedeker's *Guide to Russia,* and helping us even to find the jails and interrogation rooms where my grandfather spent the loneliest hours of his life in 1918. The Soviet guides admired my father's slightly old-fashioned Russian, so much softer and gentler in enunciation than their own, and they were puzzled but polite when I said I understood not a word of my father's native tongue. There were a few sites that it was not possible to visit: Kroupodernitsa, the Ignatieff estate in the Ukraine where my great-grandfather and great-grandmother are buried, seemed to be off limits, though for reasons that were never explained. Yet the authorities sent a photographer to the village church and took pictures of the family graves, dressed with bouquets of fresh flowers. We were told the estate is now a village school. Of Doughino, the eighteenth-century estate near Smolensk where my grandmother grew up, there was no trace. It was burned to the ground in 1917. My father wept when he left Russia, and I left dry-eyed.

There must be something to the superstition that by returning to a place one can return in time to the self one once was in those places. My father was six when he left Russia in 1919, and his memories are few and indistinct. Yet he found a catharsis in returning, a rounding out of his life. For me, the trips to the Soviet Union redoubled my sense of the irrecoverable distance of my family past. But by a paradox that must be at the heart of writing itself, the more distant everything became, the more urgent it became to get the story down before the death of my generation broke the last living links.

My father and his brothers gave me every kind of help, but they could not conceal their misgivings. I was like an auctioneer sent to value their treasures for sale. Our long sessions together over the tape recorder were harbingers of their mortality. I often thought that it would be better if I left the project aside until they were safely dead and buried. Then I would be free to say it all. But what kind of freedom is that, the freedom to say everything one never dared to say in person? Who is not haunted by the silences, the missed chances for truth that slip between father and son, mother and daughter, the chances that slip finally into the grave? I do not want to miss my chance.

I have done my best to disentangle history from myth, fact from fancy, but in the end I cannot be sure of the truth, either of what happened or what is remembered. I wasn't there. I can only register the impact of their struggle to remember: I can tell them the wave did reach the shore. Because Paul and Natasha managed to remember what they did and passed it on, I owe to them the conviction that my own life did not begin with my birth, but with hers and with his, a hundred years ago in a foreign land, and that now as the last of the generation who knew what life was like behind the red curtain of the revolution begins to depart, it is up to me to pass on their remembering to whoever comes after.

After all these years spent searching for their traces, I can hear their voices at last as if they were in the room. This is how Natasha began her memoirs, her first sentence:

> I decide while I am still in my fresh mind to put down
> all dates and years of main episodes of our lives, my dear
> husband's and mine, so that when we pass into eternity our
> sons and their families may have a picture more or less of
> interesting episodes of our lives, colorful lives, thanks to
> so many striking events and in the middle age of our lives
> tremendous upheavals we had to pass through and which
> left a totally different side of our further existence.

Angels Gather Here

VANESSA SMITH

*Eight months pregnant when her grandmother dies, Vanessa Smith
remembers the spirited Italian grandmother who emigrated in 1935
from Italy with her five sisters. Vanessa recalls playing with her dolls
at the garment factory where her grandmother worked as a seamstress, going to Mass, playing Briscola—and a darker history caused
by her grandfather's gambling debts. Now Nonie is an angel, surely
watching as Vanessa ushers in a new soul.*

THE DAY MY NONIE—MY GRANDMOTHER, my friend—passed on, I was nearly
eight months pregnant. It was October 2008.

My husband Lance and I were late to our birthing class. "I didn't catch
the instructor's name," I whispered on our way across the room to two
empty seats in the semicircle of chairs. He shrugged. We'll ask her at
break, I thought.

From birthing balls and uncomfortable squatting positions to rolled-
up towels and deep breathing exercises, after eight solid hours of encouraging coaching from my husband, I was ready. The sun was setting,
streaming a mid-October orange glow into the windows of the hospital
classroom through the half-opened blinds. I slipped into a daydream,
drifting off in thought about how much our lives were about to change.
My rumination was quickly interrupted.

"If you need to reach me with any questions about the birthing process, please call me anytime. Again, my name is Theresa," she said pointing to the white board where she had written her name in capital letters.

An hour later my feet were propped up on the couch, and I began
decompressing from the overwhelming, yet incredibly exciting day. The
phone rang. I picked up and heard my brother's voice on the end of the
line, shaky and hesitant. "V," he said, "it's Nonie."

I stood up, holding the weight of my belly with one arm, the weight of the phone with the other, and the weight of deep sorrow in my heart. "No, no, no, no," I moaned, falling to the floor.

Twenty minutes later we were in the car on our way to Santa Cruz. The car sped along, and the blur of the lights of the cities going by lulled me into a calm, sedative state. It was at that moment when I realized the instructor's name was Theresa. My Nonie's name is Theresa. I spent the whole day learning how to bring a life into the world by a woman named Theresa. Nothing could have prepared me for a life, her life, leaving my world.

Mass candles lit the room where my mom kept her body until I arrived. It took me awhile to work up the courage to go into that room. When I did, I found my mom kneeling on the floor, holding my Nonie's hand. Her face was pale and lifeless. Nonie looked as if she was in a deep sleep.

In life, my grandmother prayed every day. I went to church with her, mostly on holidays and random Sundays, in true modern Catholic spirit. I could hear her whispering her prayers, turning her worn gold band on her ring finger, chanting her prayer roll in Italian. During communion, she refused the wine—doctors had told her no alcohol some fifty years ago, and she rarely disobeyed. As a child I learned never to take the wine, and figured I was too young. As I grew older, I halfheartedly wanted to try it, and suspected that the dry wafer would pair well with a swish of backwashed red wine. But I never did, not while I was with Nonie, I suppose simply out of respect.

That night, next to her lifeless body, I prayed. Through tears and anger, I asked God, why, why now? I prayed for Him to take her into his care but give her the freedom in heaven that she didn't enjoy on earth. Let her spirit be free, I said; let her be with her sisters in heaven. Don't hold her back, I pleaded. She's been a prisoner far too long in a world she didn't understand.

My grandmother was the second youngest of seven children. She came to the United States at the age of fifteen in 1935 through Ellis Island with her five sisters and father, leaving her mother and eldest brother behind in a small village in northern Italy. In the 1930s, America was the promised land, even though the nation was still in the midst of the Great Depression. New York City was the final destination for believers and dreamers willing to gamble on what life had to offer on the other side of the Statue of Liberty.

When first arriving in New York City in her teens, she worked in a bakery near the family apartment near Hell's Kitchen, where the owner often made sexual advances toward her while she was sweeping the floors at closing time. When she continued to refuse him, he fired her. For most of my memory, she worked with women in a dimly lit garment factory in the Bronx as a seamstress, spending twelve hours a day trimming threads on sundresses and smocks.

She rode two trains and a bus to get to work each day, leaving by 5 a.m. to get there by 7 a.m. When I visited her in the summers around the age of seven, she'd bring me to the factory, and I'd sit on the table out of her way taking it all in—I was allowed to be there as long as I was quiet and didn't interrupt her work. Some days I brought coloring books and crayons, on others I'd bring a shoe box with my Strawberry Shortcake dolls and all their clothes and accessories. Fabric lined the sides of the box to make a one-room dollhouse. I played for hours, making up stories about my dolls and their lives, from what they'd have for dinner, to what they'd wear to their make-believe ball.

Even at high noon, the lighting in the factory was limited to the low-hanging fluorescent lights above each workstation. The ladies on the sewing machines hunched over to see their work more closely in the dim lighting. My grandmother's hardworking hands wielded scissors so nimbly, trimming excess threads on each seam of the dress in seconds, then piling them in bins on each side of her. At break time, we'd sit with the other ladies and eat our salami sandwiches on white bread, drinking sweet iced tea from a thermos. At the end of the day we'd walk back to the bus stop, passing fire hydrants spewing water into the street, letting off steam from the thick, humid air of summer.

I don't remember how old I was when she told me what happened to her. My Nonie told me she was in the "hospital" as a young woman. I later came to learn that she was committed to Bellevue Hospital in New York, a hospital historically synonymous with shock therapy and harsh treatment during an era when mental health was largely misunderstood and any unexplained ailment, especially in women, was labeled as a mental illness.

Family stories vary, but the common theme is that my Nonie had a nervous breakdown. The cause was my grandfather's unpaid gambling debts. Threats were made on my grandfather's life, and Nonie sold heirloom furniture, begging and borrowing the rest to produce a large sum of money, in the thousands, I was told, to spare his life. I will never know if she made the deadline and paid off the debts; I assume so, because my grandfather lived on, but the stress from the ordeal was too much for Nonie to bear.

When I was a teenager, I learned from my mom that Nonie had undergone a partial lobotomy while at Bellevue. They removed her tear ducts, so she couldn't cry. She'd had experimental shock therapy. While Nonie was alive, I never had the courage to ask her more details. It was too painful for her to talk about and for me to hear. I knew she was robbed of crucial years when she should have been carefree and enjoying her life.

She was prescribed heavy barbiturates upon release from the hospital, mainly to treat anxiety. She was not monitored by doctors following her release and ultimately became addicted to the medication. Nonie would fly off in fitful rages brought on by small things. This behavior went on until my mom intervened as a teenager and took a bottle of Nonie's pills to an older nurse friend to ask what the pills were. Shortly after my mom's discovery, Nonie got help, stopped her medication, and slowly came back to reality.

Nonie never wore makeup or colored her hair like her sisters did and never drove a car. She used a rotary dial phone, and hand-washed her curtains in the kitchen sink, hanging them on the clothesline to dry. She read at an elementary school level, if that, and spoke very broken English. Nonie thought soap operas were real-life situations playing out before her. "These people—it's terrible what happened to them," she'd say, adding, "It never ends."

She may not have enjoyed life the way I would have liked her to, but she lived each day the only way she knew how, her spirit unbroken.

My mom brought Nonie to California from New York to live with her when Nonie was nearly eighty. She lived her final years near the beach, taking in sunsets, breathing in the fresh, salt sea air. In her later years, she regularly made pesto with too much garlic, but it was the best pesto I've ever eaten. She played a mean game of Briscola, an Italian game similar to the card game War. She could count up her points more quickly than anyone she played with.

Though very simple in her ways, my Nonie taught me how to trust my maternal instincts and be a better mom. Being with her, watching her struggle with basic tasks was a lesson for me about how to slow down and be patient—the kind of patience needed with children—I see that, now that I have one. I practiced, though I didn't know it was practice for anything, with her. She taught me how to persevere when faced with a sharp learning curve, and how to have compassion when another is faced with adversity. I saw how hard she worked, and it gave me an early understanding of hard work.

I don't know whether she wrestled with the things I do, for instance how to not work so hard you have nothing left to give your family at the end of the day. That factory job didn't have much leeway in terms of how hard she worked—and how dispiriting to be so locked-in, to not be able to move on to something else when the job became intolerable.

"Don't work too hard," she'd say as I headed out to my high-pressure job in corporate communications, "it doesn't pay."

"I know, I know," I always replied.

When she was with me, I became a mother to her. I'd cook for her, paint her toes, and pluck her stubborn Italian chin hairs.

In return, she prayed for me.

"Vennie, I prayed for you today, so you would have a baby," she said, every time we spoke on the phone.

Nonie would stay weeks at a time when she came for a visit, giving my mom needed time to herself. My husband grew very fond of Nonie early in our relationship. She visited us in our small apartment where we lived before we were married. She'd walk around the neighborhood and, more often than not, end up lost. We'd drive around looking for her, and sometimes she'd get rides back from people who recognized her and knew what house she belonged to. I think that's where she found her peace—out on those walks.

After several years of trying to have a child, it ultimately took three things for me to get pregnant—what I now refer to as the perfect calm: patience with the power of modern medicine, faith that things would end up just as they were intended for us, and my Nonie's prayers.

The day after Nonie passed away, I kicked into event planning, emotionless work to get things done. I had to be the strong one in the family to make arrangements for two services, one on each coast, select a casket, make travel arrangements, plan her burial, and make banking arrangements. My mom and brother would fly with her body from California to New York, since I was eight months pregnant and considered high risk, unable to fly. I felt at ease knowing my mom, brother, and our entire New York family contingent—Nonie's nieces and nephews and all the cousins—would be there to welcome her home to her final resting place.

It wasn't until a week later, when the arrangements were complete, that I stopped and realized she was gone. This would be my final offering.

I would be taking care of her one more time. My task was to make sure she was placed in the ground next to her husband, who had laid in rest since she was thirty-two years old.

When I became thirty-two, she reminded me often that she was a widow at my age. I would stop and look at her, seeing the worry in her furrowed brow, and assure her that I knew how hard it must have been. But I couldn't really fathom the depth of that hardship. My grandfather died when my mom was only six months old. Nonie said he called my mom his "mousie." I like the thought of my grandfather being kind and gentle, though given the gambling debts and the situation he put his family in, I don't usually think of him like that.

The doctors released Nonie from a hospital in upstate New York where she was transferred after Bellevue. If calculations serve me correct, it was late 1951 and she was thirty-one years old. The doctors advised her to ease back into life, take her medicine, not to drink alcohol, and recommended she not get pregnant right away. Despite these recommendations, only a few months after her release, she and my grandfather learned they were pregnant. In 1953, when my mom was only six months old, my grandfather died suddenly from leukemia. Nonie was widowed at age thirty-two.

My great-grandmother, Nonie's mother-in-law Pierina, helped raise my mom. Though Pierina passed away when I was just five years old, I remember her as a frail but tenacious woman. I believe my great-grandmother was Nonie's angel. They lived in the same apartment on the Upper West Side of Manhattan together, the same apartment where Nonie hand-washed and hung that laundry for more than fifty years of her life.

A photo of Nonie, her husband, and my great-uncle hung prominently in that apartment and now hangs in my guest room, where Nonie stayed when she came to visit. When my son was just learning to crawl, we'd spend a lot of time in that room looking at her picture. Though he never met her, he calls for her, pointing, while I tell him stories of her.

"She would make you pesto, teach you how to play Briscola, and make you laugh," I said. "You would have been good friends, I think." Maybe they already are, I thought.

Two weeks before she passed on, with the help of my mom, my Nonie finished a needlepoint project of an angel flying through the air. Above the angel it reads, "Angels Gather Here" in an arc across the top. She gave it to me the day of my baby shower. I remember picturing her hands stitching it with the same zest that she used to trim those threads in the factory so many years ago. The angel now has a home in a wooden frame in my son's room. I know for certain that one angel lingers there.

The last time I saw her alive was four days before she passed. I was leaving the house in the morning for work. I kissed her forehead while she sat at the kitchen table eating her cereal. I told her to kiss the baby goodbye. She leaned over and kissed my belly and said, "Bye-bye, baby."

From the other side, my Nonie watches over me and my family and the great-grandson she never held in her arms. She's my angel. We all have one, and she is mine. Not a day goes by without my thoughts straying to her.

Now I know why they say if you love something, set it free.

I hope you're free, my Nonie. Bye-bye, old friend.

Obaachan: What Do *You* Want to Do?

STEPHEN MURPHY-SHIGEMATSU

*To move an elderly person far from his or her native country is difficult
for everyone, though this is often the best choice. Murphy-Shigematsu
shows how difficult it is for a woman brought up to please others to
articulate her own wishes. The author's grandmother is so accustomed
to adapting to others, it is impossible to help her voice her own wishes.
They may be lost forever, in the past of a submissive girlhood and wife.*

WHEN MY MOTHER, TWO OLDER sisters, and I realized that my grandmother
could no longer live alone in Japan, we brought Obaachan to the United
States to die. No one actually said that, but we all knew it was true. After
all, Grandma was ninety-nine. How many more years could she possibly
live? Better to die among those she loved the most, we reasoned. She
could pass her few remaining years in peace and would be able to die
surrounded by her only child and grandchildren.

So my mother and I went to her home in Matsuyama on the island
of Shikoku, a provincial city famous for its hot springs—one of several
in Japan that locals in each area claim is the oldest in the country. We
needed to help her to clean the house and sell it. This was an arduous
task, as Obaachan had lived there for nearly fifty years. She had returned
to her birthplace after my mom (her daughter), dad, and we three kids
left Yokohama in the spring of 1953 on a huge ship and sailed to our new
home in the United States of America. I don't think she ever recovered
from the loss of her only child and grandchildren. Part of her heart remained frozen in time in those golden years.

We started throwing things out, asking Obaachan what to do with
each item. But almost everything, she said, was too precious to be discarded. Those things we threw out without asking kept reappearing back
in the house.

"Didn't we already throw that out?" we asked each other. Then we noticed Obaachan going through the garbage.

Since she had never actually lived anywhere else in the world for ninety-nine years, we figured it would be safer to call it a trial. We told her that she could return to Japan if she desperately wanted to. But as she could no longer live alone, should she go back, she would have to enter a nursing home there.

"What are you doing?" we challenged her.

"Oh, I couldn't throw that out, that was a gift from so-and-so," or "I want to give that to so-and-so."

My mom became exasperated and argued futilely with her. Finally we became exhausted from moving things back and forth from the house to the garbage cans. One day when Obaachan was at the doctor's, we hired a truck to come and take things away.

My mom and sister gave Obaachan her own room in their American home in Massachusetts, near the ocean on Cape Cod, a summer vacationland of beautiful beaches. Her room was small. Obaachan was small too, shorter than five feet and seemingly tinier every time I saw her. Every day my sister took her in the car to look at the ocean, cooked her fish, and made a bath for her at night. She tried to make up for fifty years of separation by spending time with her, talking with Obaachan in her childish Japanese, and giving her warmth and comfort. We subscribed to a Japanese newspaper, which came a couple of days late, and tried to get Japanese cable television, but Obaachan insisted it was not necessary.

Once she was settled in, I flew back to Tokyo, where I worked as a college professor. Obaachan settled into her new life in her new country. Whenever I called, my sister reassured me that all was well. Obaachan couldn't understand anything anyone said, but didn't seem to mind at all. She kept talking anyway as if people could understand her, and maybe sometimes they did. She smiled a lot. Occasionally, Mom's one

Japanese friend, the only other Japanese person in the whole county, would come over and chat with Obaachan for a while.

The only one who understood was Mom. So Obaachan followed her around the house all day, chattering and giving orders. Mom called me one morning to complain that Obaachan had woken her up early and told her that my sister's husband was awake and waiting for his breakfast. Mom sleepily told her that he made his own coffee and ate only cold cereal for breakfast, which he was capable of making himself, but Obaachan insisted that Mom needed to make breakfast for the man of the house.

Mom told me that she was getting tired of Obaachan's antics and worried how she could maintain her own health. After all, she herself was eighty, and Obaachan, now one hundred, still treated her like a child. I became concerned that being the caretaker was now too much for Mom. She had fulfilled this duty for years, going back and forth from the East Coast of the United States to western Japan, a grueling journey she could no longer manage. My sisters and I wondered if the stress of Obaachan's dependency was too great and worried about Mom's health. We agonized over how we could keep both our treasured matriarchs alive as long as possible.

Having lived with both of them, I know they can be difficult. Put them together and they're like cats and dogs. They are strong, willful, and stubborn—like mother, like daughter. The similarities seemed to provoke them into exchanges like this:

"You are like a man!" Obaachan scolded. "Can't you be more ladylike?"

"What do you expect?" Mom retorted. "I had to raise three kids in America and work in a man's world. I had to be tough."

"Why can't you talk gentle and sweet, not so rough?"

"I don't need to act phony, like some women do."

Obaachan teased Mom mercilessly about her weight. Looking at her rear end, Obaachan could not resist saying, "It's really big, isn't it!"

Mom wheeled around quickly. "Why do you always have to criticize people?"

"No one else would tell you. I am the only one. I do it for your own good. You are too big because you are eating too many sweets."

"So stop bringing them home."

"But you like them so much. Here, have one."

"I don't want it."

"Come on, you know you want it."

"I don't want it!"

"Then just eat half."

Despite their crazy behavior with each other, they were boundless in their generosity to others. But while Obaachan gave to everyone, Mom extended herself most, giving to her own kids first. There are other differences—Obaachan spent money like a drunken sailor; Mom pinched pennies on her own desires so she would have more for her children. Obaachan likes presents; Mom thinks about how the money could be better spent. Obaachan loves jewelry; Mom would rather pawn the jewels. Obaachan chatters constantly; Mom is quiet—except when she's yelling at Obaachan.

Maybe it's just too hard for them to live together. For years after my dad died, Mom would return to Japan to care for Obaachan. Three months later she would leave, explaining that her visa was up. Since Mom was an American citizen now, she needed a visa to be in Japan, and it was only good for ninety days. That was about all she could take anyway, so it was the perfect excuse to leave. After reviving herself for a few months at her home in Massachusetts, she would return for another stint with Obaachan. This lifestyle continued until Mom reached eighty and announced she could no longer do it and brought Obaachan to Massachusetts. Obaachan now faced a choice: stay with her and my sister in the United States or return to Japan and enter a nursing home.

Days passed and tensions mounted. As the day approached for a decision to be made, I received a phone call from my sister. She does not speak Japanese, and requested that I ask Obaachan what she wanted to do.

"OK," I said, and when the phone was passed, asked, "What do you want to do, Obaachan?"

"I think I should go back."

She gave the phone to my sister and I translated into English.

"She thinks she should go back."

This answer did not satisfy my sister who insisted, "I want to know what she wants to do, not what she thinks she should do."

"OK, let me ask her again."

"Sister wants to know what you want to do, Obaachan, not what you think you should do."

"Well, I think your mother wants me to go back."

I passed this on to my sister, "She thinks Mom wants her to go back."

My sister said, "That might be true, but I want to know what *she wants* to do."

"OK, I'll try again."

"Obaachan, don't worry about what you think Mom wants. What would *you* like to do?"

"I think your sister's husband is not comfortable with me here."

Obaachan passed the phone to my sister, and I told her, "She thinks Tom is not comfortable with her in your house."

"Don't worry about Tom. He's fine with whatever we decide. In fact, he wants her to stay. What does *she* want to do?"

"Sister says her husband is fine with you there. She wants to know what you want to do."

"It's probably better for everyone if I go back."

"She thinks it's better for everyone if she goes back."

My sister was getting a little frustrated with my answers. "I'm not asking her that. I want to know what she wants. Tell her that if she wants to stay, we will take care of her."

"Sister says if you want to stay she will take care of you."

"I appreciate it, but I should probably go back."

"She thinks she should go back," I told sister, realizing we were back where we started.

My sister was becoming exasperated. "I just want to know what SHE wants to do."

I also was becoming frustrated. "I know you do, but maybe she just can't answer your question in the way you want her to."

There was a silence. Then my sister said, "OK, let's stop asking her."

Obaachan went back to Japan a month later. She moved into the nursing home without complaint and got her own room. She filled it with her few remaining possessions, an old chest of drawers, a favorite chair, and the clothes we had not thrown out. On top of the chest, she put a few photos of her grandchildren and great-grandchildren, but the rest she gave to me, afraid that they would be lost in the chaos following her death.

Obaachan is now 106. Though she broke her hip when she was 103, she has not slowed down. She moves around in a wheelchair. Her brain has slowed but remains clear. Sometimes she expresses regrets.

"I should have had an operation to repair my hip."

"Why didn't you?" I ask.

"I didn't want to use up all the money. I wanted you kids to have something."

Another regret: "I should have stayed in the United States with your mother and sister."

"Why didn't you?"

"Your mom told me everyone was embarrassed that my nose was too small, so she ordered me to have plastic surgery. Isn't that awful! That's why I came back." I want to challenge her story but stop myself and just say, "That's too bad."

I visit Obaachan when I can, two or three times a year, just for a few days. On those precious days I sit with her for hours and get her talking by showing her old photos. She reminisces about things that happened at least half a century ago. I have heard most of the stories already but feign interest and pretend it is the first time she has told me. Although we never touched when we were younger, I hold her hand, softer and thinner with each passing year. I kiss her on the forehead. Occasionally she says something startling like when she told me, "After you kids left Japan, I cried every day for two years."

Once in a while something shocking buried deep down erupts. Her face brightens, and she smiles like a young girl recalling the man she loved at eighteen, the only love of her life, but darkens when she tells of how her father rejected him and forced her to marry someone she did not love. Other stories are even more painful. Sometimes I have to turn away. I encourage her to try to recall happy moments. And once in a while something slips out of my mouth too, like when I asked her if she regretted having half-blood grandchildren. She didn't hesitate to answer, "You were my treasures."

Would she have been happier in the United States? I don't know. We painted a happy picture of an ideal ending, but there were undeniable and seemingly irresolvable tensions and stress for our mother. There could have been incredible problems with health insurance that would have exhausted all her savings before the bills were passed on to us. And how would she have communicated with doctors, nurses, and caregivers?

In Japan, she laments, there is no one to care for her. This is not what she expected. How could it be this way after she cared for so many people? Why is there no one to care for her? It isn't fair, I agree, but those who would have cared for her are now in their eighties and nineties and living out their last days the best they can. "I could do it if I was ten years younger," her little sisters say, and we look at each other thinking that long life is a mixed blessing. No one wants to say that Obaachan has lived too long.

Now she may die surrounded by strangers. True, they are not family, but are they really strangers? These are the people she lives with and eats and sleeps with, who bathe her, take her to the toilet, give her medicine, and change her sheets. She has grown fond of some of them. After seven years her room really has become her room. She has passed many days and nights there. And in Japan, at least she has the power of language; she knows what is being said and can say what she wants. The staff tells me that this is important for her to be in control, as it fits with her fighting personality.

Because of her advanced age, I no longer cling to her. I have had her long enough. I want her to go when she is ready. She tells me that she is ready, but that God never calls her. She even asks me to help her leave this world: "You're a doctor, don't you have anything in your bag?"

Though I feel sad, and imagine that she is lonely, this is the way she will live out her last years. Maybe she really did want to come home to Japan, where she was born, where her mother died, where she herself wanted to die. Maybe she could never express her desire, but perhaps she needed to be where things were familiar—the way things looked, smelled, the natural world of home. Maybe she couldn't stand losing memories. It was her choice, I say to comfort myself. But what does this mean?

Could she ever really choose what she wants—a woman raised at a time in which a woman's desires did not matter, a woman raised in a society where she could only see herself in a contextual web of relationships? When we asked, "What do *you* want to do?" she could not see her wishes simply as personal, individualistic desires.

What Obaachan wants and has always wanted is what is best for all her loved ones.

Contributors

Tissa Abeysekara was born in Colombo, Sri Lanka, in 1939. A fiction writer since the 1950s, he became one of Sri Lanka's most respected screenwriters and directors. The novella *Bringing Tony Home* won Sri Lanka's esteemed Gratiaen Prize. He was director of the Television Training Institute at the time of his death in 2009.

After graduating from Colorado College, **Lauren Aczon** worked as an au pair in Turin, Italy. She is a barista at La Note, in Berkeley, California, and an assistant ballet instructor at an El Cerrito studio. Through her firm Quickening Force, she does assorted letterpress and illustration work (embellishments, notecards, advertising) for clients. Her work can be seen on www.etsy.com/shop/Quickeningforce.

Gloria Avner is a batik artist and painter; for forty years she has been a purveyor of indigenous artifacts at her summer shop, Aquarius Artifacts, in Bar Harbor, Maine. In Key Largo she teaches art, exhibits mixed media, and is ritual director of her Jewish Community Center.

Joanna Biggar is a writer, journalist, teacher, and world traveler. She directed the Writing Center in Washington, DC, for many years and worked as a reading specialist for the Oakland, California, schools. She lives in Oakland, and her most recent book is *That Paris Year*.

Avery Bradford is the mother of three grown children and one grandchild. She teaches elementary school in California's Central Valley and is married to a special education teacher and musician. They enjoy spending time with family and friends, traveling, and discovering new and out-of-the-way places.

Sharon Bray is a writer, teacher, and author of two books on expressive writing during cancer. She leads regular writing groups for men and women living with cancer at Scripps Green and Stanford Cancer Centers and is an instructor for the UCLA extension Writer's Program, where she teaches creative nonfiction. She lives in San Diego.

Bridget Connelly is a scholar, folklorist, and emerita professor of rhetoric at the University of California at Berkeley. Her book on her own family history, *Forgetting Ireland: Uncovering a Family's Secret History,* was cited as a best book by *The Irish Times.*

David Jackson Cook teaches democracy, civil rights, and U.S. history at the high school level and Peace Studies at the college level in Chattanooga, Tennessee. An activist in local human rights movements, he has published in *The Sun, Geez,* and commondreams.org. He lives with his wife and two small children on a mountain in a log cabin, near parents, grandparents, aunts, uncles, and cousins.

Keith Dalton brought early theater skills to a communications career in corporate and educational television. His life has been a spiritual quest to understand the nature of reality, about which he has published several books. He homeschooled his three children near Toronto and now lives upriver from Vancouver, British Columbia.

Donne Davis has been a speech therapist, writer, college outreach counselor, and speaker, sharing information to enrich people's lives. She founded the GaGa Sisterhood, a national social network for grandmothers. She writes about the joys and challenges of being a grandma on her blog, www.gagasisterhood.com.

Nancy Hathaway is a Zen teacher in the Kwan Um School of Zen. She has studied extensively in the Zen, Tibetan, and Vipassana traditions and founded the Morgan Bay Zendo in Surry, Maine. Her private practice in Mindfulness-based counseling is in Blue Hill, Maine.

Lindy Hough (editor) is a poet and fiction writer whose most recent book is *Wild Horses, Wild Dreams: New and Selected Poems, 1971–2010*. Cofounder and publisher emerita of North Atlantic Books, she is finishing a novel about a Colorado family during the uranium boom in the 1950s. She divides her time between Mt. Desert Island, Maine, and Berkeley, California.

Kitty Hughes is a writer and local history researcher who manages neighborhood history projects for the City of Oakland, among them the historic markers telling Oakland's cultural history for the San Francisco Bay Trail. Her new novel is *Rendezvous*.

Famed historian and writer **Michael Ignatieff** stepped down from leadership of Canada's Liberal party in May 2011, after defeat to the Conservatives. He is the author of novels, history, and nonfiction about Canadian and international studies, including *The Russian Album*, about his family's life in Russia, excerpted here. He is currently a fellow and senior resident at Massey College in Toronto, where he lives.

Jane Isay (foreword) is a prominent human science editor in New York publishing who developed major authors at Basic Books and other leading publishers. She left her position as editor-in-chief at Harcourt Trade Books in 2008 to write her own books. *Walking on Eggshells: Navigating the Delicate Relationship between Adult Children and Parents* was a smash hit, as the first thoughtful analysis of the negotiations parents and adult children struggle with. Her latest book is *Mom Still Likes You Best: The Unfinished Business between Siblings*. Isay's territory is intergenerational and family life, to which she brings detailed research, understanding, and humor. She lives in New York City, where she takes the subway to spend time with her five grandchildren.

Joan Steinau Lester has published essays in many publications, including the *Huffington Post, Common Dreams, Marie Claire,* and *Essence.* She is the author of five books, including a biography of Congresswoman Eleanor Holmes Norton, *Fire in My Soul.* Her newest book is the young-adult novel *Black, White, Other: In Search of Nina Armstrong.* She lives in Berkeley, California.

Saphira Linden is a transpersonal therapist and Sufi senior teacher with a background in theater. She cofounded and is director of Omega Theater, a transpersonal drama therapy program in Boston, where she designs and leads workshops in visioning, team building, and empathy training.

John Lunn is a master flute maker, award-winning silver and gold artist, and young-adult science-fiction author of *The Mariner's Curse* and *The Aquanauts.* An accomplished video artist, he visits classrooms in New England and Canada. He lives in Newport, New Hampshire.

Singer and songwriter **Jay Mankita** performs throughout the Northeast at music festivals, fairs, and many schools. His songs embrace social change as much as the concerns of children and the spirit. The father of a toddler, he lives in western Massachusetts, and travels in a touring van powered by recycled vegetable oil.

After many years in Prince George, **Joanne Maurits** moved to Kamloops, British Columbia, where her husband took a university job. She has three grown children and four grandchildren in Edmonton, Alberta, and Prince George. Her working life was in patient care. Now she volunteers with university ESL students and writes. Her blog about raising her grandchildren is *A Nana's Journey.*

Gill Wright Miller is an associate professor and chair of dance and dance studies at Denison University in Granville, Ohio. She is a coauthor of *Exploring Body-Mind Centering: An Anthology of Experience and Method,* about the work of Bonnie Bainbridge-Cohen published in spring 2011 by North Atlantic Books.

Stephen Murphy-Shigematsu is a psychologist who teaches at Stanford and Fielding Graduate University. The director of Multicultural Leadership, he helps organizations and individuals dealing with diversity and globalization. He is the author of *Amerasian Children* and *Transcultural Japan: At the Borderlands of Race, Gender, and Identity,* recently published by Routledge. He lives in Palo Alto, California.

Nadia Natali is a clinical psychotherapist and dance therapist emphasizing somatic work. She does trauma work with clients and hosts DanceProcess workshops and DanceMedicine events in Ojai, California. She wrote about the Zen retreat center she founded in the hills above Ojai with her husband in *The Blue Heron Ranch Cookbook.*

Lenora Madison Poe is a licensed Marriage, Family, and Child therapist and clinical psychologist in private practice in Berkeley, California. She has been active nationally and on a grassroots level as an advocate for grandparents raising grandchildren. She founded the Grandparents As Parents support group at The Church by the Side of the Road in Berkeley, now in its twenty-second year. The author of *Black Grandparents As Parents,* she has been honored with many awards for her work with grandparents raising grandchildren in the African American community.

Karine Schomer was raised in France and Switzerland. A professor of South Asian studies at the University of California at Berkeley for a number of years, she was a dean and provost at several Bay Area colleges before starting the India Practice in 1997, a corporate training consultancy. She is married to writer-photographer Raphael Shevelev and lives in the Bay Area.

Douglas Silsbee has worked as an independent consultant and executive coach since 1986. He has coached Fortune 100 and nonprofit executives, business school faculty, and entrepreneurs in his Presence-Based Coaching, which was published as a book by Jossey-Bass in 2008. He lives north of Asheville, North Carolina, where he and his wife run a retreat center.

Vanessa Smith is a second-generation Italian American and native New Yorker who lives in Sacramento. She studied journalism at San Francisco State University and now works in communications for a global client services firm.

Judyth O. Weaver is a body/mind integrative therapist with specialization in prenatal and perinatal therapy. She is the creator and founding chair of the Santa Barbara Graduate Institute PhD Program in somatic psychology and teaches there, in the somatics program at the California Institute of Integral Studies in San Francisco, and around the world.

Salle Webber is a grandmother of four and postpartum doula who helps families with newborn babies throughout Santa Cruz County, California. A passionate student of hula and Hawaiian culture, she is working on a book for aspiring doulas.

Karen Best Wright is a writer and Internet marketer for SeniorPro Marketing. She is working on a master's in psychology with a focus on health communications. Karen has one of the most well-known blogs for Grandparents Raising Grandchildren, www.grandparentingblog.com. She lives in Richmond, Virginia.

JoAnn Wynn was raised in Arkansas and came to the Bay Area nine years ago. She has been employed by IBM, most recently in information technology. She is active in the Berkeley Grandparents As Parents support group and her Richmond, California, church, and lives in Richmond with her two grandchildren.

About the Editor

PHOTO: RAPHAEL SHEVELEV

Lindy Hough was born in 1944 in Denver, Colorado. She graduated from Smith College and earned an MFA from Goddard College. A journalist and dance critic, she has taught writing and literature in colleges and universities in Michigan, Maine, Vermont, and California. She cofounded the Berkeley-based mind/body/spirit publishing company North Atlantic Books with Richard Grossinger in 1974, and was publisher and editorial director for many years. She coedited *Nuclear Strategy and the Code of the Warrior: Faces of Mars and Shiva in the Crisis of Human Survival* and is the author of five books of poetry, including the recent *Wild Horses, Wild Dreams: New and Selected Poems 1971–2010.* For more information, visit her website at www.lindyhough.com.

Permissions and Copyrights

"Hark, the Moaning Pond: A Grandmother's Tale" is excerpted from *Bringing Tony Home*: Stories by Tissa Abeysekara, published by North Atlantic Books, copyright © 2008 by Tissa Abeysekara. Reprinted by permission of the publisher.

An excerpt from *The Russian Album* by Michael Ignatieff, published by Macmillan and Picador, is copyright © 1987, 1997 by Michael Ignatieff. Reprinted by permission of Picador Press.

The lyrics of the song "Wild Thing Baby" by Jay Mankita are copyright © 1996 and used by permission.

The foreword is copyright © 2012 by Jane Isay.

"Calling Clotilde" is copyright © 2012 by Lauren Aczon.

"In and Out of Step" is copyright © 2012 by Gloria Avner.

"Twins—Day and Night" is copyright © 2012 by Joanna Biggar.

"A Heart's Perspective" is copyright © 2012 by Avery Bradford.

"Confessions of a New Step-Grandparent" is copyright © 2012 by Sharon Bray.

"The Collapse" is copyright © 2012 by David Jackson Cook.

"Following Fifi" is copyright © 2012 by Kitty Hughes and Bridget Connelly.

"Loving through the Distances" is copyright © 2012 by Keith Dalton.

"Four Generations of First-Born Daughters" is copyright © 2012 by Donne Davis.

"Grandmother's Lap" is copyright © 2012 by Nancy Hathaway.

"Listening to Leo" and the introduction are copyright © 2012 by Lindy Hough.

"Talking about Race and Gender" is copyright © 2012 by Joan Steinau Lester.

"The Whirling Heart Dance of Grandmothering" is copyright © 2012 by Saphira Linden.

"The Grampy Diaries" is copyright © 2012 by John Lunn.

"An Explosion of Love" is copyright © 2012 by Joanne Maurits.

"Carving Paths in Snow" is copyright © 2012 by Gill Wright Miller.

"Obaachan: What Do *You* Want to Do? is copyright © 2012 by Stephen Murphy-Shigematsu.

270